# Digital Judaism

Drawing on many of the most established scholars studying the impact of new media on the Jewish faith and tradition, this volume presents a detailed examination of both how and why different Jewish groups adapt, embrace, or reject, developing Internet technologies within their communities. Addressing the nuances of the social shaping of technology, this book significantly contributes to our understanding of the complex relationships between religious beliefs and practices and the fast paced developments of the online world.

—*Christopher Helland, Dalhousie University, Canada*

In this volume, contributors consider the ways that Jewish communities and users of new media negotiate their uses of digital technologies in light of issues related to religious identity, community and authority. *Digital Judaism* presents a broad analysis of how and why various Jewish groups negotiate with digital culture in particular ways, situating such observations within a wider discourse of how Jewish groups throughout history have utilized communication technologies to maintain their Jewish identities across time and space. Chapters in this volume address issues related to the negotiation of authority between online users and offline religious leaders and institutions not only within ultra-Orthodox communities but also within the broader Jewish religious culture, taking into account how Jewish engagement with media in Israel and the Diaspora raises a number of important issues related to Jewish community and identity. Featuring recent scholarship by leading and emerging scholars of Judaism and media, *Digital Judaism* is an invaluable resource for researchers in new media, religion and digital culture.

**Heidi A. Campbell** is an associate professor of communication at Texas A&M University and the director of the Network for New Media, Religion and Digital Culture Studies. She is author of *Exploring Religious Community Online* (2005) and *When Religion Meets New Media* (2010) and the editor of *Digital Religion: Understanding Religious Practice in New Media World* (2013).

## Routledge Studies in Religion and Digital Culture

**Edited by Heidi Campbell, Mia Lövheim, and Greg Grieve**

1 **Buddhism, the Internet, and Digital Media**
The Pixel in the Lotus
*Edited by Gregory Price Grieve and Daniel Veidlinger*

2 **Digital Judaism**
Jewish Negotiations with Digital Media and Culture
*Edited by Heidi A. Campbell*

# Digital Judaism

## Jewish Negotiations with Digital Media and Culture

**Edited by Heidi A. Campbell**

Routledge
Taylor & Francis Group
NEW YORK AND LONDON

First published 2015
by Routledge
711 Third Avenue, New York, NY 10017

and by Routledge
2 Park Square, Milton Park, Abingdon, Oxon OX14 4RN

*Routledge is an imprint of the Taylor & Francis Group, an informa business*



*Library of Congress Cataloging-in-Publication Data*

Digital Judaism : Jewish negotiations with digital media and culture / edited by Heidi A. Campbell. — First edition.
pages cm — (Routledge studies in religion and digital culture ; 2)
Includes bibliographical references and index.
1. Internet—Religious aspects—Judaism. 2. Digital media—Religious aspects—Judaism. 3. Cyberspace—Religious aspects—Judaism. I. Campbell, Heidi, 1970– editor.
BM538.I58D54 2014
296.3'76—dc23 2014027791

ISBN: 978-0-415-73624-4 (hbk)
ISBN: 978-1-315-81859-7 (ebk)

Typeset in Sabon
by Apex CoVantage, LLC

Printed and bound in the United States of America by Publishers Graphics, LLC on sustainably sourced paper.

# Contents

# Acknowledgments

This volume would not have come to fruition without the input and assistance of a number of scholars contributing to the development of my research on Jewish negotiations with media over the past decade including Yair Amichai-Hamburger, Menahem Blondheim, Oren Golan, Gustavo Mesch, Rivka Neriya-Ben Shahar, Sheizaf Rafaeli, Michele Rosenthal, Rivka Ribak, Batia Siebzehner, Limor Shifman, Jeremy Stolow and Nurit Stadler. I am grateful for the encouragement of Mia Lovheim and Gregory Price Grieve, my coeditors in the Routledge Studies in Religion and Digital Culture series in this project. I am further indebted to my graduate students Aya Yadlin-Segal and Ruth Tsuria for their editorial assistance and feedback, as well as my Routledge editor Margo Irvin. Thanks also to Emily Berglund, Heather Elmatti, Kathy DiSanto, John and Gigi Greene, Connie Merhley, Suzanne Ousley and Iris Villareal, for their friendship and support during the writing and editing process.

# 1 Introduction

## Studying Jewish Engagement with Digital Media and Culture

*Heidi A. Campbell*

The study of new media, religion and digital culture has been in existence for almost two decades. During this time scholars have explored a wide range of religious group's engagement with the internet, yet it is clear that some religious traditions, such as Christianity and Islam, have received much more attention than others. As Campbell and Lovheim (2011) noted in their assessment of the study of religion and the internet, there is still a need for a more nuanced understanding of the negotiation of the internet as a medium for religious practice within some religious groups. Also more careful consideration is called for regarding what some scholars have described as "digital religion"—the relationship between the online–offline religious contexts—within some religious traditions. This chapter argues that the study of Jewish groups and the internet has arguably been an understudied area in need of more significant attention and critical examination.

While the study of Judaism and digital culture is gaining momentum, to date much of this work has often been limited to individual case studies mostly focused on the study of the ultra-Orthodox sector's response and use of the internet. However, some recent studies have begun to highlight how the internet raises important issues related to the negotiation of authority between online users and offline religious leaders and institutions not only within ultra-Orthodox communities but also broader Orthodox contexts (i.e., Campbell and Golan, 2011; Y. Cohen, 2012). Among the studies that currently exist, a number of overlapping observations and claims about Jewish negotiation with digital culture can be seen, pointing to a need for a more systematic study of Jewish engagement with new media. What is needed is scholarship that moves beyond a focus on ultra-Orthodox communities to compare the strategies and responses to digital technologies emerging within broader Jewish religious culture. Also lacking are interpretive categories for describing these common responses emerging from diverse groupings within this religious tradition.

*Digital Judaism* is an edited volume that seeks to map the range of responses taken by different groups within religious Judaism in relation to the rise of new media technologies and the environments they create. The purpose of this book is to gather the work of scholars who are exploring different aspects of the relationship between various Jewish communities and digital culture. Through spotlighting how different Reform, Orthodox and Haredi groups in American, Israeli and other settings have approached and adopted new media technologies, this book seeks to highlight a number of key issues. Specifically *Digital Judaism* spotlights different religious Jewish groups' perceptions of digital media and the implications technology use may raise related to the outreach goals and moral or religious patterns of life for such sectors. Before we enter this comparative exploration it is important to consider how different Jewish groups have responded to media technologies to see what general concerns and approaches have previously been noted in studies of Jewish engagement with media technologies. This leads to an exploration of trends in current research on Judaism and the internet, with current findings and approaches being noted. This sets up a framework for understanding the unique contribution offered by *Digital Judaism* in the subject and themes covered that seek to provide a map of common approaches taken and how this volume seeks to broaden our understanding of decisions made regarding Jewish negotiations with new media in a range of different religious sectors.

## APPROACHING JUDAISM

It is important to note that this book approaches Judaism by focusing on its religious identity and groupings. The definition of what it means to be a Jew or to be Jewish is a highly contested issue, as Judaism simultaneously encompasses a cultural, racial, ethnic, political, religious, and national identity (i.e., Boyarin and Boyarin, 1993; Herman, 1989). Here Judaism is approached in terms of its religious communities and institutions, focusing on the social and cultural issues, as they relate to the life practices of specific religious sectors of the Jewish community. This text provides a mapping of how a variety of religious Jewish groups, which can be linked to broad categories such as Orthodox and Reform Judaism, negotiate their use of and beliefs about new media. While these broad categories such as Orthodox Judaism are used, it is done so to identify different distinct sectors with Judaism rather than to make overarching claims about groups, such as the Orthodox as a single or wholly cohesive group.

Chapter authors recognize this complexity in their individual work, noting that while Orthodox or Haredi/ultra-Orthodox groups may share some common practices and beliefs, different communities within these groupings have distinctive histories and ethnic connections that translate into unique life practices and authority structures for different sectors (i.e., Orthodox Judaism encompasses such diversity as the Sephardim, Ashkenazi, Hassid and National Religious). Therefore, authors seek to identify and clarify the specific Jewish contexts they are investigating in order to make claims about how distinct groups within religious Judaism respond, and what specific factor are tied to their larger tradition shape these responses.

For example, discussion of ultra-Orthodox groups response to the internet recognize that communities in this grouping exhibit conservative social behaviors and religious practices based on a strict adherence to traditional understandings of religious law, coupled with a rejection of the values of modernity (Stadler, 2009). This is in contrast to the Modern Orthodox, or Israeli National Religious groups, that are typically more flexible in such interpretations and engagement with modernity (such as technology) but are still bounded by specific ideological and religious constraints, such as a belief in the religious significance of the state of Israel, and a strict adherence to *Halacha* (Y. Cohen, 2005). By acknowledging the diversity that exists within religious Judaism, authors of this volume seeks to demonstrate how specific groups within Judaism and their use of the internet and other digital technologies illuminate key facets that influence and shape religious negotiations with new media. This includes investigating response to digital technology by the American Lubavitch, Israeli National Religious and Modern Orthodox (Dati Leumi); Israeli ultra-Orthodox/Haredi groups such as the Belz and Gur communities; members of the American Reform movement, as well as the international Aish HaTorah movement; and those who would call themselves "Progressive" and "Post-denominational" Jews in Britain and the United States. Overall, this book documents a variety of social agendas and moral boundaries have an impact on community-affiliated technological enterprises and highlights the commonalities as well as their unique negotiations.

## ENGAGEMENT BETWEEN JUDAISM AND MEDIA

In recent years increasing attention has been given to the relationship between Judaism and the media. Since the late 1980s, scholars have paid serious attention to how contemporary Jewish media rhetorical strategies may be informed by traditional religious communication patterns in Israel (Cromer, 1987), especially in relation to textual media (Blondheim, 1997; Blondheim and Blum-Kulka, 2001; Jaffe, 2001). Many of these studies demonstrate how religious Judaism has shaped media discourse within Israel, such as the argument that current political discourse is shaped by historic Jewish religious argumentation found in Talmudic exchanges, seen in examination of speech used in synagogues and yeshivas (i.e., Blum-Kulka, Blondheim, and Hacohen, 2002). Other work has looked at how religious values and distinctive community affiliation may guide the extent to which different groups may engage with certain types of media (Jacobson, 2004).

In the past decade, there has been an increase in scholarship on the characteristics and importance of religious media, especially for Orthodox and Haredi groups (Caplan, 2001). These studies have noted the value of embracing these tools for enhancing group solidarity and values. Issues under investigation have included how Haredi use audio-taped sermons as a mechanism for building community consensus (Blondheim and Kaplan, 1993; Caplan, 1997) and how popular literature can serve as a tool for "imparting everyday life instructions" for religious practice within the ultra-Orthodox community (Stadler, 2002). These studies have addressed various forms of media, from the use of texts for the construction of religious and community authority (Stolow, 2006) to religious engagement with electronic media. This is seen in Lehmann and Siebzehner's (2006) study of how religious pirate radio has become a vibrant tool for communication within the Israeli Sephardic community or how Lubavitch in New York deploy video media for outreach campaigns. Bagad-Elimelech's (2009) study of ultra-Orthodox produced feature films distributed on CD and DVD revealed a reframing of rabbinical authorities and ultra-Orthodox men in ways that both challenge and affirm traditional literary troupes of good vs. evil and communal ideals. A. Cohen, Lemish, and Schejter's (2008) study of cell phone usage in Israel found that debates within the ultra-Orthodox community about the social and moral implications of cell phones led service providers to develop special services to cater specifically to religious Orthodox users. The rise of the "kosher cell phone" within Israel has also been explored, noting the role and influence Orthodox communities can play as media consumers (i.e., Campbell, 2007; Rashi, 2013), as well as intercommunity religious debates about the implication of media appropriation (i.e., Deutsch, 2009).

Some work has also been done looking at how the intersection of religious communities with media technologies and culture illuminates who religious Jewish groups are perceived within the broader society and the extent of this engagement with secular contexts. How religious Jews have been represented within mainstream media has been closely studied, especially in relation to how Orthodox communities have been framed within Israeli new coverage (i.e., Y. Cohen, 2005, 2012). Scholars of Judaism and media have further noted that the analysis of religious media and related productions processes can help illuminate broader cultural shifts at work in the authority and public influence of religious communities in contemporary society (i.e., Shandler, 2009; Stolow, 2010). Still most of this work tends to focus Orthodox groups, with much less work being done on Modern Orthodox and Israeli National Religious engagement with media. However, the few studies available suggest that while they may more openly and readily engage media than the ultra-Orthodox, they still encounter similar questions regarding how media aesthetics and technological affordances may pose challenges to community values (Baumel-Schwartz, 2009; Rosethal and Ribak, 2006). In these discussions, questions of community and authority are clearly highlighted as central debates within Judaism regarding how media is viewed, used and regulated. Such studies highlight a need for more inquiry on the religion plays in shaping media within the Judaism in other context and communities.

## STUDIES OF JUDAISM AND NEW MEDIA

To date most research on Judaism and new media has focused on Orthodox Judaism, and specifically ultra-Orthodox groups negotiations with such platforms (Campbell, 2011). Within this work most studies have centered on a few select themes, namely, (a) ultra-Orthodox engagement online (i.e., Caplan, 2001; Horowitz, 2000) and particularly (b) female use of the internet, allowing them to bypass or negotiate with traditional authority structures (i.e., Baumel-Schwartz, 2009; Bazalia-Nahon and Barzalia, 2005; Livio and Tenenboim-Weinblatt, 2007). These studies of Judaism online have recognized that the internet is an interesting and important sphere because it allows for studying the inner workings and communication practices of these traditionally closed religious communities (Tsarfaty and Blais, 2002), especially highlighting communal discourse, policies and rabbinical responses to engagement with modernity via technology (Ben-Shahar and Lev-On, 2009). Since the 1990s many Orthodox Jewish rabbis and religious leaders have spoken out about the potential landmines along the information highway (Herman, 1995).The internet is often described as a potential threat to be avoided.

Researchers have noted several key objections often voiced by Orthodox groups and leaders, especially rabbis, regarding the internet. These include framing the internet as a gateway for immoral content, a structure encouraging problematic social behaviors for members and a sphere facilitating the secular invasion into sacred sphere of the community. First, scholars have noted that internet, like the television before it, is seen as a device ushering problematic moral and ethical content into the community. The internet is equated by some Orthodox rabbis and users as a gateway technology leading to modern decadence and potential moral contamination. A key concern is the extent to which the internet may serve as a gateway to sin, providing easy access to sexually explicit materials that can lead to transgressions in thought and action. In this sense, the internet is perceived as a dangerous influence that can hamper the moral codes and boundaries upheld by an enclave society such as the Haredi (Caplan, 2001). This is comparable to other practices such as limiting interactions between the sexes (i.e., chaperoned courtships) or forbidding watching television. The concern is over visual aspects of the internet where users may be exposed to immodest images of women or sexually content. Thus, the internet is often framed as dangerous for male members of the community who is may be susceptible to such sin (Campbell, 2007; Y. Cohen 2012).

Second, the internet is often framed within studies, especially focused on ultra-Orthodox users, as encouraging the violation of communal behavioral controls and protocols. Thus, it is framed as an instrument that leads to the disintegration of the community's social fabric. It is seen as source dispersing disruptive or false information within their own communal parameters. Researchers often highlight religious leaders' concerns that the internet increases community member's exposure to secular messages that can endanger their moral codes (Horowitz, 2000), such as its ability to spread *Lashon H'ra* (gossip or slanderous information) and traditional social expectation or patterns of life (Baumel-Schwartz, 2009). Also the internet represents a solitary activity that cannot be as easily monitored by family or community members (Ben Shahar and Lev-On, 2009). As such, internet engagement is framed as enabling the transgression of long-established community boundaries, avenues of social control and recognized religious authorities.

Third, the internet is seen to transgress established Orthodox boundaries between the sacred and secular worlds. They fear of exposure to information generated outside the community, because the internet becomes a channel for interacting with the secular world. The internet challenges accepted foundations of the sacred and established divisions between piety and profane aspects of life. In this sense the internet impinges on their basic ideals and goals and may be seen as a *moshav letsim* (a seat of scorners), a social gathering where no matters of Torah are discussed (El-Or, 1994). They fear the internet may facilitate a transgression between sacred-secular community divides, running counter to daily rituals that seek to maintain clear distinction between the sacred and secular aspects of life. Therefore, access to unmonitored secular and sinful content online is seen as highly problematic, which individuals may easily and unintentionally access (Tsarfaty and Blais, 2002).

Because of these critiques, scholars have also noted that religious Jewish internet users within Orthodox groups and those involved in website production feel as if they must justify their use in the face of these fears, articulating how internet engagement by internet users can be cultured in light of religious boundaries and expected codes of practice (Barzilai Nahon and Barzilai, 2005). This means that scholars studying different Orthodox communities' relationships with the internet have tended to focus on users' perception of technology and internet use in the face of critiques from religious leaders (see Baumel-Schwartz, 2009; Horowitz, 2000; Livio and Tenenboim-Weinblatt, 2007). Recent work has sought to investigate the functional and symbolic choices made by views of religious website developers to show how they seek to frame relationship with the internet in light of their offline communities' dictate (Campbell and Golan, 2011; Golan, 2013). Scholars have also begun to note how the internet may challenge religious authorities and leaders through the innovation of traditional religious practices in online environments and how rabbis part an important role controlling the attitudes toward the internet (Steinitz, 2011; Pitkowsky 2011).

What this brief literature review shows is that much of the work to date on Judaism and the internet has focused on Orthodox, specifically ultra-Orthodox and female members, negotiation of digital media and how they seek to develop a unique discourse to justify their use and practice (i.e., Livio and Tenenboim-Weinblatt, 2007; Pitkowsky, 2011). Scholars have noted the development of both apologetic discourses and resistance narratives, which perform similar roles in seeking to frame internet use as acceptable. In the apologetic discourses, religious users frame their online engagement as in line, rather than in opposition to, religious values and boundaries, thus trying to justify that internet use can be seen as acceptable if engaged in regulate ways. Resistance narratives seek to confront opposition towards the internet, by stressing how the internet can support religious goals and values if used in prescribed ways. Such narratives are raised by groups such as Chabad.org to frame their online work as acceptable as it is centered on meeting community goals for outreach and religious education rather than on catering to individual needs for communication or socialization.

Currently most research has focused on the internet and websites, overlooking other important digital platforms and innovations such as social media and mobile telephony. There is also a lack of comparative work looking at Jewish new media use across different communities and national contexts, because most of work has focused on Israeli ultra-Orthodox Jews internet use with some exception focusing on the American Chabad movement's use of the internet. Few studies exist that have focused on grouping such as Conservative (i.e., Nevins, 2010), Reform (i.e., Frost, 2013), Progressive and non-Israeli or American (i.e. Abrams, Baker, and Brown, 2013). These points to the need for a more comprehensive exploration of religious Judaism, which explores the media technologies and groups underrepresented in current scholarship.

## OVERVIEW OF *DIGITAL JUDAISM*

*Digital Judaism* is an edited volume that maps the broad range of responses and approaches within religious Judaism to new media technologies and environments. The purpose of this book is to gather the work of key scholars exploring the relationship between various Jewish communities and digital culture. The book begins with an important chapter by Menahem Blondheim that traces the historical evolution of Jewish thinking about media and Jewish practices of communication, in order to critically review what is and is not new about "new media" technology and Jewish response to it. "The Jewish Communication Tradition and its Encounters With (the) New Media" traces shifts in the practice of Jewish communications through processes of social and technological change, focusing on three dimensions: ideology, media infrastructures and institutional arrangements anchoring communicative practices. Blondheim carefully outlines the historical, religious, legal and social sensibilities that have shaped responses to communication processes and technologies and what this means for an age of digital technologies.

*Digital Judaism* explores how Jewish communities and users of new media negotiate their uses of digital technologies, and broadly takes a religious social-shaping to technology (RSST) approach (as developed by Campbell, 2010). RSST argues religious user communities adopt, integrate and adapt new media technologies in particular ways so that they fit more cohesively with the moral life and cultural and social expectations of the communities with which they are affiliated. However, because of the diversity of interpretations of religious texts and of institutional structures and the understanding of what constitutes authentic community and religious adherence that exists among different groups within a particular tradition, the responses to a given technology can vary greatly. This is especially true within Judaism, in which some groups have ardently embraced the internet while others have vehemently opposed the use and integration of computers and the internet into the lives of their communities. Scholars using an RSST approach pay special attention the history and background of their religious tradition and highlight to specific values that have impact on and inform their media choices. This helps scholars to better understand the technology choices religious groups make and they ways they frame and talk in order to justify their decision making in light of their community values and constraints. By investigating the negotiation process undertaken by various Jewish groups in light of the current research, two broad strategies are identified and explored: "innovation and appropriation" and "resistance and reconstruction."

In the first section of the book, the ways in which religious Jewish groups innovate and appropriate digital media is explored in order to explain these choices coalesce with their core values and communal goals. This is done through a series of case studies looking at a range of digital media from social media to websites and gaming. In "Appropriation and Innovation: Facebook, Grassroots Jews and Offline Post-Denominational Judaism" Nathan Abrams shows how Facebook empowers young Jews in Britain to form what he calls "pop-up" post-denominational congregations that also allow them to experiment and create new Jewish gathering that are both online and offline. Social media thus allow networked young British Jews new ways to gather outside any existing synagogue building and infrastructure, creating new forms of religious community.

Michal Raucher, in her chapter "*Yoatzot Halacha*: Ruling the Internet, One Question at a Time" explores the ways in which Jewish women use the internet to affirm and challenge Orthodox rabbinic authority offline. Studying Yoatzot.org, an online Q&A platform, run by and for Orthodox Jewish women, shows how the internet can increase women's authority in limited areas of Jewish law and alters the practice of Judaism for halachically observant women. Thus, this chapter shows the ways in which the internet affords women in Orthodox Judaism access to positions of authority in certain areas of Jewish laws. This echoes findings that show how the internet provides valued opportunities to have a voice within male-dominated Orthodox Jewish authority structures.

Heidi A Campbell and Wendi Bellar investigate Aish HaTorah's website and digital strategy in "Sanctifying the Internet: Aish.com's use of the Internet for Digital Outreach." Here we see an Orthodox group focused on bringing secular Jews back into a religious lifestyle integrate their outreach goals with their internet work. By functioning under a set of self-imposed rules and carefully monitoring that web content to Aish.com, staff members are able to make sure that the content and images on their website are edifying and support their values. Through a structured approach they seek to sanctify the internet, bringing a Torah-base lifestyle into the digital realm. This shows that concrete strategies used by some Orthodox groups to balance their internet use and to demonstrate that online presence can not only be seen as acceptable within a halachic lifestyle but as an essential part of a religious mission as well.

Entering the world of gaming, Owen Gottlieb demonstrated how Jewish designed digital games can become space for building fruitful relationships between traditional modes of Jewish learning and interpretive practice. "Jewish Games for Learning: Renewing Heritage Traditions in the Digital Age" shows how strategic games can be a conduit for Jewish learning that extend ancient learning practices into the digital age. Through a focused case study of current trends in Jewish Games for Learning genre within progressive Judaism, Gottlieb argues that Jews can adopt and adapt modern Games to religious ritual, sacred text and sacred study.

Finally, Aya Yadlin-Segal in "Communicating Identity through Religious Internet Memes on "Tweeting 'Orthodoxies' Facebook Page" shows how Jewish internet memes focused on Jewish religion are able to communicate religious humor that also validate the beliefs of the religious community. Through a study of the "Tweeting Orthodoxies" Facebook page and the memes it hosts and produces in relation to National Religious communities, we see how religious internet memes can be important vehicles to negotiate and represent the core cultural layers of their religious identity.

Through this first part, we see various Jewish groups and user communities utilize and create new media forms with a variety of goals and motivations. One constant issue discussed in these studies is the recognition that choices related to digital technologies and online engagement are informed by their users in beliefs, practices and expectations and are grounded in the offline communities and traditions with which they affiliate. We see that Reform, Modern Orthodox and Progressive/Open Jewish groups may consciously bridge between the online and offline contexts, as social media affordances are seen to complement and extend traditional practices in ways that can be contextualized within larger historical traditions or religious and communal goals. These groups have a positive or at least more open relationship with technology than do many other Orthodox/ultra-Orthodox groups previously studied, because they see digital media as a tool enabling them to extend their religious practices and values into another realm of the contemporary world. Having a positive or neutral view of the nature of digital technology allows them to engage and play with different digital media first, and evaluate its impact on the community second. Through bridging the offline and the online religious Jews, these groups are able to experiment and live out religious patterns of life in a new sphere while reflecting on the broader communal and religious implications.

In Part II of this book, strategies involving how different Jewish groups seek to "resist and reconstruct" particular aspects of new media are investigated. Attention is given to consideration of the reactions and discourses that emerge about problematic aspects of new media within some Jewish communities. Here the ways in which Jewish users and designers negotiate what may be perceived to be problematic aspects new media in light of the social affordances they offer or moral boundaries they may impinge upon are identified. Through this we see that new technologies often become consciously domesticated or cultured in light of community boundaries and expectations.

In "Legitimation of New Media and Community Building Among Jewish Denominations in the US" Oren Golan compares three Jewish denominations—the ultra-Orthodox, the Chabad and the Reform movement—and their use of new media. Based on interviews with webmasters, digital creative and analysis of online and offline texts, three distinct patterns emerge regarding to how different groups seek to legitimate their internet use: dualist, purposeful and inclusive adoption. Each scheme of legitimation reflects the different religious group's outlook toward modernity, perception of the "other" and religious authority and the extent to which religious webmasters and app developers can or should serve as powerbrokers within their respective religious groups.

Michele Rosenthal and Rivka Ribak explores how National Religious families in Israel negotiate the internet in their everyday practice through the use of a commercial internet service provider *Rimon*, which filters contents according to selected religious criteria. "On Pomegranates and Etrogs: Internet filters as Practices of Media Ambivalence among National Religious Jews in Israel" is based on a study of young National Religious couples and their choices concerning media adoption and use in domestic environment. While most of the participants expressed ambivalence about television, they embraced the internet, at least in its filtered version as provided by Rimon. This highlights how National Religious negotiations strategies with technology become important identity makers, how these markers are used to help frame and communicate their unique religious identity and how they seek to distinguish themselves from other Israeli religious groups.

Hananel Rosenberg and Tsuriel Rashi offer an analysis of *Pashkevil*, opinion posters, and the public discourse emerging around the rise of kosher cell phones in "*Pashkevilim* in Campaigns Against New Media: What Can *Pashkevilim* Accomplish That Newspapers Cannot." Through analyzing how Haredi-oriented *Pashkevil* operate and the distinct messages communicated about mobile technologies in the 2005 public campaign over the kosher cell phone, they show how these posters seek to support rabbinical leaders' rhetoric about cell phones and exalt the ban on Internet use among the ultra-Orthodox community. Here they demonstrate how *Pashkevil* provide insights into key debates offered by Haredi about how mobile media transgress the sacred-secular boundaries of the community, and can be seen a public performance of beliefs about the role and problems created by new technologies for devout "Torah-observant" Jews.

Finally in "The Israeli Rabbi and the Internet" Yoel Cohen investigates in details the attitudes of Israeli rabbis in Israel to computers and the internet. By promoting a philosophy of withdrawal from modernity, and seeking to maintain religious values in a cultural ghetto framework, ultra-Orthodox or Haredi rabbis have issued religious decrees against computers and the internet as being threat to Torah family values. By comparing the responses of different Orthodox, and National Religious groups and investigation the tension created by computer being presented as a tool for work and even for religious study, this chapter attempts to draw out a thorough picture of the range of rabbis' attitudes to computers and internet based on extensive survey research of Israeli rabbis carried out by the author. This work reveals important insights about Israeli rabbis' evaluations of internet regarding its impact on religious values, the family and the religious community.

In this part, authors investigate a variety of religious groups whose response to digital media range from hesitant to fearful, in relation to the perceived impact it can and does have on the religious and social life of the community. Some groups such as the National Religious and Chabad are more open to the Internet while still articulating perceived problematic affordance. This leads them to culture the technology in distinct ways through filter or sophisticated rhetoric's that set self-imposed limitations around the technology to avoid moral and ethical transgression facilitated by use. Other groups such as Haredi or ultra-Orthodox groups seek to draw a tight fence around the technology from the outset, lest new media technologies become a gateway to sinful content or behaviors. These chapters highlight strong resistance narratives employed in relation to digital media, focusing on resisting content through controlled media use, or even using restructure or specially designed media to resist or block media content. Here we see more conservative and tightly bounded religious groups' first response to resist rather than engage technology and, after critical reflection and careful evaluation, to allow for limited interaction and monitored use.

Overall *Digital Judaism* presents a broad analysis of not only how and why various Jewish groups negotiate with digital technologies and culture in particular ways but also how such observations are situated within a wider discourse of the ways in which Jewish groups have utilized communication technologies throughout history to maintain connection and their identity across time and space. By highlight interesting and important recent scholarship from leading and emerging scholars of Judaism and media in a cohesive collection, the text offers an invaluable resource for scholars who research and teach in the areas of new media, religion and digital culture.

## CONTRIBUTIONS TO THE STUDY OF JUDAISM AND NEW MEDIA

*Digital Judaism* makes an important contribution to the study of Judaism and New Media in several ways. First, it moves beyond the narrow focus of current research by investigating a number of important understudied religious Jewish communities including Cohen's and Rosenthal and Ribak's investigations of National Religious groups in Israel, Golan and Gottlieb chapter's exploring the Reform movement in the United States and Abrams's work on groups aligned with Progressive or Post-Denominational Judaism. Second, it expands attention beyond an interest in just religious websites and internet use to consider how different groups engaging other popular digital media platforms as Facebook (i.e., Abrams and Yadlin-Segal), gaming (i.e., Gottlieb), mobile phones (i.e., Rashi) and even mobile application (i.e. Golan).

Third, it spotlights a range of new theoretical and methodological approaches that can be useful in studying religious Jewish groups' engagement with digital technology. Rosenthal and Ribak illustrate how religious groups can be studies through actor network theory to investigate how National Religious shape internet practice in line their desire open to modernity while remaining "halachically observant." Campbell and Bellar uses an RSST approach to show how web innovation can be framed in a way that allows Orthodox Jews to justify their online presence as not only acceptable but also as essential to their religious mission. Gottlieb employs game theory, specifically taking a serious games approach, to show how explorations of digital and strategic religious games mirror continuous with ancient religious learning and textual engagement practices. These studies also show that diverse methodologies, from Textual analysis (i.e., Rosenberg and Rashi) and surveys (i.e., Cohen) to ethnography and interviews (i.e., Campbell and Bellar, Golan) and case studies (Raucher, Gottlieb), can lead to more nuanced and comparative investigation of the intersection between Jewish communities and digital media.

Fourth, it pushes the study of Jewish interactions with digital media beyond the simple focus on how or why religious groups accept or reject certain digital media toward identify the specific factor influencing positive and negative responses leading to innovations in practice, framing narratives and even the technologies themselves. Golan's investigation of different modes of legitimacy enacted in relation to the internet identifies three distinct negotiations strategies—Dualist, purposeful and inclusive adoption strategies—religious user may employ within their respective communities to contextualize digital practices while seeking to mitigate the technology's potential threat to religious values a communal solidarity. Blondheim shows how a historically grounded approach exploring traditional view of orality, text and Jewish law can be seen to foreground contemporary theological responses and critique of digital technology highlighting how ideology, media infrastructures and institutional arrangements enable the people of the book to perform as people of the network. Campbell and Bellar show the importance of identifying distinct rhetorical argument enacted by religious groups to contextualize and justify religious practice within the secular sphere of the internet, such as using a "prescriptive discourse" to frame internet use as acceptable because its primary target is to engage unaffiliated Jews. This draws attention to the need to pay careful attention to narratives and rhetorical patterns employed about digital media by religious users and communities.

In summary, *Digital Judaism* provides scholars with models for number of useful research approaches and areas of inquiry for doing focused and comparative work about the motivations behind how and why religious Jews in Israel, America and beyond consume, critique and create digital media for religious purposes. It also illustrates that studying Jewish engagement with digital technology can illuminate how digital culture serves as an important sphere for religious identity performance for many religious communities, whether this is to affirm traditional religious identification or construct new relationship among cultural, political and religious factors in the public sphere (i.e., Yadlin-Segal, 2014). By looking at a range of responses and innovations produced by religious Jewish groups we see the continued importance of fleshing out connections between religious tradition and new media practice.

These studies also highlight emerging research trends within the study of Judaism and digital media, which coincide with broader work occurring within Digital Religion studies. These include the importance of doing comparative work studying multiple groups across diverse religious sectors to more fully map the commonalities and disparities among different religious groups' strategies and reactions toward new media. Also we see a similar attention to research that compares online and offline religious practices, to show how offline beliefs and traditions inform online engagement and technology or platform design as well as how online discourse and behavior impact upon broader community boundaries, structures and expectations. *Digital Judaism* thus reflects the "fourth wave" of religion and internet studies (Campbell and Lovheim 2011), which notes the importance of studying online and offline practices and relationships together as religious groups, even those who see to resist digital technology, find themselves in a world increasingly influenced and shaped by the digital. Overall, the studies contained within *Digital Judaism* offers media, religious and Jewish studies scholar important models of how to conduct such research and consider the religious, cultural and broader social implications of different form of Jewish engagement with new media for the tradition as a whole.

## REFERENCES

Abrams, N., Baker, S. and Brown, B.J. (2013). Grassroots Religion: Facebook and Offline Post-Denominational Judaism. In: M. Gillespie, D. Herbert and A. Greenhill (Eds.), *Social Media Religion and Spirituality* (pp. 143–163). Berlin: De Gruyter.

Bagad-Elimelech, V. (2009). From the Far Past to the Present: Rabbinical Figures in Haredi Films. In: K. Caplan, and N. Stadler (Eds.), *Leadership and Authority in Israeli Haredi Society* (pp. 99–126). Jerusalem: Van Leer and the Hakibbutz Hameuchad (in Hebrew).

Barzilai-Nahon, K. and Barzilai, G. (2005). Cultured Technology: Internet and Religious Fundamentalism. *The Information Society*, 21(1), 25–40.

Baumel-Schwartz, J. (2009). Frum Surfing: Orthodox Jewish Women's Internet Forums as a Historical and Cultural Phenomenon. *Journal of Jewish Identities*, 29(1), 1–30.

Ben Shahar, R. and Lev-On, A. (2009). Forum of their Own: Studying Discussion Forums of Ultra-Orthodox Women Online. *Media Frames*, 4, 67–106 (in Hebrew).

Blondheim, M. (1997). Cultural Media in Transition: From the Traditional Sermon to the Jewish Press. *Kesher*, 21, 63–79 (in Hebrew).

Blondheim, M. and Blum-Kulka, S. (2001). Literacy, Orality, Television: Mediation and Authenticity in Jewish Conversational Arguing, 1–2000 CE. *The Communication Review*, 4(4), 511–540.

Blondheim, M. and Kaplan, K. (1993). Media and Cassettes in the Ultra-Orthodox Society. *Kesher*,14, 51–62 (in Hebrew).

Blum-Kulka, S. Blondheim, M. and Hacohen. G. (2002). Traditions of Dispute: From Negotiations of Talmudic Texts to the Arena of Political Discourse in the Media. *Journal of Pragmatics*, 34(10–11), 1569–1594.

Boyarin, D. and Boyarin, J. (1993). Diaspora: Generation and the Ground of Jewish Identity. *Critical Inquiry*, 19(4), 693–725.

Campbell, H. (2007). "What Hath God Wrought": Considering How Religious Communities Culture (or Kosher) the Cell Phone. *Continuum: Journal of Media and Cultural Studies*, 21(2), 191–203.

Campbell, H. (2010) *When Religion Meets New Media*. London: Routledge.

Campbell, H. (2011) Religious Engagement with the Internet within Israeli Orthodox Groups. *Israel Affairs*, 17(3), 364–383.

Campbell, H. and Golan, O. (2011). Creating Digital Enclaves: Negotiation of the Internet Amongst Bounded Religious Communities. *Media, Culture & Society*, 33(5), 709–724.

Campbell, H. and Lovheim, M. (2011). Studying the Online-Offline Connection in Religion Online. *Information, Communication & Society*, 14(8), 1083–1096.

Caplan, K. (1997). God's Voice: Audiotaped Sermon's in Israeli Haredi Society. *Modern Judaism*, 17(3), 253–280.

Caplan, K. (2001). The Media in Haredi Society in Israel. *Kesher*, 30, 18–30 (in Hebrew).

Cohen, A. (2005). The Knitted Kipa and What Lies Beyond It. *Academot*, 15, 9–29 (in Hebrew).

Cohen, A., Lemish, D. and Schejter, A. (2008). *The Wonder Phone in the Land of Miracles. Mobile Telephony in Israel*. Cresskill: Hampton Press.

Cohen, Y. (2005). Religion News in Israel. *Journal of Media & Religion*, 4(3), 179–198

Cohen, Y. (2012). *God, Jews and the Media*. London: Routledge.

Cromer, G. (1987).The Polluted Image: The Response of Ultra-Orthodox Judaism to Israel Television. *Sociology and Social Research*, 71(3), 198–99.

Deutsch, N. (2009). The Forbidden Fork, the Cell Phone Holocaust, and Other Haredi Encounters with Technology. *Contemporary Jewry*, 29, 3–19.

El-Or, T. (1994). *Educated and Ignorant: Ultra Orthodox Jewish Women and Their World*, trans. H. Watzman. Boulder: Lynne Reinner.

Frost, J. (2013). *Online Communication Practices of Reform Judaism Congregations*. Auburn University, PhD Thesis. Available at: http://hdl.handle.net/10415/3744 [Accessed October 2011].

Golan, O. (2013). Charting Frontiers of Online Religious Communities: The Case of Chabad Jews. In: H. Campbell (Ed.), *Digital Religion: Understanding Religious Practice in Media Worlds* (pp. 155–163). London: Routledge.

Herman, S.N. (1989). *Jewish Identity: A Social Psychological Perspective*. New Brunswick: Transaction Publishers.

Horowitz, N. (2000). The Ultra-Orthodox and the Internet. *Kivumim Hadashim*, 3, 7–30.

Jacobson, D. C. (2004). The Ma'ale School: Catalyst for the Entrance of Religious Zionists into the World of Media Production. *Israel Studies*, 9(1), 31–60.

Jaffe, M.S. (2001). *Torah in the Mouth: Writing and Oral Tradition in Palestinian Judaism*. Oxford: Oxford University Press.

Lehmann, D. and Siebzehner, B. (2006). Holy Pirates: Media, Ethnicity and Religious Renewal in Israel. In: B. Meyer and A. Moors (Eds.), *Religion, Media & the Public Sphere* (pp. 91–111). Bloomington: Indiana University Press.

Livio, O. and Tenenboim-Weinblatt, K. (2007). Discursive Legitimation of a Controversial Technology: Ultra-Orthodox Jewish Women and the Internet. *The Communication Review*, 10(1), 29–56.

Nevins, A.J. (2010). Rabbinate and Laity in the Internet Age. *Conservative Judaism*, 61(3), 65–75.

Pitkowsky, M. (2011) "Dear Rabbi, I Am a Woman Who . . .": Women Asking Rabbis Questions, from Rabbi Moshe Feinstein to the Internet. *Nashim: A Journal of Jewish Women's Studies & Gender Issues*, 21, 134–159.

Rashi, T. (2013). The Kosher Cell Phone in Ultra-Orthodox Society: A Technological Ghetto Within the Global Village? In: H. Campbell, (Ed.), *Digital Religion. Understanding Religious Practice in New Media Worlds* (pp. 173–182). London: Routledge.

Ribak, R. and Rosenthal, M. (2006). From the Field Phone to the Mobile Phone: A Cultural Biography of the Telephone in Kibbutz Y. *New Media & Society*, 8(4), 551–572.

Steinitz, O. (2011). Responsa 2.0. Are Q&A Websites Creating a New Type of Halachic Discourse? *Modern Judaism*, 31(1), 85–102.

Shandler, J. (2009) *God, Jews and Video Tape: Religion and Media in America*. New York: New York University Press.

Stadler, N. (2002). Is Profane Work an Obstacle for Salvation? The Case of the Ultra-Orthodox. *Sociology of Religion*, 64(4), 455–474.

Stadler, N. (2009). *Yeshiva Fundamentalism: Piety, Gender, and Resistance in the Ultra-Orthodox World*. New York: New York University Press.

Stolow, J. (2010). *Orthodox by Design Judaism, Print Politics, and the ArtScroll Revolution*. Berkeley: University of California Press.

Stolow, J. (2006). Communicating Authority, Consuming Tradition: Jewish Orthodox Outreach Literature and Its Reading Public. In: B. Meyer and A. Moors, (Eds.), *Public in Religion, Media and the Public Sphere* (pp. 73–111). Bloomington: Indiana University Press.

Tsarfaty, O. and Blais, D. (2002). Between "Cultural Enclave" and "Virtual Enclave": Ultra-Orthodox Society and the Digital Media. *Kesher*, 32, 47–55 (in Hebrew).

Yadlin-Segal, A. (2014). *"Fighting the War of God"—Religious Authority Affirmation Online: The Case Study of Our Future Website*. Conference paper presented at the Association for Israel Studies 30th Annual Meeting, Ben Gurion, Israel, June 23.

# 2 The Jewish Communication Tradition and Its Encounters with (the) New Media

*Menahem Blondheim*

Judaism, like digital technology, is binary. Unlike other religions, it is a nationality, and unlike other nationalities, it is a religion. Put positively, Judaism is the religion of a distinct people, and it is the core of that nation's peoplehood. This duality shapes the approach taken in this chapter to understanding digital Judaism: It traces the evolution of both Jewish religious thought about communications and unique aspects of its practice by Jews, from Genesis to the digital age. The purpose of this dual enterprise is to establish a basis for considering what is and is not unique about the Jewish contemporary encounter with "new media."

In what follows we divide the survey of approaches to new media in the Jewish past and present into two major parts. The first focuses on the religious aspect, outlining the development of Jewish media theology from the earliest layers of the Bible, through the emergence of the oral law and down to the ways Jewish law understands digital media. The second part focuses on the social history of Jewish communication, with an emphasis on its Diasporic phase, particularly since the Jewish Middle Ages and up to the present. Given this very ambitious agenda and the limited scope allotted to it, what follows can only be suggestive and exploratory. It is attempted with the Jewish sages' well-known caveat: "It is not incumbent upon you to finish the task, but neither are you free to absolve yourself from it" (Mishnah, Ethics of the Fathers, II 19).

## PART I: JEWISH MEDIA THEOLOGY

### The Biblical Era and Antiquity

A fundamental tension between and within world religions concerns the relation of the deity to humankind. Transcendence of the deity, its utter distance from the physical and human, represents one pole of this theological axis. The opposite pole is immanence, the notion of God being present in the physical reality of the world and in the lives and minds of its inhabitants. One way of charting the tension between transcendence and immanence is by reducing it to a question of communication: Can God and humankind establish, and possibly even maintain, communications? If so, what can mediate between the eternal, omnipresent and unalterable, on one hand, and the shifting time- and space-bound, on the other hand?

Theologies tending toward immanence, to include major trends in the Abrahamic religions, have responded to these quandaries by shaping media theologies (Blondheim and Blum-Kulka, 2001). Revelation—the godly presenting itself to the human in time and in space—and its media are the key theme here, and scriptures represent a dominant component of it. On the return path, religions have launched and shaped ritual as media by which humans may seek and engage the divinity, transcending the spatial and temporal limits of their world in the process.

Theorizing the supposed communicative encounter between God and man should be of interest not only to theologians but also to communication scholars, for at least two clusters of reasons. The first emerges precisely from the problem of God's transcendence—the fundamental challenge to which media theology is a response. The mere idea of transcending transcendence by media and establishing communications with God tests the limits of human communicative practices. It also sets the outermost frontiers of the idea of communications, as it gives way to abysses that cannot be bridged (Peters, 1999). This stretching of the horizon takes communication to places that mundane thinking about workaday media would never reach. Viewed from these extreme outposts, our thinking about communication may be richly complicated.

The second cluster of considerations is methodological or, in this case, historiographical: Media theology is the site of millennia of purposeful thinking about communications. In that thinking, the problem of mediation between heaven and earth touches the core of human existence, and thus, as a fateful, urgent quest, it received sustained and enormously intensive scrutiny. The resulting acumen, compiled over millennia, may be tapped by media scholars with profit.[1]

As noted, revelation stands at the center of the religious quest for understanding media. We argue that it has a crucial impact on its counterpart, ritual, and further afield, on a surprisingly large repertoire of communicative practices. In Judaism, as in the other Abrahamic religions, revelation is understood as the miraculous transmutation of the divinity from eternity and omnipresence to a kind of focused worldly presence limited in time and space. That kind of presence was inevitably understood by humans as a radical reduction of the deity, and it was only an aspect of it that was crowded into time and space—most commonly God's communiqué, complete with the agent or medium delivering it. But the reduction could not be complete; some residual attributes of the divine remained through the process of revelation, and they could be found in both the message and the medium.

When revelation took the shape of sharing a message with people, by its godly nature this message would inevitably retain some attributes of the sender. The message would be good for all times, reflecting God's eternity; it would have universal relevance, reflecting God's omnipresence; and it would feature performative power, reflecting God's omnipotence. The same would hold for the media of revelation: God's words and altars, angels and tablets, shrines and books would remain sacred. Humans could conceivably sanctify such media generically, but particularly when using them to try to engage God, turning revelation on its head.

Indeed, the early ritual of the Hebrews, as exposed in the Bible, appears to have been an attempt to emulate the media they understood God to use in addressing man, for communicating a response. In fact, we argue that it was the mere adoption of God's media, not the conveying of any particular message, which formed the core of early Jewish ritual. First, humankind adopted the visual media of fire and smoke to address God, extending the celestial sun, moon and clouds. Then people used sound as produced by instruments and, finally, the word: written and spoken. With the use of the word as an element of ritual, messages and meaning would come into play too, as they were conveyed to God by the same type of media the deity was believed to use in addressing humans.

### *The Media of Jewish Ritual: The Tabernacle*

The early institutionalized ritual of the Hebrews, according to the biblical account, focused on the tabernacle built in the desert after the exodus. Recent critical studies of the Bible point to two layers of text describing this phase of ritual. While both reflect priestly traditions, one, focused on Leviticus 17–26, is known as "the book of holiness." It pertains mainly to the temple's rites, and its main protagonists are Moses and God. Nevertheless, this layer's God is shrouded in holiness and is distant and transcendent. Paradoxically, this god dwells in the worldly tabernacle, and his nature emerges from verses that have the tabernacle as their focus and the priests as a sidekick to God and Moses.

According to these verses, there is a striking feature to the mobile Sinai tabernacle that differentiates it form other sanctuaries of the ancient Near East—or for that matter, from our contemporary shrines and temples. This feature is silence. As Yehezkel Kaufmann (1955) pointed out in the mid-20th century, and as highlighted by Israel Knohl (2003, 2007) in his recent studies of the priestly sections of the Bible, the tabernacle is a silent shrine, off limits to God's people and with but minimal presence of priests. These priests utter no words and sing no songs. In this silent temple the Holy of Holies is something of a hiding place for a distant, unsocial God who cannot be approached but who dwells for some unknown reason amid the Israelites, at the center of their mobile desert camp.[2]

This does not mean, however, that there was no reciprocity of messages in the silent tabernacle. In fact, reciprocity seems essential to the tabernacle, and a distinct linguistic feature points to this essential facet. An outstanding feature of the lengthy and somewhat redundant texts describing God's instructions for building the tabernacle, then their execution, and finally the description of the completed shrine, is the preponderance of the root *panim*—"face." The word appears in the context of the temple project numerous times. For instance, the tabernacle's table is built to hold twelve loafs of *lechem hapanim*, literally, "bread of the face," apparently because two sets of six loaves faced each other on either side of the table. The candelabrum's seven candles are to shine across "the face of the candelabrum." Most important, the two golden, winged cherubim positioned on the top of the ark in the Holy of Holies are to "face" each other, and God's voice emanates from between the cherubim facing each other.

Symmetry, reciprocity and facing thus seem to be the tabernacle's fundamental blueprint and, by extension, its purpose and function too: The tabernacle was constructed, and was intended to serve, as a grand interface. It would appear that just as people face each other, and as the temple's loaves of bread, candles and cherubim are to face each other, the temple's plan and purpose were to facilitate God's interfacing and communicating with people (Goffman, 1967).

### *Fire and Cloud*

The reciprocity model of face structuring the architecture of the tabernacle may possibly point to a more specific process of communication between God and man in the Temple of silence. The fundamental rituals performed every morning and evening at the temple were the lighting of candles and, in close association with it, the burning of incense on the gold altar. The burning of incense, morning and evening, is to result in "a perpetual incense before the Lord" (Exod. 30:8; see also 30:1–10). The two daily sacrifices were an extension of these rituals of fire and smoke.

The silent rituals of fire and smoke appear to have had a deep communicative significance underscoring reciprocity. For fire and smoke appear in the Bible as God's media par excellence. The earliest message from God to all mankind reported in the Bible, and referred to as a "sign" (literally a "letter"), is the rainbow in the cloud, and God's revelation to Abraham in the covenant was by "a smoking furnace and a burning flame" (Gen. 15:17). Subsequently God would appear to Moses in the fire of a burning bush. Then, after the exodus, pillars of cloud and of fire serve not only as a God-sent navigation device guiding the children of Israel out of Egypt, they are presented as a habitus God actually dwells in: "And the Lord went before them by day in pillar of cloud to lead the way, and by night in a pillar of fire to give them light" (Exod. 13:21). Subsequently God "looked down upon the army of the Egyptians through the pillar of fire and cloud" (Exod. 14:24, cf. Deut. 1:33: "who goeth before you . . . in a fire by night . . . and in a cloud by day"). Later, in the key interface of presenting the Ten Commandments, God will appear through a fire covered by a cloud (Exod. 19:16; 19:18; Deut. 5:4; 5:20).

According to these descriptions preceding the tabernacle, fire and cloud are God's media and signs. And indeed, in the tabernacle, the initial fire that lit the candelabrum is God given. This fire is guarded by the priests, who are to rekindle the lamp every morning and evening perpetually. That same fire is used, two times a day, to burn the daily ration of incense. The burning incense, in turn, creates a cloud of smoke that covers the shrine. This, its burning, as the high priest enters the Holy of Holies on the Day of Atonement, is described as creating a cloud: "for in a cloud I shall be seen" at the ark (Lev. 17:2).

God and man thus flash the same signs at each other: fire and cloud—they interface and interact using the same silent media. Underscoring the sanctity of the shared media is the terrible outcome of their unauthorized use, tantamount to breaking into a sacred conversation. Nadav and Avihu, the sons of Aaron the high priest, brought unauthorized fire to the temple and were burned alive (Lev. 10:1–2; Num. 3:4). The ordeal of Korach and his clan that ended when "the earth opened its mouth and swallowed them up" occurred when God rejected the incense they offered and accepted that of Aaron the high priest (Num. 16:1–24). But besides sharing a language of "signs" and "letters" of smoke and fire with humankind, the Bible's god also talks to man, in sounds and words, and a selected few could also answer by these same media.

### *Sounds and Words*

The first hint of sound in the Tabernacle emanates from the bells attached to the rim of the high priest's garments. Then, another sound would be heard in or near the Tabernacle: the sound of the ram's horn—the shofar. The ram's horn is God's veteran wind instrument. He sounded it on Mount Sinai when giving the Ten Commandments, but then God commands his people to sound it on special occasions, such as holidays and over sacrifices. The sound of the ram's horn may say very little, but by moving from sight to sound, it opens up an entirely new universe of communications between God and man while retaining "face"—the reciprocity model of the fire and cloud. The acoustic sphere gives rise to the potential of words (spoken or silent) and ultimately to verbal prayer, mediating between humans and their God.

Yet the theological significance of the silent phase of ritual communications cannot be exaggerated. Sharing a medium gives rise of the possibility of God and man communicating with each other. It represents a theological breakthrough, signifying that the Bible's God is not only the creator of man, and not only mindful of humankind, but seeks a living relationship, even a rudimentary conversation with his creatures.

The sharing of the same medium, language and meaning is what James Carey (1989) called, many years ago, the ritual model of communication (i.e., Peters 1999). The ritual model is opposed to the "transmission" model, which implies the conveying specific messages between parties. Carey's ritual model referred to the kind of commonness that unites people such as those praying together or sharing in the performance of other rituals. The Bible, however, suggests that it is in fact an aspect of transmission—the mere reciprocal sending of messages through the channel—that establishes "ritual" communications between heaven and earth. But the reciprocity of visual symbols and sounds, in revelation as in ritual, would ultimately be swamped by literary texts. These texts, written and oral, would become the center not only of Jewish ritual but also of Jewish religious culture.

### *Enter Script*

If the light of the candelabrum and the essence burned on the gold altar took center stage in the tabernacle, and God's words and the shofar were sounded there, another divine medium was also lurking in the Tabernacle. It had the potential to subvert the tabernacle, even to replace it. The cherubim facing each other, even as they served as the gateposts between which God's words entered the human world, were positioned on the cover of the "ark of testimony/covenant," as though standing guard over its interior. Guarded in the ark were supposed to be the tablets on which the commandments were inscribed (Deut. 10:1–5; Haran, 2009, pp. 146–154).

The ark and its cherubim thus represented a nexus of the orality and literacy of God's message. His evanescent utterings could be perpetuated by their being etched in stone and, by extension, inscribed on papyri or parchment (Haran, 2009, pp. 187–301). This modulation of the word, enabling continued presence, could transform verbal revelation, delivering it from present to future. This potential would demonstrate the far-reaching implication of the word only after the demise of the Tabernacle, and then the Temple, and the decline of revelation once the visions of the prophets were no longer reported (Zeligman, 1996).

With the eclipse of the prophets' visions, the scripted word became paramount in the religious universe as the vestige, in effect the continuation, of the history of revelation. The word would follow, however, the hallowed tradition of ritual employing the media of revelation. And indeed, henceforth the word would become paramount in Jewish ritual. As the center of ritual, the word became dominant, shaping a religion of prayer but, more important, of study of the scriptures, God's continuing revelation. Script thus became the center of the religious heritage of those who would come to be tagged "the people of the book."

### *Orality as a New Medium*

But before long the dominance of script in the religious heritage was challenged. A new medium emerged within the scripted, testament-based religious culture of the Jews, and it developed into the core of post-Temple Judaism. Ironically, this new medium was the old medium of revelation, and of man: the spoken, oral word. The reemergence of orality within text-based Jewish culture may be considered a surprising turn by the standard of traditional understanding of the dynamics of literacy and orality (Olson, 1994; Ong, 1982). Nevertheless, the latter reentered the cultural scene with gusto and carved out a dominant place for itself in parallel to, but as distinct from, the Jewish literate tradition.

Indeed, from the middle of the first millennium BC there is evidence that a body of oral law had developed among the Jews and, moreover, that a clear distinction was made between the written text of the Pentateuch and this body of oral supplements and interpretations. With the gradual canonization of the 24 books of the Old Testament, the distinction between the scriptures and the oral tradition became sharper and better defined (Leiman, 1991; cf. Demsky, 2012).

Since both the written and the oral bodies of teachings were attributed to God, his wish to distinguish his messages by the medium of their delivery implied no less than a divine theory of orality and literacy. Notwithstanding the assumed godly origins of both bodies of law, the role of human agency was acknowledged as much greater in the case of the oral law. This agency had two aspects: One was the transmission of the divine teachings not committed to writing from one generation to the next by word of mouth. The other was the derivation of the oral law from the written text of the Testament by means of God-given exegetical tools.[3] According to both aspects, God's original intent became subject to the human mind—to its powers of memory in transmitting oral edicts in the first case, to its intellectual powers to divine the "true" meaning of the texts in the second and, in both cases, to man's competence in applying the principles of the law to changing circumstances. Either way, an important implication of an oral law was the notion of accommodation—of God empowering the products of human intellectual processes (Funkenstein, 1993, pp. 88–121; Scholem, 1995, pp. 284–291).

Ultimately, God's supposed intent of having his messages deliberately divided between the oral and the written called for a careful and creative differentiation between the two, as well as other media. In particular, once the oral law was redacted, it was imperative that it be carefully distinguished from the texts of the scriptures. Two distinct sets of safeguards were created to ensure that the divine distinction between the oral and the written would be maintained. One concerned the strict preservation of the exact text of the written law, in its most minute detail (Spiegel, 1996). This would effectively prevent the infiltration of the developing oral law into the scriptures. Ironically, this elaborate body of oral law was dedicated to this mission. It included the strict regulation of the content of the written law, as well as of its form, to include the surface, ink, and process of scripting the texts, let alone regulations for their storage and handling (e.g., Maimonides, *Mishneh Torah, Ahava, Hilchot sefer torah* [laws of the Torah scroll]; Haran, 2009). The machinery for ensuring the exact preservation of the written law's content was ultimately incorporated in the *messoratic* system.[4]

But no less effective were elaborate mnemonic techniques for preserving the other part of the law while keeping it oral. The key to conserving the oral law without committing it to writing was an innovative process of oral "publication" (Lieberman, 1950, pp. 20–46; Sussman, 2005). These orally published texts took the form of mnemonic-rich sequences befitting oral rendition (Neusner and Chilton, 1997) and remained close to the life world of their contemporary Jewish society (Faur, 1986; Zlotnick, 1988). However, with time, these techniques were in danger of faltering, and gradually, in late antiquity and the early Middle Ages, the oral law was scripted. Then, early in modern era, it was printed (Heller, 1993). Once it entered the universe of script and subsequently print, the challenge of keeping the oral law distinct from the written law became much more serious, and it required most imaginative solutions.

The overall strategy that was shaped to face it seems to have been retaining the flavor of oral transactions—scholastic, sermonic or judicial, even as they were committed to writing. Thus, for instance, the Passover Haggadah (literally "saying") became, in essence, a written document that in itself said little other than serve as a menu framing and structuring oral discourse. But more dominant, and even more striking, was a literary contrivance that presents itself fully developed in the written text of the Talmud. This strategy was scripting the text as though it were a transcript of an oral transaction, giving the written text the look and feel of a conversation, commonly an argument or a debate. The Talmud in particular gives its readers the distinct notion of eavesdropping. Its editors throw open the doors to a virtual, but distinctively oral, study hall, in which the sages are energetically engaging each other in reciting, debating, and disputing the law. In this form, the orality of the law, even as it was frozen into script, remained distinctive (Blondheim, 2001).

## Jewish Religion as Law

Moving from antiquity to modernity, that the high sensitivity to the oral–written divide as an element of Jewish media theology would continue to condition approaches to the word as shaped by new technologies was inevitable. It was also inevitable that in diagnosing the religious implications of the electric, then digital representation of words, the test would be a legal (halachic) one, at least within traditionalist circles, that became known since the emergence of the Reform movement as "Orthodox" Judaism.

### *Jewish Law and the Media of Modernity*

Traditional Judaism stands out among the world's religious denominations in the sharp contrast between its relative indifference to theology and dogma and its engrossment in the religious significance of mundane praxis. Consequently, Jewish orthodoxy applies an elaborate body of religious law to the detailed analysis of real world performances, not least among them the practice of communication, and the use of media. The careful legal codification of communicative institutions, such as witnessing, vowing and even excommunicating, reveals characteristic, and occasionally surprising, perceptions and conceptions of media and communications in the ages of the Mishnah and Talmud as well as in subsequent epochs of Jewish history. The resulting legal construction of communicative tools and practices enables a particularly keen analysis of the meaning of new and transformed means and processes of communication. We have seen it in action, earlier, in the negotiation of orality and literacy in terms of religious law. This cumulative legal and historical acumen was a key to subsequent negotiation and regulation of new media, as they historically imprinted, and currently have an impact on, the Jewish experience.

In this tradition, problems such as the status of the electric and digital word require a halachic response, and at least nominally, religious leaders have the privilege and the duty of shaping it. These leaders—who are primarily legal scholars—are expected to consider the new technologies in detail as well as the legal implications of their use, in the process of shaping a halachic response to them. Rabbis had a relatively limited problem when it came to electric words conveyed as telegraph, radio or television signals and recorded on appropriate devices. They decided, for instance, that words stored or conveyed electronically could not stand for words uttered live in cases in which hearing a text recited was a religious requirement. The same would apply to sound more generally, as in the case of the obligation to hear the blowing of the ram's horn on New Year: Electric delivery would not suffice. However, the digital word and, more generally, the digital environment posed a much broader and more complex legal challenge.

When rabbinical authorities address the digital word, they inevitably address in depth some of the most fundamental issues emerging from the digital experience, even if in halachic terms. They must perform a rigorous deconstruction of digital communications, to apply the *Halacha*'s analytical categories to it, and on the basis of that application, shape an authoritative response. Two aspects make this process particularly fascinating from the perspective of new media studies: One is the highly detailed (one might say pedantic) and complex "external" analysis of the new media and their implications. The other is their consequent interpretation in terms of general principles and categories of religious law that dates back to antiquity. The analysis and the interpretation go beyond theory, or theology in this case. They have considerable practical implications in a religious culture that attributes paramount religious significance to workaday behavior and action.

### *The Case of the Digital Word*

A good example of this dual process is the case of the ontology of the digital word, a case that has received considerable rabbinic attention. Mainly in the form of digital responses to queries by laypeople, rabbis pondered whether the digital word should not be considered a material entity to which the elaborate legal framework governing religious texts would apply. At issue here is an elaborate set of halachic rules governing religious texts. They range all the way from the proper location and handling of the textual artifacts, to the problem of discarding them. A particular aspect of this overall issue is the problem of the permissibility of writing, and particularly of erasing, God's name: It is considered a Biblical prohibition. In practical terms, the distinct issues of handling canonized text and writing and deleting God's name overlap (Blondheim and Jackson, 1998; Cohen, 2012).

Responses by rabbis have been surprisingly uniform. They tend to make a sharp distinction between the written and digital word and the rule that the digital word is not considered to be in existence until it is printed. When it comes to digital devises such as CDs, discs, or media players, rabbis in their rulings acknowledge that they are material artifacts, yet because they depend on codes that only the CPU and operating system of the computer—its "brain"—can translate into letters, voices and colors, for humans the digital file is not a text.

Given the deep schisms crisscrossing the Orthodox community, the near consensus among rabbis concerning the nonexistence of the digital word is quite surprising. This broad agreement is particularly striking given that the ruling is not self-evident and that it is lenient: In cases of halachic doubt it has become standard to adopt the strict ruling. However, in this case it may be that leniency was perceived as imperative, and to sustain it, rabbis had to tend in the same analytical direction. There is a strong exegetical strain that views script as existing even when not affixed to a material object. Thus, according to Midrash, the Bible was given to Moses in the form of "white fire over black fire," that the holy writing on a burned scroll "ascends into the air" and that the *Halacha* even acknowledges writing on sand as writing, even if not permanent. In other words, there are grounds to consider digital texts as "real" ones.

In parallel, an extensive corpus of research into digital culture discusses the halfway status of the electronic word. In Brenda Danet's (2001) apt phrasing, it is not only an attenuated form of script but also an enhanced form of the oral utterance (Nayar, 2006). The near consensus of rabbis embracing the attenuation rather than the enhancement pole seems to be driven by the external rather than inherent merits of the issue. A decision that the electronic word was similar to script, would have led to activating a massive set of religious regulations that would complicate, even obstruct, the use of digital media, at least for religious purposes. For instance, no religious text could ever be deleted, and the PC would have to be dealt with as a sacred artifact (for instance, it could not be taken into a bathroom and nothing could be placed on it). By opting for attenuating the significance of digital script, these rabbis consciously made it possible for Jewish textual practices to exist in cyberspace.

However, by deciding leniently on the status of the digital word, the rabbis are forced into a problematic theoretical position with regard to a lingering problem affecting the observant, as well as other social groups. The problem concerns copyright, and a common dilemma is whether it is permissible to freely download copyrighted music files and streaming video, to copy protected software and so on. From the almost universal ruling that the electronic signal has no actual existence, it would follow that neither does it have any legal status (such as property, including intellectual property) that can be infringed. Simply put, if God's name—in digital—cannot be attributed to Her or Him, how could a music file be attributed to a musician? Moreover, the halachic notion of intellectual property is extremely prescribed and very minimal: In Jewish law, cultural production tends to be considered collective and communal. Yet the law of the land, and international law too, considers digital wares to embody real property rights. How then are the rabbis to rule concerning IP issues?

This latter horn of the dilemma is what gives many of the rabbis responding to such queries over the internet their solution. Rather than decide on the issue of IP rights in cyberspace in halachic terms, rabbis simply defer on these issues to the law of the land and instruct their flock to do likewise and to follow secular law on copyright issues. This is a legitimate and well-established halachic strategy in civil law cases, known as *dina demalchuta dina*—"the law of the kingdom is the law."

## Summary

Jewish theology is founded on the interaction between humans and God, based on shared media. In the latter phases of this religious media history, God is understood to reveal himself through scriptures. This gave texts and their processing paramount significance in Jewish culture, and it carried over to assessing the meaning of the media embodying them. The tradition of giving theological significance to media provides an important heuristic of novel media technologies, as illustrated by the case of halachic interpretations of digital technology. But Judaism is not only a theology and religion but also a social entity. Accordingly, attitudes to new media in Jewish culture are derived not only from their religious interpretation but also from an analysis of their social functions. This analysis is based on the unique traditions and structures of communications in Jewish society over the ages and down to the present.

# PART II: THE SOCIAL HISTORY OF JEWISH MEDIA

## From the Middle Ages to Modernity

The entrenchment of the oral law paralleled the continuing exile of Jews from Palestine and the building-up of the Jewish Diaspora. In this phase of their history, communications between Jews formed a unique challenge of connecting a people scattered over ecumenical space. That space shrank and stretched, its geographical contours changed continuously and the networks connecting individuals, groups and communities tended to be in flux. Yet from the book of Esther to the Wandering Jew, Jews found ways to maintain communication with each other. Quite remarkably, the extent of communication, contact and solidarity between Jews and Jewish communities was maintained even after the disappearance of a recognized Jewish religious center, with the turn of the first millennium.

Thereafter, a centerless Jewish people would live on through lateral communications in space as a flat virtual network, some nodes of the network better connected than others. This network would transcend geographical barriers and political borders. In the process it would adopt, adapt and devise novel communicative arrangements, demonstrating how the will to communicate creates ways of communicating, whether physical or systemic. One can indeed identify these three necessary dimensions of lateral communications—ideology driving to communicate, infrastructures for communicating, and institutional arrangements for carrying communications out, even after the fall of the centers of Jewish authority in early Middle Ages.

These three fundamental components of Jewish Diasporic communications—ideology, media infrastructures and institutional arrangements—can be anecdotally illustrated through three medieval episodes. The will to communicate emerges from a story, well known because of its relevance to the ongoing debate over the emergence of Jewish mysticism. The story has a 13th-century scholar from Acre, Rabbi Itzhak, hearing about the discovery of the foundational ancient text of Jewish mysticism. However, Itzhak also heard doubts as to the authenticity of the discovery. He therefore immediately sailed to Spain and met in Valladolid with the manuscript's purported finder, Moshe de Leon. Itzhak's self-appointed mission of verifying the authenticity of the discovery would ultimately fail, but that is beside the point, and so is the wide agreement that many elements of the story are apocryphal. For the fiction could only work if a Jew in Palestine could realistically be expected to hear conflicting scholarly news reports from as far as Spain and on the inspiration of a moment set sail and travel there from city to city, meeting and engaging local scholars and laypeople. The relevance of scholarly happenings in Spanish Jewry to a local Palestinian rabbi made embarking on an expedition to the end of the settled world both realistic and reasonable.[5]

When it comes to media—the physical layer of communications and their arrangement— Responsa from Europe in the 11th and 12th centuries, taken together, would seem to point to the existence of systematic, professional mail services arranged by Jews, serving Jews and operated by Jewish riders covering France and the Rhineland. These mail services included regular routes along which mail was delivered at a uniform price, as well as much more costly "express" services (*Tshuvot Rashi*, 241). This was a particularly outstanding enterprise when considering its environment—the inward looking, geographically static populations of feudal Europe. As historian Marc Bloch (1962) noted, "the last attempts to maintain a royal posting-service on the model left by the Roman government, had disappeared with the Carolingian empire . . . The relative slowness of messengers, the mishaps that at every stage threatened their progress, meant that the only effective authority was the one on the spot" (pp. 61–65). But the trans-local orientation of Jews seems to have overcome those localizing obstacles.

An illustration of the institutional layer of medieval Jewish communications emerges from famous ordinances (*takanot*) attributed to Rabbi Gershom of Mainz (ca. 960–1028), "the light of the exile." Of some 20 statutes commonly included in this corpus a large majority are communication relate, such as a ban on reading someone else's mail without permission. The general thrust of most of the corpus is international private law, regulating the legal relations between the localized Jewish communities that by Rabbi Gershom's time had become the focus of decentralized legal authority and between them and wandering Jews. It should be noted, parenthetically, that Rabbi Gershom's bans were to be enforced through punishing offenders with "excommunication." Taken together, this body of communication regulations demonstrates both the great challenge and the great resourcefulness in efforts to keep the Diaspora together, at least virtually.

## The Media of Modernity

The dispersed, centerless Jewish world remained connected and in many ways intact into the modern era, based on innovative and effective media arrangements and communication strategies. However, developments sweeping the Western world—where most Jews resided—in the modern era would pose new challenges as well as novel opportunities to Jews and Jewish society. Here, too, as in the logic of the medieval response to the challenges of Diasporic connections, one can discuss these responses on three levels: ideology, media infrastructures and institutions.

### *The People of the Network*

In the modern era, the ideological aspect of Jewish connectivity appears to drive social and communicative change. A series of revolutionary ideological movements, to include the Jewish Enlightenment, Hasidism and anti-Hasidism, Zionism, Socialism and the Reform Movement, among others, had profound effects on the Jewish mind, identity and social organization. These changes would inevitably correspond to highly significant shifts in the modes of Jewish communications.

The enlightenment and secularization presented a radical shift in European sensibilities and with them in Jewish ideological and social traditions. Early Jewish adopters of these ideas (*maskilim*) piggybacked on the infrastructures of the preexisting Jewish communication network to spread the new discourse and the new ideas to the most remote Jewish communities and hamlets (Feiner, 2011; Soffer, 2007). Indeed, the Jewish Enlightenment would develop as a movement existing mainly in a new discourse and in the media sustaining and carrying that discourse—books, pamphlets, newspapers, lecture circuits and meetings, often clandestine. It was a movement in the air, in the mind and in the media, not much of a movement on the ground.

The Jewish network also sustained a traditionalist parallel to the enlightenment and secularization: Hasidism, then the counter-Hasidic movement, and its influential satellite, the Mussar movement. These movements had greater physical presence in the community: Synagogues, courts, schools and Talmudic academies (*yeshivot*) served to ground their ideas. Yet similar to the Jewish Enlightenment, these new ideas spread through the Jewish world of Europe, creating contending supra-local movements. Although staunchly traditionalist in their rhetoric, they did not hesitate to adopt some of the same novel media used by the proponents of the Enlightenment to diffuse their ideas. However, the media mix of these countercultures also included well-embedded traditional media. They spanned the erstwhile underground Jewish mail, and all the way to the combination of the *balegula* (coachman) and his transport, the grand tradition of hospitality for travelers and the indefensible, but universal practice of synagogue and study-hall whispers and chat, together enabling rapid circulation of gossip and information, stories and ideas (e.g., Agnon, 2000).

Before long another pan-Jewish ideological movement would present itself—the proto-Zionist movement (*Hovevei Zion*), and following it, mainstream Zionism. It would compete with the socialist movement, also making major inroads in the Jewish community of the latter 19th century. Zionism, its later mainstream movement headed by a Viennese journalist, would launch a creative combination of new media and the veteran Jewish communicative apparatus. With all the variety in the media mixes of the major pan-European Jewish ideological movements of the modern era, in their institutional strategy these ostensibly revolutionary movements would prove staunchly traditional. They would try to unite scattered enclaves spread over the entire scope of the Jewish world, in a coherent network that would form a virtual supra-local community.

In the process, a further institutional implication of the ideological shattering of the premodern Jewish community was the breaking up of the formerly cohesive local Jewish community. Now Jews in local nodes of the network would be divided along the lines of Orthodox versus secular, and in some countries Reform too; they would be divided into congregations of Hasidim and Mitnagdim; some groups would be Zionist, and others not. In every city, town and even village, Jewish groups would form their own institutions, be they synagogues or schools, libraries or salons.

### *The Broadcast Option*

The Enlightenment had other implications too for Jews in Europe, and emancipation—the granting of individual rights of citizenship and political rights to Jews—was particularly significant among them. Jews could now have a political and social existence beyond the Jewish community. As individuals they could now become part of their national societies, and this novel option opened to them a new world of communicative encounters and activities that formerly could not have been thought of. Most significant, they could now be part of national communications that covered a continuous and coherent national space, characteristically by means of mass media. This kind of "broadcast" orientation challenged the Jews' traditional network orientation. Individual Jews could now address a mass national society, not only target messages to groups of brethren within it and in other national societies beyond it.

These dramatic ideological and social developments paralleled the emergence of new media, some based on novel technologies. Among these, perhaps the most radical even if not much noticed was the telegraph. It was a network medium par excellence, but one that also enabled broadcast-like applications. The news wire service interfaced between these ostensibly conflicting but in fact compatible potentialities. It served as a gigantic funnel, having a network of reporters spread over vast expanses send news via the sprawling telegraph network to the wire service nerve center. There the news gathered by the network of reporters was edited and integrated.

Given the network nature of telegraphic news gathering, it is perhaps not surprising that the founders of the European wire services were all Jewish: Havas in France, Wolff in Germany, Reuter in England and Stefani in Italy.[6] But not only were the wire service founders Jewish; their network of reporters was mainly Jewish too. This composition of the wire service's network of reporters was anticipated by Havas's Paris office early personnel list, which included Reuters and Wolff. The wire services thus represented a new type of institution that in turn integrated two major endowments: the ideologically connected Jewish Diasporic network together with the new infrastructure of the telegraph network (Blondheim, 1988).

But the other end of the wire service funnel followed a completely different logic, one John Peters considered a "gentile" orientation of "speaking into the air" (Peters, 2006). It employed the telegraph's potential as a broadcast medium. Once the telegraph network connected all its circuits, the wire service's report could be received, simultaneously, in all other stations on the telegraph system. Thus, from the wire service nerve center the integrated news report was broadcast by telegraph to the editorial sanctums of newspapers far and wide and, in a second step, to a national audience of readers.

The broadcast mode of telegraphy converged with other significant developments in mass communication, most prominent among them the rise of the cheap, mass-circulating dailies, and national magazines. Employing in turn new technological developments in the production of paper, printing and cheap, rapid distribution, combined with a new fascination with speed, the new popular press gained tremendous circulations. These new broadcast media of Europe and the United States came into their own in the mid-19th century, just as enlightenment and secularization were bringing about Jewish emancipation and participation in the affairs of the public in Western Europe. Just as in the case of the wire services, Jews could find in the new media of the times—most prominently the mass-circulating press—new sources for employment and wide open business opportunities, as well as the release of pent-up energies. Here Jews would appear to have been abandoning their historical communicative tradition of the network and joining the Christian and Gentile communicative orientation to mass, society-wide communications.

### *Between Two Worlds*

Many observers have suggested fundamental affinities between the new of modernity media and uniquely Jewish sensibilities (e.g., Peters). To point out only one, the fundamental function of the "professional communicator" an employment type that emerged, according to Carey (1989), in this historical epoch, was the translation of information from one world to another—usually from a specific, inner-looking context to a broader and more universal one. The journalist represents precisely such a "translation" model: delivering local news from a prescribed, parochial environment to a national one, from circles of political insiders to the masses and from the heart of economic decision making to markets, delivering and deciphering foreign news from one country to another. This type of "translating" was based on understanding and rendering events between two worlds or sets of mind, by a player conversant with both. Modern Jews, who tended to constantly translate experiences between two sets of identity, experience and consciousness were fundamentally prepared for a calling of this nature.

The most outstanding case, perhaps, for the adaptation of the people of the network to the new media of modernity would be the film industry. The hub of the industry, Hollywood, was composed, ethnically, very much like a *shtet*,with immigrant Jews dominating it (Gabler, 1988). The economics of the film industry were based on massive consumption: Only products appealing to millions, throughout the United States, would justify glitzy productions and bring windfall profits. The point was making films for everyone, and that required in turn understanding that which was generically American. Immigrant Jews, who inevitably looked at the new country, like they had looked at their European homeland—from the outside in—proved successful at that task, ultimately building a celluloid empire of their own. Just as Pulitzer, Ochs and many other "outsiders" in the newspaper industry had managed to make their products appeal to a heterogeneous, supra-local audience, the film industry managed to amass audiences on a new order of magnitude. Its product was ultimately based on crystallizing what was, as Carl Laemmle's studio would tag itself, *universal.*

The institutional dimension of communications in a modern world thus represented trends of both continuity and change. On one hand, the erstwhile Jewish network provided an infrastructure for new supra-local movements such as Hasidism and Enlightenment, Zionism and the Mussar movement, and they anchored new media projects such as telegraphic news gathering. But in parallel, the formerly coherent Jewish network gave way to competing socio-ideological networks. The rise of national mass media and Jewish participation in the new industry both reflected and affected the discarding of the old ethnic and religious ties by Jews in the Western world and their gradual assimilation into mainstream national cultures they helped imagine and shape. Yet a common sense of marginality and ambivalence may have united these Jewish practitioners and consumers of the new mass national media in the various nations, just as it could shape the experience of Jews joining supranational movements such as socialism, masonry, professional and academic organizations or even the promotion of Esperanto.

### *The People of the New Media*

The exciting swirl of the Jewish encounter with modernity—its ideas, its social transformations, and its media—would reach a tragic climax in the Second World War.[7] Other significant developments would follow in its aftermath, in particular the establishment of the state of Israel. These developments would shatter Jewish social and cultural traditions (e.g., Soloveitchick, 1994). Later yet, in the generation straddling the turn of the millennium, media would enter a phase of dramatic change. Perhaps in no other era in history had change in everyday life focused so sharply on one aspect of life as change, in the past generation, has focused on communication and information. The dovetailing of these two histories—the history of post-Holocaust Jews and the history of digital media—yields a striking complex.

The emergence of a Jewish state signaled a new turn in the communicative history of the Jews since antiquity. Although they had previously participated in national media, they did so not as Jews but as members of their host societies. Now, as Israelis and Jews, they would have to adopt the Gentile broadcast orientation, albeit in the interest of Jewish nationalism. Yet even though European Jewry was practically wiped out, Israeli Jews remained, until quite recently, a minority among the Jews of the world. Side by side with national broadcast media—in print, over the air, and through a variety of cables—the Diasporic communication traditions would have to be maintained. State-focused media were no more than part of the broader Jewish media environment.

There was more to maintaining the network orientation than the continued existence of a Diaspora, now homeland centered. Unlike shifty political and technological environments, ideological and cultural traditions tend to be persistent. Even with the launch of state-focused media systems, the Israeli context would provide glimpses of the Jewish religious and cultural communicative traditions. As a conclusion to the journey of Jewish communications from antiquity to the present and from Zion and back, two aspects of the encounter between tradition and the digital world are highlighted: One relates to mainstream Israeli society; the other, to a social enclave within it (Sivan, 1991). Both are merely illustrations of directions for further inquiry into digital Judaism.

## Adopting and Creating New Media

The engagement of Israelis with recent media technologies is unique, both as adopters and users and as creators and producers. When it comes to new-media use, an assortment of indicators from the latter 20th century shows a consistent pattern of extremely rapid, epidemic-like diffusion of the new media technologies to the household in Israeli society. In most measures of diffusion and use, Israel handily led the world, notwithstanding a per capita income much lower than in Western Europe and the United States. For instance, by 1995 Israel led the world in the penetration of cellular telephones. But while its margin over the United States (and Finland) in overall penetration was not dramatic, airtime use per customer was four times higher in Israel than in the United States. At least as striking was the diffusion of the PC in Israel. If in 1993 30% of Israeli households owned one, the equivalent rate for France was 11%; Germany, 12%; the United Kingdom, 18%; and Japan, 7%. The per capita income in all these countries was more than double that of Israel (Blondheim, 1997).

On the supply side, Israel's role in developing new communication basic-technologies, products and applications was at least as anomalous. Aspects of this phenomenon have been recently popularized in Senor and Singer's (2011) *Start-Up Nation*; however, little noticed has been the outstanding predominance of information and communication technologies in the overall output of Israeli high tech. History may be a key to this striking emphasis on media. The deep cultural investment in the word, in the diffusion of sacred texts, memories and ideas from one generation to the next and from one part of the world to others, to brethren scattered far and wide, may help explain this preoccupation with media technologies. So would the drive to transcend real and invisible barriers—religious, ideological, social and cultural—and, in the case of the state of Israel, geographic and geopolitical. These historical and cultural factors could be the deep roots of the ungainly involvement and innovativeness of Israelis and Jews in the new media industry.

Then, too, the start-up structure has dominated the development of Israeli high tech, unlike high-tech development in many other countries. This pattern is quite surprising, given the deep involvement of Israel's only two large organizations—the military-industrial complex and the government—in developing the new media technology industry. It appears that the explanation for the start-up phenomenon is to be found in deep cultural and social traditions, among them the social sanctioning of questioning, disagreement, even iconoclasm, high mobility and propensity for change, fluidity of life-style, social admiration for innovation and pioneering—one could go on. At least as important are dense social networks that allow rapid, multidisciplinary, organization building and aggregation. Even the unique patterns for recruiting investment and of marketing in the start-up milieu appear to echo Jewish network traditions: Both financing and early marketing of start-ups tend to be based on wide and sprawling networks of social connections, local, national and international, applying the best traditions of historical Jewish networking.

### *The Media Mix of Social Enclaves*

Another aspect of contemporary Israeli communications that may illustrate the role of longstanding communicative traditions is the resurgence of the ideologically defined community within the broader tapestry Israeli society. The focus here is on the ways Israeli cultural enclaves build communication environments of their own. We have seen that European Jews responded to the Enlightenment, to Hasidism, Socialism and Zionism by joining relevant breakaway local communities. In the process they splintered the formerly cohesive local community and linked their breakaways to like-minded communities at a distance. Israeli society seems to be experiencing a similar process, complete with new media solutions to sustain this kind of social dynamic.

While this tendency can be demonstrated through numerous ethnic, social, linguistic, religious, class and ideological clusters of communities crisscrossing the fabric of world Jewry and Jewish Israeli society, the most intensively studied case relates to the ultra-Orthodox segment. Numerous studies have traced specific aspects of the ultra-Orthodox (Haredi) media practices (a literature well documented in H. Campbell, 2010; Lev-On and Neriya Ben-Shahar, 2009), yet it would seem that taken together, this diverse catalog of communicative practices points to a more general strategy, or logic, that fits a deep historical pattern.

To trace it, it is useful to recall Tomita's discovery concerning the evolution of the media technology map in late modernity (Tomita, 1980). His discovery was the "Media Gap": While technologies such as telephony, wireless, fax and telex dramatically enhanced dyadic communications in real time, and while the likes of radio, television, and film dramatically expanded mass communications—both in real time (e.g., CNN) and in a delay (e.g. books, movies), nothing new was happening in the "communal" sphere. Media serves not dyads or masses, but communities and groups, and not necessarily in real-time or in great delay, but in intermediate intervals of hours, days and weeks remained stagnant (Russell Neuman, 1991). The new media of the past three decades would appear to be mainly oriented to filling in the media gap: From the web to Facebook, the focus of the new digital media is asynchronous, communal connectivity.

The media mix created by the Haredim can be similarly seen as effort to fill the media gap. As such, it coheres with the affordances provided by many of the new digital media. Seen this way, the media environment created by the Haredim represents a traditionalist response to the new social reality and new media environment. They have been creating a media environment that, while limiting dyadic media and bringing them under control, is rich in communal media that enhance internal discourse, and with it social control and social cohesiveness (H Campbell, 2010). Bulletin boards and mobile loudspeakers in the neighborhood, regular sermons and special mass assemblies, voice cassettes, CD newsreels, stand-alone computer software, kosher telephones and other elements of the Haredi communication repertoire all represent media that enhance communal integration and connectivity, blocking in the process the infiltration of mass society and its media.

This is in line with the cherished traditions of Jewish communication, translated from a global to a national environment. At the same time, unique communicative arrangements such as V-SAT broadcasts, wired telephone-based national and international networks maintain connections between Haredi communities over national and international space. These arrangements emerge from close scrutiny of media technologies and their affordances, according to the best halachic traditions that evolved from the ancient Jewish media theology.

## FINAL THOUGHTS ON JEWISH RESPONSES TO MEDIA

There appears to be a fundamental affinity between the new media environment—with digital affordances at its center—and the Jewish historical communicative experience. This affinity has a dual core: One relates to new possibilities in formulating content, affecting its creation and consumption, meaning and significance. The other concerns the communicative plans and systems that digital media enable. These two trajectories correspond to the two fundamental dimensions of Judaism: its being a religion and being a nationality.

As we have seen, the origin of Jewish ritual was the sharing of media, not messages, with God. This tremendous theological emphasis on media would be carried over to the era of scriptures, in which religious development was founded on a productive and highly conscious contrariety of written and oral media. The subsequent legalistic turn in Jewish religious life brought issues of media and communication generally and new media in particular to a very careful analysis by an elaborate and venerated system of religious law that came to subsume theology. This media-centric religious heritage inevitably imprinted Jewish culture with considerable attention and acumen in understanding media. One may see its implications in the complex religious construction of our contemporary digital media.

But at least as important as religious traditions in shaping Jewish cultural attitudes to new media was the unique social experience of Jews. "One people, scattered," the unity of the nation and the integrity of its heritage was challenged by plenty of time and plenty of space. But connectivity and unity could potentially be maintained by new media technologies, and plenty of new media technologies, infrastructures and institutional arrangement if engineered correctly.

The lessons of theology and history appear to have prepared Jewish communications for the media environment of the 21st century. Its core is the resurgence of the notion of society as comprised of individuals and minority communities scattered over national and ecumenical space. These global virtual communities are founded on shared content—words, memories, ideas, texts and often ethical or legal systems. At least as important to their survival and well-being is the communication system enabling connectedness and maintaining the group's coherence and solidarity. This notion of people existing as a network, scattered over space is in complete accord with the historical experience of the Jews and the media traditions they developed in its course.

## NOTES

1. Given the centrality of religious thinking to the historical development of ideas and sensibilities, theological understandings of communication may well have affected our contemporary sensibilities, whether religious or secular. Thus, reconstructing the process of theologizing media may help uncover biases as well as blind spots in our media common sense. Conversely, given the great temporal and geographic scope of religious thinking about media, their intensity and their consequent multiplicity and variety, media theologies are a potential source for what to us may be novel, even exotic ideas about communication and media. They hold the promise of challenging and complicating our present ways of thinking on these issues.
2. It would appear that Kaufmann, and particularly Knohl, take the theme of silence a bit far. For even if the priests are practically silent, God is not: The text has God speak to Moses repeatedly, just as it did when instructing him about every detail of building the Tabernacle, and then of its worship. But on the return path, from man to God, there is indeed only silence. Other layers of the biblical text include three recitations that are associated with the temple, but only one of them is relevant to the tabernacle, and that recitation is not addressed to God. This is the recitation of the Sota (Num. 5:11–31). The two other recitations in the temple are those on bringing the first fruits (Deut. 56:5–10) and on the periodic clearing out of tithes (Deut. 56:13–15).
3. The literature on the original nature of the oral law is vast. It features differing opinions as to the relative importance of the tradition as opposed to the derivation aspect of the oral law. See discussions in the sources quoted in the previous note; for a recent discussion placing an unusually strong emphasis on derivation see Harris (1995); for more general analyses see Silman (1999, pp. 11–38).

4. Scholar David Stern sees a connection between the development of the Messorah and the appearance of the codex. Supposedly, the Messorah was a response, intended to assure the accuracy of the text in the new medium. Yet an opposite construction is possible too: Many massoritic features can be construed as tools intended to preserve the insights generated by oral association and to assure their survival in an age of proliferation of scripted texts.
5. I wish to thank Aryeh Edrei for bringing this incident to my attention. By comparison see Gerber (2013, p. 1).
6. In the United States the early wire service—the New York Associated Press—was a cooperative arrangement of New York's leading newspapers. At the time of its founding (1846) none of the editors of those newspapers was Jewish, and the entire population of Jews in the United States was only about 25,000. Later in the 19th century Jews would become dominant in the Associated Press, prominent among them, for example, Ochs, Rosewater, de Young, Carvalho and Pulitzer (should he be considered Jewish; Blondheim 1988).
7. The total failure of Jews to muster help or even sympathy to their terrible plight, let alone wield the power to prevent it, was the ultimate and tragic answer to anti-Semitic accusations of their wielding great subversive power through their prominent role in the media. More fundamentally and as we have seen, Jews' prominence in the media reflected a desire to assimilate into the mainstream national society, not to subvert it or promote ethnic goals. When Jews did use media to promote their national aspirations, such as in the case of Zioninism, their goal was to leave European society, not to change or control it.

## REFERENCES


Agnon, S. Y. (2000). *The Bridal Canopy*. Syracuse: Syracuse University Press.

Bloch, M. (1962). *Feudal Society*, vol. 1, *The Growth of Ties of Independence*, trans. L. A. Manyon. London: Routledge and Kegan Paul, Ltd.

Blondheim, M. (1988). Jews in the Telegraphic News Agencies: From Wolff and Reuter to Pulitzer. *Kesher*, 3, 19–29.

Blondheim, M. (1997). Communication Technologies and the World of Knowledge: The Universal Construction and the Israeli Anomaly. In: D. Caspi (Ed.), *Communication and Democracy in Israel* (pp. 47–70). Jerusalem: VLJI and Hakibbutz hammeuchad.

Blondheim, M. and Blum-Kulka, S. (2001). Literacy, Orality, Television: Mediation and Authenticity in Jewish Conversational Arguing, 1–2000 AD. *Communication Review*, 5, 499–527.

Blondheim, M. and Jackson, T. (1998). *Mundane Religion, Sublime Technology: Performativity of the Digitally Communicated Word in Jewish Law*. Association of Internet Researchers (AoIR), Maastricht. Paper available upon request.

Campbell, Y. (1976). *A People That Dwells Alone*. London: Widenfeld and Nicolson.

Campbell, H. (2010). *When Religion Meets New Media*. New York: Routledge.

Carey, J. W. (1989). *Communication as Culture: Essays on Media and Society*. New York: Routledge.

Cohen, Y. (2012). Jewish Cyber-Theology. *Communication Research Trends*, 31, 4–14.

Danet, B. (2001). *Cyberplay: Communicating Online*. Oxford: Berg.

Demsky, A. (2012). *Literacy in Ancient Israel*. Jerusalem: The Bialik Institute.

Faur, J. (1986). *Golden Doves with Silver Dots*. Bloomington: Indiana University Press.
Feiner, S. (2011). *The Jewish Enlightenment*. Philadelphia: University of Pennsylvania Press.
Funkenstein, A. (1993). *Perceptions of Jewish History*. Berkeley: University of California Press.
Gabler, N. (1988). *An Empire of their Own: How the Jews Invented Hollywood*. New York: Crown Publishers.
Gerber, N. (2013). *Ourselves or Our Holy Books? The Cultural Discovery of Yemenite Jewry*. Jerusalem: Ben Zvi Institute.
Goffman, E. (1967). *Interaction Ritual: Essays on Face to Face Behavior*. New York: Doubleday.
Haran, M. (2009). *The Bible and Its World: Selected Literary and Historical Studies*. Jerusalem: Magnes Press.
Harris, J.M. (1995). *How Do We Know This? Midrash and the Fragmentation of Modern Judaism*. Albany: SUNY Press.
Heller, M.J. (1993). *Printing the Talmud: A History of the Earliest Printed Editions of the Talmud*. Brooklyn: Im Hasefer.
Kaufmann, Y. (1955). *The Religion of Israel, From Its Beginnings to the Babylonian Exile*. Jerusalem: Mossad Bialik and Dvir.
Knohl, I. (2003). *The Sanctuary of Silence: A Study of the Priestly Strata in the Pentateuch*. Jerusalem: The Hebrew University Magnes Press.
Knohl, I. (2007). *Biblical Beliefs*. Jerusalem: The Hebrew University Magnes Press.
Leiman, S. (1991). *Canonization of Hebrew Scripture: The Talmudic and Midrashic Evidence*. New Haven: CAAS.
Lev-On, A. and Neriya Ben-Shahar, R. (2009). A Forum of Their Own. *Misgarot Media*, 4, 67–106.
Lieberman, S. (1950). *Hellenism in Jewish Palestine*. New York: JTS.
Nayar, P.K. (2006). *Virtual Worlds: Culture and Politics in the Age of Cybertechnology*. Thousand Oaks: Sage.
Neusner, J. and Chilton, B. (1997). *The Intellectual Foundations of Christian and Jewish Discourse*. London: Routledge.
Olson, D. (1994). *The World on Paper: The Conceptual and Cognitive Implications of Writing and Reading*. Cambridge: Cambridge University Press.
Ong, W.J. (1982). *Orality and Literacy: The Technologizing of the Word*. London: Methuen.
Peters, J.D. (1999). *Speaking into the Air: A History of the Idea of Communication*. Chicago: Chicago University Press.
Peters, J.D. (2006). The Part Played by Gentiles in the Flow of Mass Communications: On the Ethnic Utopia of Personal Influence. *The Annals of the American Academy of Political and Social Science*, 608, 97–114.
Russell-Neuman, W. (1991). *The Future of the Mass Audience*. New York: Cambridge.
Scholem, G. (1995). *The Messianic Idea in Judaism*. New York: Schoken Books.
Senor, D. and Singer, S. (2011). *Start-Up Nation: The Story of Israel's Economic Miracle*. New York: Twelve.
Silman, Y.D. (1999). *The Voice Heard at Sinai: Once or Ongoing?* Jerusalem: Magnes Press, Hebrew University.
Sivan, E. (1991). The Culture of the Enclave. *Alpayim*, 4, 45–98.
Soffer, O. (2007). *There Is No Place for Pipul! HaTzfira Journal and the Modernization of Sociopolitcal Discourse*. Jerusalem: Bialik Institute.
Soloveitchik, H. (1994). Rupture and Reconstruction: The Transformation of Contemporary Orthodoxy. *Tradition*, 28(4), 64–130.

Spiegel, Y. S. (1996). *Pages from the History of the Hebrew Book: Proofs and Proofreading*. Ramat Gan: Bar Ilan University Press.
Sussman, Y. (2005). Oral Law in Its Simple Meaning: The Power of the "Tip of the Yod." *Mehkerey Talmud*, 3, 209–384.
Tomita, T. (1980). The New Electronic Media and Their Place in the Information Market of the Future. In A. Smith (Ed.), *Newspapers and Democracy: International Essays on a Changing Medium* (pp. 49–62). Cambridge: MIT Press.
Zeligman, I. A. (1996). *Studies in Biblical Literature*. Jerusalem: Magnes Press.
Zlotnick, D. (1988). *The Iron Pillar—Mishnah: Redaction, Form, and Intent*. Jerusalem: Bialik Institute.

# 3 Appropriation and Innovation

## Facebook, Grassroots Jews and Offline Post-Denominational Judaism

*Nathan Abrams*

While research into digital religion, including Judaism, has been growing, its scope of reference is still restricted in both geographical and denominational terms. The available scholarship, for the most part, continues to be confined to the United States and Israel and primarily focused on Haredim.[1] By far the most research in the area of digital Judaism, as Campbell (2011) has noted, has been conducted in terms of the Haredi engagement with the internet, which has overwhelmingly focused on the Israeli and US contexts (Barzilai and Barzilai-Nahon, 2005; Livio and Tenenboim Weinblatt, 2004). The problem is that such studies of digital use within Jewish religious communities in Israel and the United States are limited by their specific focus on Haredi denominations since Haredim have a fraught relationship with new digital technologies such as the internet and mobile phones (Campbell, 2010). Consequently, their use in generalizing overall patterns to fit non-Haredi Jews' relationship to such media, therefore, is limited. Furthermore, other work has been done exploring how Judaism has been/is done online (Brasher, 2001; Voloj, 2008), but this has not been extended to the offline or social networking spheres. In addition, the lack of cross-cultural comparative work and even less work that examines and compares Jewish self-definition globally has frustrated the overall picture. As a consequence, to date, non-Haredi digital offline Judaism in the Diaspora, beyond the two poles of American and Israeli Jewry, is virtually ignored. This chapter hopes to rectify these gaps through a case study of how young Diaspora British Jews, from across the religious spectrum, have developed their offline (as well as online) sense of religious self-identity through their interaction with digital media.

The specific focus of this chapter is on how Facebook has allowed new forms of Jewish practice to emerge, unshackled from the constraints of denominational control, or at the very least reinventing and reviving earlier forms. In this chapter, it is shown how Facebook has empowered young Jews, primarily based in London, to form "pop-up"—that is, small, emergent, labile congregations (Abrams, Baker and Brown, 2013)—in a post-denominational environment that has also allowed them to experiment with Judaism to a certain extent. Previous work has shown how

Facebook facilitated the creation of offline communities and, in so doing, helped to address feelings of alienation or disenfranchisement amongst post-denominational Jews dissatisfied with the existing communal and congregational infrastructure (Abrams et al., 2013). Furthermore, such communities provided greater opportunities for religious self-definition, as well as a *qualitatively* different encounter with Judaism. However, the longer term effects of Facebook are still to be examined, as the prior research, which focused on the emergence of one pop-up congregation, Grassroots Jews (GRJ) was only conducted between September 2009 and October 2010, and there were still many unanswered questions.

Grassroots Jews was chosen as a case study because it was the first completely independent post-denominational pop-up community in London that used Facebook to organize and form. This was done not within an existing synagogue building or infrastructure, nor in partnership with one, but entirely autonomously. At no point was communal approval requested or sought. In this chapter therefore, updating that initial research and undertaking the beginnings of a longitudinal study, by extending it to the present through on-going monitoring of GRJ's Facebook pages, is sought. This will be done in order to better assess the impact of this relatively young phenomenon and to ascertain what type of internal dynamic it has developed. In so doing, it will show how post-denominational Jews in Britain have responded to digital technologies by using Facebook to form pop-up offline congregations, divorced from the existing religious infrastructure. As a consequence of their negotiation with new media young British Jews' Judaism has been enabled in new and flourishing ways that very well may not have occurred in a more formal online/offline setting in which religion is dictated from above, that is, at the organizational level, rather than from below.

Data in this study was primarily drawn from online and printed sources, interviews with key participants/organizers, and ethnographic research. This took place over 2 years from 2008 to 2010, including attendance at many of these groups' events as well as the GRJ services. It included participant-observation in GRJ's Facebook group and monitored its ongoing posts.

## THE POST-DENOMINATIONAL CONTEXT

The use of Facebook has played an important role to help organize what occurred within a context known as post-denominationalism. Recent research in the United States has indicated a sense of alienation from Jewish communal organizations and experiences among 20- and 30 year-olds who perceive them to be boring and uninviting (Kelman and Schonberg, 2008). The result has been a general decline in synagogue membership and financial contributions (Cohen and Kelman, 2007b), as well as in denominational affiliation, as greater numbers of younger Jews identify as "just

Jewish" rather than Reform, Conservative or Reconstructionist than in the past (Cohen et al., 2007). Cohen and Kelman (2007a) noted that "as institutions experiment with ways to understand and engage the next generation, many younger American Jews have begun creating their own opportunities for Jewish engagement that are relatively independent of existing communal organizations and institutions" (p. 4). Many among the Jewish-educated leaders of the next generation are choosing to pursue Jewish life outside of institutional structures (Bleyer, 2007; Cohen et al., 2007; Cohen and Kelman, 2006). "Rather than following their parents into the halls of synagogues and federations, a significant segment of younger Jews are seeking to create new avenues of, and opportunities for, Jewish involvement that do not replicate older patterns of Jewish communal participation" (Kelman and Schonberg, 2008, p. 12).

Commentators have defined this experience as that of the "post-denominational Jew." The post-denominational Jew "refuses to be labeled or categorized in a religion that thrives on stereotypes. He [*sic*] has seen what the institutional branches of Judaism have to offer and believes that a better Judaism can be created" (Rosenthal, 2006, p. 20). Rather than reject Judaism wholesale, or "engage in community structures they find alienating or bland" (Kelman and Schonberg, 2008, p. 12), post-denominational Jews use their creativity and commitment to organize independently, to build meaningful Jewish experiences and to create ritual on their own terms outside of community institutions but within their own organic community of friends and family. They resist labeling by existing religious institutions and reject existing branches of Judaism to create something more fluid. This trend is seen both in American and European contexts. These Jews tend to be, but are not exclusively, those younger than 30 who often feel excluded from religious life. As Lurie (2011) put it, "justifiably so: the suburban mausoleum that is the liberal synagogue was, at best, built for a sociological reality decades out of date" (p. 25). This has become known as "*Do-it-Yourself (DIY)*" (Kelman and Schonberg, 2008, p. 12) or "empowered" Judaism (Kaunfer, 2010). Graham (2004) has drawn attention to "an ongoing process of identity development" (p. 22) in Europe, what Webber (1994) has termed "a reconstruction of identity" especially by the young (p. 22). Dencik (2005) uses the term "ethno-cultural smorgasbord" (p. 54). As early as 1977, Stein and Hill (1977) coined the term "dime store ethnicity" in which individuals pick and choose from a variety of ethnic identities. Using these observations Graham (2004) uses a more generalized term, namely "Pick 'n' mix Judaism," reflecting an environment in which European Jewry now finds itself that is "open and welcoming and encourages choice and personal preference above rules and dictates—Pick 'n' mix Judaism is European Jewry's adaptive response to this new environment" (p. 22). Pick 'n' mix post-denominational Judaism provided the essential grounding needed for the developments in offline religion enabled by Facebook.

## PICK 'N' MIX DIY JUDAISM IN THE UK

Since 2005, the British Jewish community has seen the growth of a number of self-organizing pop-up communities and congregations. These are grassroots, bottom up, young people generated activities, reflecting their rejection of institutional structures, as well as expressing the values of diversity and inclusiveness already witnessed in the United States in an offline setting. Young British Jews have been inspired by the annual Limmud conference. Founded in 1980, Limmud has grown into "a world-leader in cross-communal, multigenerational, volunteer-led Jewish learning experiences" (Simonson, 2011, p. 862). Based on their experiences at Limmud, young British Jews have followed its example to create truly grassroots, volunteer-owned and volunteer-led pop-up communities. These Jews shared a common passion for Jewish learning and engagement in its broadest sense, something they were involved with of their own volition. A group of these Jews, who were mainly friends, initiated a series of activities and events. They did so without the interference of the professionally staffed organizations around the British-Jewish community—although over the years, such organizations have carried out the important task of providing support to these growing pop-up communities. The most prominent of these groups are Wandering Jews (www.wanderingjews.co.uk/), Carlebach Minyan[2] Belsize Park, Jewdas (www.jewdas.org/) and MoHoLo (www.moishehouse.org/houses_a.asp?HouseID=22; see Kranz, 2011).

These pop-up communities and congregations pride themselves on creating gatherings that they felt were pluralist, inclusive, heartfelt, soul centered, intellectually inspiring, vibrant and full of vitality to fill the gap of what they often find so lacking in more traditional communal events (Russell, 2009, p. 11). They are self-organizing collectives characterized by their refusal to be labeled by the existing denominational tags; for example, they typically draw in participants from the existing mainstream branches of Reform, Liberal and Orthodoxy (Haredim are usually absent unless they are ex- or lapsed Haredi), as well as the religiously unaffiliated. The philosophy and principles of these collectives are to create very different Jewish spaces to the synagogues and other communal organizations, as well as to be egalitarian, democratic, peer-led, informal and inclusive. They are avowedly open, welcoming to non-Jews, organized and led by volunteers, have no paid clergy or denominational affiliation, meet at least once a month and are not linked formally or directly with any of the mainstream communal organizations in the United Kingdom. Neither age nor bank balance is a barrier to the level of involvement or to the roles that can be take on. In all of these ways, they perceive themselves to be different from the existing communal infrastructure.

These groupings subscribe to a very broad definition of Jewishness in an arena where such definitions are complex and contested. In Britain today, there are two main categories of Jewish identity: ethno-cultural-historical and religious. Within the second category, according to *Halacha* (Hebrew: Jewish law), that is, normative rabbinic Judaism there are two ways of being Jewish: being born to a Jewish mother or "by choice," that is, through a process of conversion by a recognized rabbinic authority. However, *Halachic* (Hebrew: according to Jewish law) Judaism can further be subdivided into Masorti (Hebrew: traditional), Modern Orthodox and Haredi, which may or may not agree on what constitutes Jewishness because they may refuse to recognize and sanction conversions carried out under each other's auspices. This was evidenced by a fairly recent controversy in which a Masorti pupil was denied entry to the Jews' Free School (JFS), an Orthodox Jewish school in Brent, northwest London.[3] Furthermore, normative rabbinic Judaism's privileging of matrilineal descent is being challenged by the Liberal and Progressive movements' recognition of descent through the male line only, that is, patrilineal descent. As a consequence, there is no single, common agreed British Jewish identity (Graham, 2004). Rather than take sides, these groups allow Jews to self-identify. It has been argued elsewhere that this propensity to identify as Jewish is the only genuinely common Jewish characteristic, that is, what makes a person Jewish is saying s/he is one. This approach was adopted by the European Community–funded research consortium DIALREL: Encouraging Dialogue on Issues of Religious Slaughter (www.dialrel.eu/) and the "Identity à la carte" project (2011), respectively. Both interviewed self-declared Jewish participants, that is, where the respondent and his or her relatives, grandparents, parents, partner and children were identified to be Jewish if he or she did so him- or herself. Like these models, Jewishness was defined in the broadest possible fashion, with no preconditions placed on this classification, to include anyone who self-identifies as Jewish, regardless of their actual *Halachic* or legal status. This is important here because young British Jews are not always relying on normative definitions of who is a Jew or of Judaism in constructing their offline pop-up congregations.

These groupings are, in some ways, descendants or heirs of the *Havurot* (Hebrew: fellowships), those participatory communities that sprang up in the 1960s and 1970s in the United States and were marked by a "countercultural, anti-institutional, Do-It-Yourself aesthetic" (Lurie, 2011, p. 25). What is different, however, is that each of these *offline* activities has been facilitated through extensive Facebook coordination and networking. Indeed, Carlebach Minyan is an invite-only secret group. Jonathan Boyd (2009b), the only scholar thus far to pay serious attention to this development, has argued:

> These members of the 'Net Generation' who have grown up with the internet, differ significantly from their forebears in Jewish outlook, expectations and notions of community. They have little faith in the 'authoritative' or 'authentic' view—they scrutinize information online, and decide what makes sense to them. They refuse to be passive

> consumers—they satisfy their desire for choice, convenience, customization and control by designing their own products. And they don't retreat into a lonely world behind their computers, they collaborate and network in the vast array of communities line.

It should also be added here that they also collaborate and network with a vast array of *offline* communities. The trend toward post-denominationalism directly correlates to the growth of social media usage among young Jews in Britain today. The more alienated and disenfranchised they may feel, the more likely they are to look for alternatives using Facebook (and other digital media). It is the contention of this chapter that the rise of offline pop-up communities via Facebook is a product and example of post-denominationalism.

## THE SEEDS OF GRASSROOTS JEWS ARE PLANTED

Grassroots Jews provides an illuminating case study illustrating many of the trends under discussion in this chapter: DIY Judaism, post-denominationalism, bottom up and Facebook enabled. It also took place in the Diaspora beyond Israel and the United States and involved a spectrum of religiously affiliated and unaffiliated Jews, including Modern Orthodoxy, Masorti, Reform, Liberal and Progressive, as well as those who have opted out of joining an established synagogue or movement. Furthermore, given the nature of English as a lingua franca, combined with London's function as a transnational hub for European and other Jews who move there in terms of financial markets, banking, international finance, and other employment opportunities (Kranz, 2011), the potentialities for its transference beyond Britain are heightened and more potent than if, say, GRJ had occurred in another European capital, particularly one in which there may be language limitations.

In 2009, a small group of volunteers involved in the alternative Jewish groups mentioned earlier (namely, Wandering Jews, Carlebach Minyan and MoHoLo) met, both online and offline, to organize their own offline Rosh Hashanah (Jewish New Year) and Yom Kippur (Day of Atonement) services. Feeling that their voices were not heard within mainstream British Judaism, and rather than becoming angry with the existing denominations, they decided to turn their back on them and to find or create what they liked. Consequently, using the internet in general and Facebook in particular, this group set about to produce its own alternative in which, as (2009a) pointed out, "most of all, they want to do it their way, on their terms, and with their people." They named themselves "Grassroots Jews." The group's very name encapsulates their aspirations: to build something completely new, alternative and from the bottom up, not to rely on existing choices.

Significantly, the organizers and participants were not marginalized Jews. They are what Cohen, Landres, Kaunfer, and Shain (2007) described as "groomed, not bloomed Jews." "Their renegade independence from the denominational label has been made possible by years of communal education, involvement, and training in denominational institutions," training for which the established movements have reaped little reward (Lurie, 2011, p. 28). Most of them are in the late 20s to early 40s age band and are well known for their communal activism, individuals who cut their teeth in such mainstream organizations as the Union of Jewish Students, Bnei Akiva, Noam, RSY-Netzer and Limmud, as well as the new initiatives mentioned earlier. Some of them are even the children of well-known rabbis. "In short," as one commentator pointed out, "people you would think the community would be bending over backwards to include within existing frameworks" (Schalit, 2009).

They described themselves thus: "We are a group of friends with many different Jewish backgrounds and perspectives." A blog (http://grassrootsjewishnewyearproject.wordpress.com/2010/09/03/ellul-boot-camp/), Facebook group (www.facebook.com/groups/97599398526) and website (http://grassrootsjews.org) were set up; a downloadable video (http://vimeo.com/5667190) was produced promising "the most exciting autonomous & non-hierarchical Judaism ever to surface" and a series of invitations were sent out, via Facebook. A flat fee of £45 for the services was requested; however, the inability to pay was taken into consideration, and others paid what they could afford. At the time of writing, the price stood at £37 (approximately US$55; see grassroots.org/registration). As Boyd (2009) observed, GRJ members are "largely unwilling to buy into a model of community that implicitly, if not explicitly, demands that they sign-up for the whole synagogue package at considerable expense." A second promotional video (http://vimeo.com/14154519) clearly symbolizes how GRJ members feel about the existing options. Opening with shots of a traditional Reform service, after 44 seconds it cuts to a black screen emblazoned with the large white letters "Bored of *shul* [Yiddish: synagogue]?" as a reggae soundtrack blares over a montage sequence of traditional Jewish iconography including *Haredim* dancing the *hora*, synagogue interiors, the Torah, Hebrew lettering, praying and so on. Such imagery is then intercut with a series of statements: "Looking for something new and fresh?" "A new form of community," and "Where do you belong?" Thus, the group clearly positions itself as one which would appeal to those who are seeking both novelty and a sense of belonging.

The aim of the independent High Holy Days, namely, Rosh Hashana (Jewish New Year) and Yom Kippur (Day of Atonement), services were to be as avowedly religiously inclusive, participatory, friendly and nonhierarchical as possible. There were no age restrictions, and newborn babies through to grandparents were in attendance. A guest cantor and a teacher from Israel—a musician and a professor of medieval Jewish history at the

University of Haifa—was flown in. The initial venues were a marquee in the back garden of a private home and a classical music concert hall, both in North West London. In its second year of operation, GRJ relocated to the premises of the Moishe House in North West London, where it has remained since, and prompting one participant to wonder if GRJ can continue to grow there.

GRJ services took place along *Halachic*, that is, normative rabbinic lines, but with some distinct and nontraditional differences. Women were called up to the Torah in accordance with *Halacha*, led the *davening* (Yiddish: praying), and sang the *haftorah* (Hebrew: a short reading from the Prophets following the reading of the Torah in synagogue). In fact, one of the unique features of GRJ is that where for many communities, *leyning* (Yiddish: reading from the Torah) is considered the preserve of the professional Torah reader, at GRJ the Torah reading can be done by everyone or anyone, regardless of age, experience, qualifications, and gender. In 2011, 26 people, 14 women and 12 men, volunteered to *leyn*, 15 of whom did it for the first time. Innovatively, what they dubbed a "*trihitza*," was provided. The word *trichitza* is a neologism based on the Hebrew word for a partition (*mechitza*) that traditionally segregates men and women in Orthodox and Haredi congregations. The *trichitza*, in contrast, divided the worship space into three discrete areas of seating: men, women and a mixed section along Reform/Liberal/Progressive/Masorti lines. Finally, there was an unallocated area, described as "freewheeling, open, free to come and go, chill out spaces, cushions, tents, friendly, space for mothers and babies" including "space for breastfeeding." GRJ presupposes some of "the permanence of innovations made by Reform and Conservative movements in having women lead all parts of the services, men and women [can] sit together, and both [can] count in the prayer quorum" (Lurie, 2011: 25), but at the same time, as the preceding arrangements demonstrate, it is flexible enough on these issues in order to accommodate those who are more to the right on the religious spectrum. GRJ is united in its desire to provide an egalitarian experience, "usually with the full liturgy, but with *feeling*" (Lurie, 2011: 25). Thus, GRJ's innovations rely on older, canonical and traditional religious practices.

In these ways, GRJ attempts to blend the traditional with the innovative. Its preference for Hebrew prayer and traditional liturgy is one indicator of its emphasis on the traditional but also most likely stems from the upbringing of a sizable number of attendees, United Synagogue—the British variant of mainstream Orthodoxy/American Conservatism. Drawing on the Jewish exegetical tradition, GRJ believes that exploring, questioning and challenging are important. At the same time, however, GRJ investigated alternatives to tradition not typically found in mainstream religious infrastructure in the United Kingdom, such as parallel sessions with less structure and more spontaneity, including experimental approaches to prayer, meditation and yoga. In this way, GRJ aimed to inject a more joyful spirit and sense of exploration to its services.

Another distinctive feature of GRJ is its attempt to accommodate the varying religious traditions based on country of origin. Typically, in addition to denominational distinctions, Jewish congregations in the United Kingdom are organized along lines based on origin. These include Sephardi Jews, those whose descendant hail from North Africa, southern Europe and the Asian subcontinent; Mizrahi or Middle Eastern Jews; and Ashkenazi (eastern and central Europe) Jews. Each group has its own liturgical traditions or *nusach*, which overlap with the aforementioned denominational divisions, but which are rarely blended. GRJ, in contrast, sought not to base its service on any single one of these but to allow its services to be dictated by the plurality of voices within its midst. My observation was that while the majority of attendees were British Ashkenazim, there were other participants from differing countries who were not all Ashkenazi. Israelis were few in number.

It is clear then that GRJ feel that inclusiveness, experimentation, exploration and a spirit of joy are missing from the typical communal fare in the United Kingdom and that such fare is the antithesis of "heartfelt, soul centered and intellectually inspiring." As one blogger put it, "the Judaism they find elsewhere in the community is rather dull, meaningless and stuffy" (Schalit, 2009). Have "you ever sat in Shul and thought 'there must be more to it than this?' " GRJ asked. Thus, if mainstream Jewish religious organizations are not willing or are not able to provide this outlet, GRJ will, but not by challenging the mainstream organizations to change from within but by providing their own alternatives.

Reflecting the American experience, core participants have a more serious commitment to community and to prayer than the average synagogue member/goer, who can rely on institutional staff to look after logistics and lead prayers (Lurie, 2011, p. 27). The nucleus of GRJ is predominantly, but not exclusively, single, unmarried or recently married young adults in their 20s and 30s. They represent what has been variously labeled in the United States as "the long-extended enabled adolescence," "post-college, pre-whatever" (Kaunfer, quoted in Shapiro, 2010), "emerging adulthood" (Arnett, 2004) or "the odyssey years" (Brooks, 2007). This is a 10- to 15-year post-university period in which, underwritten by their parents (or by good jobs), middle- and upper middle-class Jews postpone such responsibilities as marriage, children and supporting Jewish institutions financially (Lurie, 2011, p. 26).

Two examples from different ends of the religious spectrum illustrate the appeal of GRJ. In an interview in the *Jewish Chronicle*, 30-year-old Zoe Jankel, a Reform Jew who was a member of the GRJ organizing committee in 2009, explained the motivations for her involvement. She initially described herself as "barely religious and rarely interested in matters of the spirit." Her non-Jewish friends identify her as a "cultural Jew," and she "mainly avoids synagogue," but on the "rare occasions" she attends, she will sit, hiding her paperback inside a prayer book, "studiously ignoring the prayers" around her and hence "not an obvious contender for involvement in something such as Grassroots Jews." At the same time, however, she describes her participated for the past 10 years or so as

> both actively and passively in a number of informal Jewish organizations, most of which concentrate on the evolution of Judaism into a practice relevant to our lives today. For me this is not just a cultural affiliation—it is definitely a connection to the religious practice—one that is not synagogue-based but is fluid and changing and more in line with the world outside the walls of prayer.

Like many young Jews, Zoe enjoys the experience of *Rosh Hashanah* and *Yom Kippur* with her family but is turned off by the synagogue service, which she finds very passive ("It used to be quite a lot of looking at my watch"), "quite dry" and "boring" and denies her agency ("Last year I was a little bit annoyed with myself because I thought I could have just stayed at home"). That is one of the key reasons she became involved with GRJ because it allowed her a sense of ownership and action in constructing the sort of services *she* would like to attend ("We're all involved in creating this for the first time"), but at the same time, as many of her friends were involved, an important social aspect was also provided. Clearly she was dissatisfied with the existing religious infrastructure ("I think Grassroots Jews is a commentary on today's synagogues. It's a way to move forward and to engage in what is going on in the Jewish community"; Kasriel, 2009).

GRJ coordinator in 2011 Rachel Marcus, also aged 30, hails from a committed Orthodox family. She studied at a seminary in Israel in her gap years before university. She was drawn to the independent pop-up scene after arriving in London following her graduation from university and finding "nothing that really got me excited Jewishly." At mainstream synagogues, she found there was little to contribute "unless you are a member somewhere, you send your children to *cheder* [Hebrew: religion classes], and unless you are a man." Lack of female participation was a key motivating factor in deciding to reject the mainstream and attend the GRJ alternative: "If I was counted in an Orthodox *minyan*, I'd be there every morning." Yet Rachel did not want to reject Orthodoxy. When it came to planning the GRJ High Holy Day services, she said, "It was very important for us that those who consider themselves within the spectrum of Orthodoxy would also be able to feel comfortable" (quoted in Rocker, 2011).

As Abrams et al. (2013) noted initial participant feedback following the 2009 services was overwhelmingly positive (albeit on the proviso that the "open" nature of Facebook was likely to preclude negative comments) because GRJ was perceived as fulfilling a need that was missing. Since the services were not about providing a service to others but about creating an event for themselves, their friends and their families, there was certainly a tangible sense of ownership and empowerment among the participants.

Furthermore, as there were no elected or appointed leaders per se, the model was felt to be inclusive and participatory fully. As has been said of Limmud, but is just as appropriate here: "The agenda is not set and delivered top-down, but is created, developed and delivered bottom-up by those who wish to respond positively to the critique they have of the community" (Simonson, 2011, p. 866). Furthermore, one of the ways that GRJ has sought to counter and absorb criticism is by encouraging those with critiques to take responsibility for driving the change or fixing the problem. In this way, by responding to those with criticisms of GRJ with an invitation to become actively involved in improving it, the organizers feel that they could help facilitate the actualization of ever more people's ideas and visions (Simonson, 2011, p. 866).

It is for these reasons, then, that when negative feedback began to appear on the GRJ Facebook site, many of those who had voluntarily devoted their time, energy, and ideas to maintain the GRJ congregation became quite upset. that Since the initial two services, a vigorous debate was initiated on the GRJ Facebook page, querying some of the decisions that had been taken over the Rosh Hashanah and Yom Kippur services in the autumn of 2011, and implicitly the previous two years. The nature and the leadership of the services was increasingly called into question and criticized for being authoritarian rather than pluralist. Arguably, Facebook's features and interface facilitated this process/interaction of community building on- and offline. Crucially, participants do not have to be located in London, or attend a synagogue meeting to get involved in shaping the future direction of GRJ. Nor do they have to appeal to a religious authority who may be sole arbiter as in a more traditional congregation.

Significantly enough, given GRJ's pluralist, post-denominational agenda, the discussion was sparked over denominational lines, in particular the timing and nature of *Yizkor* (Hebrew: lit. "He will remember," but referring to the memorial service recited four times per year in synagogue), which differs between Orthodox and non-Orthodox. A representative comment from GRJ's Facebook page read:

> However, I did find both last and this year that the service is exclusively Orthodox, and, although it allows space for women to participate which is exciting, for me, who grew up in Reform synagogue, I find it quite inaccessible and confusing. For example there are many rituals that I don't know and haven't seen before, only Orthodox prayer books are used, and I also don't know many of the tunes used. In addition, I find any type of *mechitza* both visually and spiritually affronting: . . . I don't like all the divisions and find it distracting. I remember this was one of the things we debated over in the first year but it was decided it would alienate too many people to not have one. Maybe this conversation could be opened up again. To conclude, perhaps there isn't space for Reform at GRJ and that's probably fine—there are other options for

> me and there aren't other options for Orthodox women who want real involvement.

After much to and fro on the GRJ Facebook page, it was decided to hold several physical "Town Hall planning meetings" that took place over late 2011 and the first half of 2012. Again, it is interesting to note that the online nature of the discussion, which continued on the Facebook wall, was considered to be too limiting and reverting to an offline forum was considered the most efficacious route forward.

The subsequent discussion focused around the need for a single *Chazan* (Hebrew forcantor) to lead the services, the use of Orthodox tunes and prayer books, greater use of English during the services, the *trichitza* and, perhaps most controversially of all, the recital of Leviticus 18:22—the controversial text on homosexuality. Some participants expressed a desire to see a reduction in the Orthodox format, and increased meditation, chanting, *niggunim*,[4] music making and mantras. It was proposed that multiple and simultaneous services could take place with meals, breakout spaces and non-prayer based sessions available to all attendees, with the opportunity for participants to move between services should they so wish, or to remain in one particular service. Feedback showed that while some people felt very included because there was something for every level of observance, others felt that this was only the case for people who read/understand some Hebrew. Furthermore, aside from feeling religiously excluded, some people felt socially excluded, while others felt excluded by reasons of their sexual preference. A few lesbian, gay, bisexual and transgender (LGBT) and allied members of GRJ were really upset by how Leviticus 18:22 was read without proper caveat last year, implying in their eyes that GRJ endorses this verse at face value. Given the sensitivity of this issue, novel methods of communication were devised. GRJ leaders sought out small-group and one-on-one discussions with key people on this issue because, perhaps more than other questions, it was deemed so controversial that Facebook was not considered an appropriate forum to discuss it. The suggestion of doing some ritual action to subvert the reading of the text is, at the time of writing, being discussed, but there are still some who are very dissatisfied that it is being read at all.

The Facebook pages of GRJ show, then, that while participants are clearly enjoying their GRJ experiences, the process of post-denominational congregation formation is perhaps not as smooth as may have originally been anticipated. As one of the organizers admitted, "We have created a very strong pop-up community but this can make others feel shut out" (Danon, interview, August 5, 2012). Yet, as a key organizer/participant in the Town Hall discussions stated, "Having been part of a 'pluralist' youth movement where all too often the Orthodox would trump the rest, I've been encouraged by the seriousness with which Masorti, Reform, gay, allied and other contributions have been invited and welcomed" (Danon, interview, August

5, 2012). Whether positive or negative, these issues deal with the core issue at the heart of GRJ: what is GRJ? As Danon put it,

> is it a decentralized community of people who all self-organize and co-create (like a *minyan*, an ideal some still ascribe to . . .) or is it a centrally organized entity, with a committee that makes things happen through consultation with and inviting participation from the wider community (rather more like *Limmud*, or dare I say it, a traditional community).
>
> (personal communication, August 5, 2012)

Another problem is that GRJ is restricted to London. Despite being home to the second largest, and rapidly increasing, Jewish community in the UK, no such grouping exists in Manchester. Expressing a sense of exasperation, one Facebook user wrote on the group's wall, "i love you beautiful people! but we currently live in Manchester!! arrgg! do we have to move to Hampstead/London to be part of a Cool Jewish community? !?!" But given that GRJ is still in its infancy one can safely predict that these issues will continue to surface well into the future.

## CONCLUSION

This case study of the London-based GRJ demonstrates how Facebook has facilitated the construction of pop-up Jewish communities/congregations in a post-denominational era for and by young Jews who are not guided by a sole religious authority figure or lay denominational infrastructure. Without Facebook, GRJ would not have happened, according to Zoe Jankel (personal communication, 2009). Certainly, it would not have happened in the way it did. Facebook shaped the offline contours of the congregation because Facebook allows organizers to connect—as a group and more importantly personally—to those who join the group, inviting them to participate in consultation and preparation events in a way that the traditional meeting format may negate from the very outset. Someone can volunteer a comment on the group wall, and an organizer can follow up with them directly; a new participant can also see who is organizing and get in contact directly. As Debbie Danon put it, "I can't really see how an email list or similar [thing] would enable this kind of organic, casual, personal connection. I will certainly be using Facebook to recruit session presenters with whom I'm not yet personally connected" (personal communication, August 5, 2012). There is no doubt that Facebook will get people to turn up on the High Holy Day services, as inviting and accepting intensify as they come around. At other times of the year, GRJ's Facebook page signposts other activities and so has become a sort of communal notice board.

The negotiation of digital media extends far beyond the Israel/United States binary and encompasses far more individuals across the religious spectrum than just Haredim. Unlike Haredim, the Jews of GRJ see no religious conflict with their use of digital media. Indeed, the opposite is the case, because digital media such as Facebook provide qualitatively different Jewish experiences in the offline world that might not otherwise exist. Such experiences are not merely extensions of the existing denominational offerings but offer real alternatives to young Jews in London.

GRJ provides a case study for considering the extent to which Facebook is used to address, and how far it succeeds in doing so, feelings of alienation or disenfranchisement among Jews who are dissatisfied with the existing denominational infrastructure. GRJ provides a transferable model of how offline post-denominational Judaism is constructed and practiced because of the online world in one setting. While data here were exclusively drawn from the United Kingdom context, this case study opens the possibility of the mobility of Jewish self-definition across geographical boundaries by virtue of utilization of virtual networks, particularly those physically located in a transnational European hub such as London. Since participants are globally connected via the internet, they can be part of a global, post-national and post-denominational digital Jewish congregation or at least inspire analogues in other settings. Thus, it is hoped that the proposed chapter will not only interest students of Judaism but will also provide a model for the study of other transnational diasporic and religious media in a world that is increasingly globalized and ethnically fragmented while opening broader theoretical reflection on issues related to Jewish users and groups decision making and adaptation to different forms of digital media.

## NOTES

I would like to thank Isamar Carrillo Masso, Debbie Danon, Sally Baker and B.J. Brown for their assistance with this chapter.

1. *Haredism* is derived from the term *Haredi* (plural: *Haredim*), which literally means, "one who trembles." It derives from Isaiah 66:5, in which the prophet admonishes his people to, "Hear the word of the Lord, you who tremble [*Haredim*] at His word." The term is often confused with the much more common designation, in American English at least, Hasidic. *Haredi* is translated as "ultra-Orthodox" but this definition does not do justice to an extensive and nuanced term that covers a range of Jews who fall into this category but not all of whom are "Orthodox" in the strictest definition of that term.
2. Carlebach refers to the "singing Rabbi" Shlomo Carlebach and his emphasis on song. A *minyan* (plural: *minyanim*) is the minimum number of ten Jewish males over the age of thirteen required for a *Halachic* communal religious service. Some non-Orthodox denominations include women in the count.
3. In October 2006, a Jewish father applied for his son to be admitted to JFS for the 2007 academic year. Despite being a practicing Jew, the school denied the boy a place because it had twice as many applicants as it could take and

prioritized children whose mothers were recognized as Jewish by the then Orthodox chief rabbi, Jonathan Sacks. As the boy's mother had converted to Judaism through the Masorti movement, a non-Orthodox authority, he was not recognized as Jewish by the chief rabbi and was refused entry. The boy's father took the school to court, claiming racial discrimination. In June 2009, the Court of Appeal ruled in his favor, declaring that JFS, under the Race Relations Act 1976, had illegally discriminated against the child on racial grounds. The court ruled that the mother's religious status, and thus her child's religious status, had been determined using a racial criterion rather than a religious criterion. The school subsequently issued a revised admission criteria based on religious practice, including synagogue attendance, formal Jewish education and volunteering. JFS and the Orthodox United Synagogue appealed to the Supreme Court, with the support of Chief Rabbi Jonathan Sacks. In December 2009, the UK Supreme Court upheld the Court of Appeal's ruling ("The JFS Ruling," 2009; Kahn-Harris and Gidley, 2010: 106–109; ; Kossoff, 2009; UK Supreme Court 15, 2009).

4. Hebrew, meaning "tune" or "melody," pl. *niggunim*; it is a form of Jewish religious song or tune sung by groups in which formal lyrics are replaced with repetitive sounds rather than words.

## REFERENCES


Abrams, N., Baker S. and Brown, B.J. (2013). Grassroots Religion: Facebook and Offline Post-Denominational Judaism. In: M. Gillespie, D. Herbert and A. Greenhill (Eds.), *Social Media Religion and Spirituality* (pp. 143–163). Berlin: De Gruyter.

Arnettt, J.J. (2004). *Emerging Adulthood: The Winding Road from Late Teens Through the Twenties*. New York and Oxford: Oxford University Press.

Barzilai, G. and Barzilai-Nahon, K. (2005). Cultured Technology: Internet and Religious Fundamentalism. *The Information Society*, 21(1) [online]. Available at: http://www.indiana.edu/~tisj/21/1/ab-barzilai.html [Accessed September 2014].

Bleyer, J. (2007). Do It Yourself. *Tablet: A New Read on Jewish Life* [online]. Available at: http://www.tabletmag.com/jewish-arts-and-culture/books/939/do-it-yourself [Accessed September 2014].

Boyd, J. (2009a). *Grassroots Jews: UK Goes DIY*, Jewcy.Com [online]. Available at: http://www.jewcy.com/post/grassroots_jews [Accessed September 2014].

Boyd, J. (2009b). *My Way, the Sinatra Style of Judaism* [online]. Available at: http://www.jpr.org.uk/news/archive/detail.php?id=132 [Accessed September 2014].

Brasher, B. (2001).*Give Me That Online Religion*. San Francisco: Jossey-Bass.

Brooks, D. (2007). The Odyssey Years. *The New York Times*, October 9.

Campbell, H.A. (2010). *When Religion Meets New Media*. Oxford and New York: Routledge.

Campbell, H.A. (2011). Religion and the Internet in the Israeli Jewish Context. *Israel Affairs*, 17(3), 364–383.

Cohen, S.M., Kaunfer, E., Landres, J.S. and Shain, M. (2007). *Emergent Jewish Communities and Their Participants: Preliminary Findings from the 2007 National Spiritual Communities Study*. Los Angeles and New York: Synagogue 3000 and Mechon Hadar.

Cohen, S.M. and Kelman, A.Y. (2006). *Cultural Events and Jewish Identities: Young Adult Jews in New York*. New York: National Foundation for Jewish Culture.

Cohen, S.M. and Kelman, A.Y. (2007a). *The Continuity of Discontinuity*. New York: Andrea and Charles Bronfman Philanthropies.

Cohen, S.M. and Kelman, A.Y. (2007b). *Beyond Distancing: Young Adult American Jews and Their Alienation from Israel*. New York: Andrea and Charles Bronfman Philanthropies.

Cohen, S. M., Landres, J. S., Kaunfer, E., and Shain, M. (2007). *Emergent Jewish Communities and Their Participants: Preliminary Findings from the 2007 National Spiritual Communities Study*. Available at: http://www.synagogue3000.org/files/NatSpirComStudyReport_S3K_Hadar.pdf [Accessed September 2014].

Dencik, L. (2005). *"Jewishness" in Postmodernity: The Case of Sweden* (Vol. 10). Rappaport Center for Assimilation, Research and Strengthening of Jewish Vitality, Bar Ilan, Faculty of Jewish Studies.

Graham, D. (2004). *European Jewish Identity at the Dawn of the 21st Century: A Working Paper*. A report for the American Jewish Joint Distribution Committee and Hanadiv Charitable Foundation presented to the European General Assembly of the European Council of Jewish Communities, Budapest, May 20–23.

The JFS Ruling Is a Victory for Jews. (2009). *The Guardian*, December 16. Available at: http://www.theguardian.com/commentisfree/belief/2009/dec/16/jfs-supreme-court-ruling [Accessed September 2014].

Kahn-Harris, K. and Gidley, B. (2010). *Turbulent Times: The British Jewish Community Today*. London and New York: Continuum.

Kasriel, A. (2009). Getting Our Spiritual Fix. *The Jewish Chronicle*, September 17. Available at: http://www.thejc.com/judaism/judaism-features/20027/getting-our-spiritual-%EF%AC%81x. [Accessed September 2014]

Kaunfer, E. (2010) *Empowered Judaism: What Independent Minyanim Can Teach Us about Building Vibrant Jewish Communities*. Woodstock: Jewish Lights Publishing.

Kelman, A.Y. and Schonberg, E. (2008). *Legwork, Framework, Artwork: Engaging the Next Generation of Jews*. Denver: Rose Community Foundation.

Kossoff, J. (2009). JFS: Mazeltov! To the Supreme Court. *Daily Telegraph*, December 16. Available at: http://blogs.telegraph.co.uk/news/juliankossoff/100020063/jfsmazeltov-to-the-supreme-court/ [Accessed September 2014].

Kranz, D. (2011). Living Local: Some Remarks on the Creation of Social Groups of Young Jews in Present-Day London. *European Review of History—Revue europe´enned'histoire*, 18(1), 79–88.

Livio, O. and Tenenboim Weinblatt, K. (2007). Discursive Legitimation of a Controversial Technology: Ultra-Orthodox Jewish Women in Israel and the Internet. *The Communication Review*, 10(1), 29–56.

Lurie, M. (2011). Minyan 2.0. *Jewish Review of Books*, Winter, 25–28.

Rocker, S. (2011). Spiritual Pioneers or Just a Passing Trend? Are Independent Minyans Like Grassroots Jews Here to Stay? *The Jewish Chronicle*, September 15. Available at: http://www.thejc.com/judaism/judaism-features/54714/spiritual-pioneers-or-just-a-passing-trend [Accessed September 2014].

Rosenthal, R. (2006), What's in a Name? The Future of Post-Denominational Judaism. *Kedma*, 1, 20–32.

Russell, D. (2009). Why Cool Communities are Hot. *Jewish Renaissance*, July, 9–11.

Schalit, J. (2009). Grassroots Jews. Jewcy.com [online]. Available at: http://www.jewcy.com/religion-and-beliefs/grassroots_jews [Accessed September 2014].

*Shapiro*, S. M. (2010). Minyan Man. *Tablet: A New Read on Jewish Life* [online]. Available at: http://www.tabletmag.com/life-and-religion/26047/minyin-man/ [Accessed September 2014].

Simonson, R. (2011). Limmud: A unique model of transformative Jewish Learning. In: H. Miller, L. D. Grant and A. Pomson (Eds.), *International Handbook of Jewish Education* (pp. 861–877). Dordrecht: Springer.

Stein, H.F. and Hill, R.F. (1977). *The Ethnic Imperative: Examining the New White Ethnic Movement*. University Park: Pennsylvania State University Press.

UK Supreme Court (UKSC) 15 (2009). Judgment R (on the application of E) (Respondent) v Governing Body of JFS and the Admissions Appeal Panel of JFS (Appellants) and others and R (on the application of E) (Respondent) v Governing Body of JFS and the Admissions Appeal Panel of JFS and others, December 16.
Voloj, J. (2008). Virtual Jewish Topography: The Genesis of Jewish (Second) Life. In: J. Brauch, A. Lipphardt and A. Nocke (Eds.), *Jewish Topographies: Visions of Space, Traditions of Place* (pp. 345–356). Farnham: Ashgate.
Webber, J. (Ed.) (1994). *Jewish Identities in the New Europe*. London: Littman Library of Jewish Civilization.

# 4 *Yoatzot Halacha*

## Ruling the Internet, One Question at a Time

*Michal Raucher*

In the late 1990s, Nishmat, a women's seminary in Jerusalem, Israel, began training women to become advisors to other women on particular topics within Jewish law. These advisors, or *Yoatzot*, were trained to answer questions on a hotline, but the hotline quickly reached its capacity for the number of calls it could handle every week. Responding to the urgent need for *Yoatzot* to be able to reach more women, Rabbanit Chana Henkin, the founder and dean of Nishmat, created an online forum for *Yoatzot* to answer questions. This online space includes an indexed list of questions and answers—in Hebrew and English—and a space for women to write in with new questions. Their website also includes materials for women to educate themselves in areas of Jewish law, a goal of Nishmat's seminary. This chapter explores the ways in which Jewish women use the internet to affirm and challenge Orthodox rabbinic authority offline, increase women's authority in limited areas of Jewish law and alter the practice of Judaism for halachically observant women. In this way, we see that the internet has allowed Orthodox Jewish women to enhance their traditional roles while offline attempts to do so have not been accepted.

Women's participation in Jewish public life and their role as interpreters of and authorities on Jewish law has expanded in recent decades, but these changes have been limited to the more liberal streams of Judaism, namely Reform, Reconstructionist and Conservative Judaism, all of which ordain women as rabbis. In Orthodox Judaism, however, women's roles have remained largely unchanged, despite feminist contributions to Orthodox Jewish thought.[1] Although women have, in the past, played informal authoritative roles on issues related to menstruation and sex, the education of women as *Yoatzot Halacha* represents the institutionalization of women as legal advisors within Orthodox Judaism. Beyond the official status of *Yoatzot*, their growth and popularity on the internet reveals that their role is accepted widely, from both women who frequent the site and male leaders who endorse the mission. This is a significant difference from the ways in which the Orthodox Jewish community has reacted to the ordination of women as clergy by Yeshivat Maharat. In 2009, Rabbi Avi Weiss, founder of *Yeshivat Maharat*, first ordained Sara Hurwitz as *Rabbah*, a Hebrew term denoting only a gender difference between Hurwitz and other Orthodox rabbis. The reaction by the ultra-Orthodox group, Agudat Israel, and the more centrist Rabbinical Council of America (RCA), led Weiss to agree not to confer the title on further graduates of his program. Instead, after following a rigorous program of study at Yeshivat Maharat, women are ordained as clergy within Orthodox Judaism with the title of *Maharat*, a Hebrew acronym meaning "teacher of Jewish law and spirituality." Despite the change in title, however, the president of the RCA, Rabbi Shmuel Goldin, stated, "We do not accept the ordination of women as members of the Orthodox rabbinate, regardless of title" (Cohen, 2013). Despite the differences in title and function between the *Maharat* and the *Yoetzet Halacha* (the subject of another paper entirely), in this chapter, it is suggested that the internet presence of the *Yoatzot* has already laid the groundwork for female religious authorities within Orthodox Judaism.

Additionally, yoetzet.org represents an important moment of change within the practice of Judaism for many Orthodox women. Because Orthodox Judaism is predicated on the direct interpretation and application of Jewish law by rabbis, *Yoatzot Halacha* and their use of the internet changes the practice of Judaism for many women. By asking a *Yoetzet Halacha* a question that one might otherwise bring to her rabbi, a woman removes her rabbi from her observance of menstrual laws, thereby changing her practice of Jewish law. In this shift, a woman implicitly acknowledges an alternate source of authority (a *Yoetzet*), which is addressed later in this chapter, but more broadly, the presence of *Yoatzot Halacha* on the internet challenges this practice of Orthodox Judaism. Finally, this example of Jewish interactions with the internet reveals an attempt to influence Orthodox Judaism globally, as questions are asked and answered in Hebrew and English. As *Yoatzot Halacha* participate in the online Q&A, they use technology to change the practice of Jewish law for Orthodox Jewish women all over the world.

## INTRODUCING *YOATZOT* AND YOETZET.ORG

Rabbanit Chana Henkin started the training program for *Yoatzot Halacha* in 1997 when she discovered that many Orthodox Jewish women were not asking their (male) rabbis questions about menstruation or sexuality out of embarrassment. Though sometimes a woman sent her husband to ask the rabbi, Henkin found that most women were making decisions for themselves, some more stringently than the law requires, while others were taking more lenient positions. Interpreting the laws incorrectly, Henkin (1998) argued, could result in marital anguish, abstaining from marital relations, and inadvertent infertility (p. 286).[2] She commented that "needless to say, unnecessary stringency at the expense of marital harmony, or unwarranted leniency not in accordance with *Halacha*, [Jewish law] are both terribly wrong" (Henkin, 1999, p. 1). To correct this and provide women with someone with whom they would feel comfortable discussing intimate issues, Henkin created the training program for *Yoatzot Halacha*.

In order to become a *Yoetzet* (singular) *Halacha*, an Orthodox Jewish woman must study traditional Jewish legal texts on topics such as sexuality, family purity, pregnancy, birth, intimacy and menstruation. Women training to become *Yoatzot* (plural) also learn about a variety of issues in the medical and behavioral sciences to prepare them to apply the legal texts to contemporary situations. For instance, Jewish women write in to the website with questions regarding the correct way to practice Jewish law when they are undergoing medical treatment. In fact, there is an entire section of the questions online that refers to issues that might arise in the overlap of Jewish legal observance with medical procedures. Because *Yoatzot* learn about various medical procedures related to women's health, they refer to both to the medical procedure and the observance of the laws in their responses. We will see that the combination of halachic learning with medical knowledge gives *Yoatzot Halacha* a unique advantage as they field questions from women.

Significantly, and according to the website, the *Yoetzet Halacha* is not *intended* to replace the need for a rabbi's verdict on controversial issues. Her purpose is to serve as a sort of intermediary, clarifying any confusion a woman might have about the correct way to practice a particular law. For this reason, the women who pass the training program are given the title of *Yoetzet* (advisor) instead of *Posek*, which means "decisor." Henkin (1998) explained that *Posek* implies a higher level of *Talmud* scholarship and an ability to provide an original halachic ruling.[3] A *Yoetzet Halacha*, instead, provides guidance or advice for interpreting *Halacha* but cannot create laws.

Originally, women trained as *Yoatzot Halacha* answered questions on a hotline. Quickly though, the Golda Koschitzky Women's Halachic Hotline received more than 100 calls each week, a volume that has remained steady and that reveals significant gaps in women's knowledge on issues related to the laws of family purity.[4] Now, of the 60 *Yoatzot* who have completed the training program since the first class graduated in July 1999, one quarter work on the hotline. In June 2002 Nishmat launched an English website for questions directed at the *Yoatzot*, and in April 2006 it created a Hebrew website as well. Five *Yoatzot* staff the website. As of 2011, the hotline received almost 15,000 unique and distinct questions, most of which have been in Hebrew, and the website has received almost 10,000 questions, most of which have been in English (Ganzel and Zimmerman, 2011). On the website, yoetzet.org, the founders explain the purpose of their expansion onto the internet as an opportunity to "make practical information on women's health and *Halacha* quickly and easily available to a wide international audience."[5] With this goal in mind, the founders recently began offering training manuals for bridal teachers and other educational resources for

Orthodox Jewish women and medical professionals, all accessed via their website.

The home page for yoetzet.org features, side by side in Hebrew and English, links to all of the programs organized by Nishmat. A woman can gather information about various learning programs at Nishmat or click on the link for "Women's Health and *Halacha*," which will redirect her to the Q&A section of the website. Once there, she can scan the left side of the page for a list of topics, such as "Becoming *Niddah*,"[6] "Family Planning," "Fertility" or "*Mikvah*."[7] Clicking on one of these topics will lead her to a more detailed list of questions and answers. Someone needing to ask a question will easily find the phone numbers for the hotline and a link, "Ask the *Yoetzet*," which enables her to ask a question online. Once there, the website states that a *Yoetzet* will try to send an answer to a woman's e-mail address within 3 days (excluding the Sabbath and holidays), which gives the *Yoetzet* enough time to confirm her answer with a rabbinic authority. A woman does not need to identify herself, only to give her e-mail address and ask her question.

On the home page a woman can also choose to participate in two research projects organized by the directors of yoetzet.org, both about fertility and menstrual cycles among "*Halacha* observant women." She can also register for classes taught by *Yoatzot Halacha*. Visitors to the site are encouraged to learn about the history of *Yoatzot Halacha* and to make a donation. The website, yoetzet.org, provides the internet surfer with an abundance of information to access as well as opportunities to expand her Jewish education in person. The focus of this chapter, however, is on the Q&A section of the website.

As noted earlier, *Yoatzot Halacha* and yoetzet.org represent an expansion of women's leadership roles in Orthodox Judaism, but the internet has long been a site of expanding female roles in the Orthodox Jewish community. Though Orthodox and ultra-Orthodox communities in Israel had even gone so far as to ban the internet from their communities, in the mid-2000s the ban was lifted slightly because many argued it would allow for certain benefits to the community. Unlike men in these communities, women are expected to enter the workforce to support their husbands who study Jewish texts all day. Campbell (2011) points to the fact that Israeli ultra-Orthodox rabbis finally approved the internet for women so that women could work from home. Like the cellular phone, radio and telephone in ultra-Orthodox Israeli society, rabbis banned the internet until socioeconomic necessities led to its introduction (Livio and Tennenboim Weinblatt, 2007). With the allowance of internet usage, women could work from home and thus simultaneously care for growing families.

This allowance quickly spread to the growth of kosher search engines and Orthodox websites that were also approved for usage by these religious communities. Many scholars point to the proliferation of websites for Orthodox Jewish women in particular, noting the changes this may or may not have on women's positionality offline. Livio and Tennenboim Weinblatt (2007) consider the ways women who use the internet for business purposes legitimate its use for other purposes. The Orthodox Jewish women they interviewed maintain that the internet provides opportunities to expand communication and knowledge while allowing for self-expression (Livio and Tennenboim Weinblatt, 2007, p. 36). Along this vein, Leiber (2010) addresses the practice of blogging among Orthodox Jewish women who are blurring the public–private distinction through their use of the internet. Though in religious life Orthodox Jewish women are confined to the home, Leiber maintains, the internet allows them to access a more public world within a religiously sanctioned framework. Barzilai-Nahon and Barzilai (2005) found that "cyberspace has emancipated women somewhat from their inability to transcend their local communal boundaries," though it does not present an alternative to religious life. Instead, the internet provides a "platform to communicate within and outside the community in ways that empower feminine identity" (Barzilai-Nahon and Barzilai, 2005, p. 28). In a similar way, yoetzet.org provides a platform for female religious authorities that they do not have otherwise.

## AFFIRMING AND CHALLENGING OFFLINE RABBINIC AUTHORITY

Through the Q&A section of the website, *Yoatzot Halacha* uniquely affirms and challenges traditional rabbinic authority in the offline Orthodox Jewish community. On one hand, the rabbis affirm their own authority as they endorse and limit the *Yoetzet*'s authority. The website makes it clear that women have been trained and certified by well-respected rabbis in the Orthodox community. Furthermore, even before a woman submits her question, and then following each question, women are reminded that advice from the *Yoetzet* does not replace a rabbi's ruling. These steps interrupt the *Yoetzet*'s direct response and admit to the greater authority and knowledge of the rabbi. And yet, the entire premise of the *Yoetzet*'s role is to respond to women who do not *want* to turn to their rabbis for these questions. *Yoatzot* offer an alternative (or at the very least a supplement) to rabbis, thus admitting that rabbis cannot sufficiently respond to women's needs. The presumption is that women can respond more adequately to other women regarding issues of family planning, sexuality and menstruation. In this way, though a *Yoetzet Halacha*'s authority on the internet is limited by rabbis, her relevance supersedes that of a rabbi.

In light of this confusion, it is helpful to turn to Campbell's analysis of authority on the internet. Campbell (2007) suggests that the term *authority* needs to be refined when used to refer to online contexts. Based on interviews with Christians, Muslims and Jews she finds four layers of authority in the context of religion online: religious hierarchy, religious structures, religious ideology and religious texts. Each layer plays a distinct role in shaping the religious user's experience on the internet. Germane to this context, among religious Jews, traditional religious leaders' affirmation of the place of the internet plays a role in determining the individual's internet use (Campbell, 2007). Thus, the internet creates a space for affirming traditional offline authority structures and provides new roles for them: gatekeepers of the internet.[8] In a similar way, yoetzet.org acknowledges the necessity of rabbis and provides them with new role: certifying and overseeing the practices of female legal guides. In so doing, yoetzet.org affirms the hierarchy of religious authority offline.

Additionally, the rabbinic role in the establishment of *Yoatzot Halacha* contributes to *Yoatzot*'s credence in the Orthodox community online. In their study of the dynamic created between traditional and new sources of authority on the internet, Campbell and Golan (2011) consider the ways in which the internet allows some Orthodox internet entrepreneurs to gain authority and legitimacy by affiliating with offline authorities. Yoetzet.org, certified by particular rabbinic gatekeepers, has allowed women to take on a role in Orthodox Judaism that they did not have previously. Women who have trained and studied extensively can now act as guides for other women. Though there are a few *Yoatzot Halacha* who function as such in offline communities, their largest presence is on the internet.[9] In this way, the internet has created a new authority on women's issues in Orthodox Judaism, but only with the negotiation of those considered authorities offline. The negotiation between the online and offline authorities is a crucial element in their mutual reinforcement.

This paradoxical and competing authority structure is characteristic of other iterations of religion online. Dawson and Cowan (2004) suggested that there are two significant social consequences of the internet: "a crisis of authority and a crisis of authenticity" (p. 2). Because there is no tool for vetting information posted on the internet, Dawson and Cowan argued, anybody can claim an authoritative role, thus challenging the authenticity of that position. This, however, does not adequately address the situation of *Yoatzot Halacha*. Their training process consists of studying, learning and passing a certification exam offline to ensure that they are sufficiently prepared with the texts and responses that are recognized as authoritative. As the certification process shows, the women who serve as *Yoatzot Halacha* online do not claim any authority independently. Instead, their role is designed to be in complete coherence with community norms in offline religion.

Others highlight the fact that democratizing access to religious texts and giving a voice to many different sources have the potential to both challenge and affirm the authority of those on the internet.[10] This, too, however, does not apply to the *Yoetzet*'s authority online. Though particular rabbis at Nishmat may be limiting her authority, nobody else publically challenges the *Yoetzet*'s authority. In contrast to online Q&A forums staffed by male rabbis, yoetzet.org does not allow for anybody to respond to the *Yoetzet*'s answer. Steinitz (2011) studied the responses to Orthodox rabbinic answers to legal questions online and found that the casual setting of the "talkback" allows web surfers to respond to rabbis without the respect that one would usually have for a rabbinic authority. Thus, they challenge the authority of the rabbis on the internet. Because yoetzet.org does not have a "talkback" section, nobody can challenge a *Yoetzet*'s answer. The democratization of texts is clearly limited to the women who have studied and passed the certification exam offline.

Contrary to examples of online religion that challenge the offline authority[11] the Q&A on yoetzet.org actually affirms the traditional role of the rabbi in two important ways. First, as mentioned earlier, it is clearly stated on the website that the *Yoetzet* has been certified by a panel of Orthodox rabbis and that every question is reviewed by one of the rabbinic advisors of the website. Therefore, the website acknowledges that the *Yoetzet*'s answer is in line with the opinion of prominent rabbinic authorities offline. Second, after each answer the *Yoetzet* provides, the website reproduces the following statement: "This internet service does not preclude, override or replace the *psak* [verdict] of any rabbinical authority." The *Yoetzet*'s answer, then, is publicly recognized for its official limitations while the role of the rabbi is affirmed. In many ways, then, the *Yoatzot* are merely an extension of rabbis, an online method of broadcasting rabbinic positions and reaching the female audience that is too embarrassed to turn directly to their rabbis.

In this way, yoetzet.org maintains an overarching authority structure within the Orthodox Jewish community, thereby appearing to support traditional Judaism even as they challenge gender norms. Recall that the impetus for training *Yoatzot Halacha* was that women in the Orthodox community were too embarrassed to turn to the traditional religious authorities to discuss issues related to sexuality (Henkin, 1999). Women, therefore, were rejecting rabbinic authority and in turn the practice of asking a question of a rabbi. Thus, the availability of *Yoatzot Halacha* online encourages women to participate in the required practice of asking a question of a religious authority. Although their gender challenges traditional authority structures, *Yoatzot Halacha* reinforce the Orthodox Jewish understanding that an individual should not apply texts or laws without consulting a rabbi. In the following example, a woman awaits an answer from her rabbi and asks the *Yoetzet* if she can instead go ahead and make an assumption about his ruling:

> **Question**: during the 2nd day of my *sheva nekiim*[12] days, my *bedika* cloth[13] looked a little pinkish in color . . . but really very pale and just around the ends. I gave it to show to my rabbi last night, before sunset and he never got back to me. Does that mean everything is ok and go about my regular checking or am I supposed to wait for him to call me back?

**Answer:** You should make every effort to reach your rabbi for his ruling. In the meanwhile, you should continue with your *bedikot*.[14] Keep in mind that if the questionable cloth is ok, you continue your count. If the questionable cloth is not ok, then the first clean *bedikah* is your new *hefsek* [15] and you begin a new count.[16]

The *Yoetzet* reminds this woman that she needs her rabbi's answer before she can move forward; yet, the *Yoetzet* also provides this woman with an answer by clarifying what it means for her practice, whether the rabbi tells her the stain is OK or not. As Campbell (2007) states about the adaptation of the internet among Jews in Israel, a major concern is that "the community is seen to function as a single entity" (p. 1056). The practice of asking a question and receiving an answer is meant to ensure this unity in practice. Even though women are now asking questions of other women instead of male rabbis, the authority structure of the community is maintained. Yoetzet.org reminds women that untrained individuals are still unable to apply the law without consulting someone with more authority.

## THE INTERNET AS A SITE FOR THE EXPANSION OF WOMEN'S ROLES

Despite evidence that yoetzet.org reinforces traditional male authorities in Orthodox Judaism, the internet forum also challenges religious authority offline by assuming that women are more appropriate respondents to women's questions, and by showing that not all questions *need* the direct guidance of a rabbi. Despite the fact that *Yoatzot* are not ordained as clergy in Orthodox Judaism, these women learn some of the most complicated legal issues in Jewish law, and they are certified by a board of rabbis in a similar manner to rabbinic ordination. This education allows them to understand the laws, apply them in different circumstances, and importantly, recognize when a rabbi is unnecessary. As mentioned earlier, the internet provides a platform for the *Yoatzot Halacha* to broadcast their roles as legal advisors, and as women submit questions to yoetzet.org, they endorse the authority of the *Yoatzot*. When the question moves beyond the precise application of menstrual laws, we see how the internet allows for the further expansion of the *Yoetzet*'s role. In this example, a woman asks a question of the *Yoetzet* about the different legal positions of two rabbinic authorities in the Middle Ages.

**Question:** Was mainstream practice to follow Rambam or Ramban[17] in interpretation of the 7/11 cycle—i.e. continuously from first menstruation or anew each month? If it was Rambam, is this a reason the *Bnot Israel*[18] took on the extra days, because counting was so difficult? . . . If the Ramban were the mainstream, why would *bnot Israel* have taken on the *humra*[19] . . . Are there any other repercussions to this *machloket*[20] or reasons to introduce Rambam or explain him if his view is/was not mainstream (i.e. in Middle Ages)?[21]

The question is not personal and does not have any immediate bearing on the life of the person who asked it. However, the mere fact that she asked a woman for information about rabbinic legal authorities is a departure from traditional practice. Women do not traditionally learn rabbinic texts; *Yoatzot*, however, are well versed in the rabbinic sources. The *Yoetzet*'s answer to her is thorough:

**Answer:** The Ramban's explanation was accepted, largely because it is difficult to be sure of what the Rambam really meant and how it would work in practice. The difficulties of counting on a *d'orayta* level,[22] even according to Ramban, were compounded by the lack of expertise in assessing which colors of blood rendered a woman *temeiah*[23] and which did not. A woman could bleed six days, thinking she had gone through six days of *niddah* when in fact she only began having blood that would render her *niddah* on day five. Counting and differentiating between *niddah* and *zavah*[24] days would thus be more difficult. There could also be an issue in assessing *zavah* days with blood that was seen *bein hashmashot*.[25] The Rambam's view is most interesting on a theoretical level and in order to bring into relief the implications of the Ramban's view (for example, that one cannot be a *niddah* and *zavah* simultaneously).[26]

Especially because the question is theoretical, it is significant that the asker viewed the *Yoetzet* as an authority on this issue. The *Yoetzet*'s authority, then, is seen to expand beyond the practical applications of the laws.

Madge and O'Connor's (2005) application of Victor Turner's "liminal" concept to women on the internet is useful in thinking about how *Yoatzot Halacha* function on the internet. Examining the role of the internet in the life of new mothers, Madge and O'Connor argued that, "in the liminal zone of cyber/space, women 'tried out' different versions of motherhood, resulting in the production of new selves" (Madge and O'Connor, 2005, p. 84). The authors explained that this is possible because cyberspace is also a liminal zone—a place "betwixt and between"—in the case of cyberspace, between geographical and virtual space (Madge and O'Connor, 2005, p. 83). As such, they argued, "it appears that cyberspace as a liminal space and becoming a mother as a liminal life stage are particularly suited to one another" (Madge and O'Connor, 2005, p. 92).

*Yoatzot Halacha* is also a liminal group—its members are between the traditional roles of women and those of men in Orthodox Judaism. They are extensively trained in Jewish law as it applies to women's bodies and yet because of their gender they are not extended the authority that men with similar training would receive.[27] Their gender, however, is paradoxically what affords them a greater amount of respect from Orthodox Jewish women. Reporting on the status and development of *Yoatzot Halacha* on the hotline and the website, Ganzel and Zimmerman (2011) maintained that "the key advantage of the yo'atzot seems to be the comfort and openness that many women feel in discussing matters of an intimate nature with other women" (pp. 166–167). This, in addition to the fact that *Yoatzot* have the practical experience of keeping the laws of *Taharat Hamishpacha* affords female legal advisors an embodied perspective when discussing these complex issues.

Ganzel and Zimmerman continued, stating, "The prolific use of the services of *Yoatzot* seems to indicate that it is important to many women to have access to a professional that can understand both the *halakhic* [Jewish legal], medical and practical aspects of keeping *taharat hamishpacha* [family purity laws] from a feminine perspective" (p. 166). This "female" perspective is an important part of the *Yoetzet*'s role, as women ask questions that are not always legal questions but necessitate the response of someone who can speak from experience and a position of authority.

*Yoatzot Halacha* have also received a level of training that most rabbis do not receive. They possess a specialty in laws of *Taharat Mishpacha*, or family purity, an expertise many rabbis do not possess, and they have studied the overlap between women's health and *Halacha*. Because *Halacha* as it applies to women regarding their bodies and menstruation, having medical training is a crucial element of applying Jewish law to these circumstances, but most rabbis do not have this training. Ganzel and Zimmerman (2011) found that "women are turning to *Yoatzot* for this advice because they want input on both the medical and the Halakhic issues. Physicians and rabbis can often offer guidance on only one aspect or the other" (p. 167).Online, a Yoetzet's unique skill set can be showcased and appreciated. The liminal status of *Yoatzot Halacha* fits well within the liminal space of the internet and allows for these female legal guides to fill a void in women's observance of Jewish law.

## PUBLIC RELIGION AND PRIVATE ISSUES

The literature considering the resonance between online and offline religion is vast[28]; here I consider the role that yoetzet.org has played in Orthodox Judaism offline. Chana Henkin did not imagine that *Yoatzot Halacha* would have a place in offline religion; at least initially, the *Yoatzot* were not intended to replace rabbis but rather to facilitate more interactions with rabbis on topics pertaining to women (Henkin, 1999). *Yoatzot Halacha*, then, trained to work online so that they could solve a problem occurring in offline religion. In the process, however, they have become more skilled at answering questions regarding the practical application of female obligations in a way that the rabbis are not trained to answer, and in this way

*Yoatzot Halacha* have altered the nature of this intimate interaction. In this section I argue that the internet facilitates the type of service *Yoatzot Halacha* provide, and I consider the impact this might have on offline religion for Orthodox Jewish women.[29]

For many Orthodox Jewish women, the internet allows sharing private concerns and thoughts in an anonymous way. Based on her investigation of blogs maintained by American Orthodox Jewish women, Leiber (2010) argued that blogging "enables an expansion of the private sphere" for those who write them (p. 622). Though the blogs are a public forum, women view them as part of their private sphere and thus feel comfortable expressing themselves in ways that they may not otherwise, Leiber claimed. Similarly, women write in to *Yoatzot Halacha* knowing that their private question might be posted online for all to see, but they write private (and potentially embarrassing) questions such as this one:

> **Question:** My husband and I have been married for 10 months, and during this time we have strictly kept to the *hilchot niddah*. This month, during the seven clean days, we were talking before falling asleep—as we usually do—(our beds completely detach from one another, but are in the same bedroom) and eventually the conversation turned sexual. Despite efforts to stop the conversation, it eventually led to my husband sitting on my bed, which then led to kissing and other inappropriate *niddah* behavior . . . What does this mean as far as counting clean days and going to the *mikveh* are concerned? And how can we prevent this happening again, or even worse—going all the way?[30]

A woman would most likely be too embarrassed to admit to a friend or a rabbi that she and her husband violated the fundamental laws of marriage, but as long as she remains anonymous, she can describe the situation in detail online.

This kind of sharing can be understood as anonymous intimacy. The internet allows for anonymity and distance from some of the most private and personal questions an Orthodox Jewish woman has. Precisely because women writing in are not identified, they feel more comfortable sharing personal details; their community cannot judge them if they cannot be identified. Some women, like the one who has the following question about a medical condition, admit explicitly that they are not comfortable asking questions in person:

> **Question:** This is not a question I am capable of discussing with someone face to face yet. I am coming to terms with my condition, but am not ready to discuss it with anyone I have to look at, especially a male.[31]

This questioner repeatedly states her discomfort about facing anyone, particularly a man, when asking this question. The internet allows her to ask her question of a woman who she does not have to look at or talk to, an option she did not have before the establishment of yoetzet.org.

Women feel this distance most poignantly from their interactions with internet, even though the hotline provides them with the same amount of anonymity. In Ganzel and Zimmerman's (2011) comparative analysis of questions asked on the hotline and those posted on the internet, they found that women were more likely to ask about intimate topics on the website. About 9% of the questions asked on the English website were about topics of sexuality and intimacy; these questions, however, are almost completely absent from the hotline. Zimmerman (2011) explained, "with very sensitive topics, anonymity alone is not enough. Women seemed to prefer the added distance provided by virtual communication" (p. 166). This distance and anonymity of the internet facilitates a level of intimacy that is not possible offline.

As *Yoatzot Halacha* respond to important and sensitive issues in the lives of married Orthodox Jewish women, one has to ask what impact this has on Orthodox Judaism. Charlotta Fonrobert and Ilan (2001) insisted that the efforts of the *Yoatzot Halacha* are, in fact, changing the face of rabbinic authority in Israel. She means that through their participation in the discourse, a discourse that has long been dominated by male voices, women are changing the interpretation of the text and the implementation of the law. Fonrober and Ilan (2001) argued that women trained at the Nishmat Seminary are "picking up the threads that have been left hanging and continue to spin with them, adding different colors and textures to the web" (p. 10). Thus, it is not so much that *Yoatzot Halacha* might replace rabbis when it comes to topics relevant to women but rather that their mere involvement in the discourse changes the nature of legal reasoning. In turn, the practices demanded by these texts change.

Though I cannot say whether or not the role of the *Yoetzet* online affects the role of the rabbi offline,[32] it is the case that the online presence of *Yoatzot Halacha* and the various services offered by the broader website is intended to increase women's education in areas of Jewish law that affect them. To be sure, this is one of the primary goals of Nishmat—to encourage women to educate themselves and make sources available to women around the world. A woman approaching the website with a question is *first* encouraged to read other answers to see if her question has already been addressed. In other situations, women are instructed to read articles on the website and then gather more information themselves in order to answer her question. This is significant, since women writing in with questions could have just received their personal answers without any public forum for the display of these answers. Instead, Nishmat decided to make these answers available to all who visit the site. Ganzel and Zimmerman (2011) have described this as a nonhierarchical structure of guidance. This approach, they claim, is appropriate for the modern Orthodox audience of women seeking guidance from *Yoatzot Halacha*, since they would be more attracted to the personal autonomy that the approach requires.

Nishmat has also created a variety of manuals for other female authorities to freely download and use in their classes. In order to help women understand the laws regarding marriage and their bodies, Nishmat educators created an online curriculum for bridal instructors. As a supplement to traditional marriage education that is provided separately to men and women, yoetzet.org also offers a course for a husband and a wife to participate in together. In a seminar for marriage instructors that I attended, one of the directors of the organization explained that the internet is helpful for educating both men and women. She continued:

> The benefit of the internet is that individuals can learn some things alone, and one can do that wherever and whenever one wants. The discussion pieces and activities [she is referring here to the marital companion materials], however, should be done together as a couple—building their relationship together.

Indeed, the *Yoatzot Halacha* website facilitates the discussion of topics previously avoided by providing and responding to the privacy characteristic of this community. With the help of yoetzet.org, an Orthodox Jewish woman need not turn to her rabbi or marriage teacher with questions. All the resources are online for the individual to find. It would seem, then, that Nishmat and yoetzet.org are attempting to significantly change the authority structure and procedure characteristic of Orthodox Judaism by slowly eliminating the need for rabbinic authorities and encouraging the individual to educate him- or herself.

## CONCLUSION: WOMEN AND RELIGION ON THE INTERNET

Using yoetzet.org as a lens through which to view women in religion, we see that this negotiation with the internet allows for two significant changes in Orthodox Judaism: (a) the expanded roles of women as legal authorities, and (b) women's exploration of topics otherwise not discussed, thereby changing the practice of Orthodox Judaism. In this conclusion I address each of these innovations and how the internet has enabled both.

Women's roles in Orthodox Judaism have expanded in the last 40 years, as women's education in traditional texts has increased and schools dedicated to women's education have gained prominence, thus allowing women to hold unofficial leadership roles and serve as informal advisors. Significantly, the certification of women as clergy by Rabbi Avi Weiss has represented the institutionalization of the expansion of women's roles in Orthodox communities. The training of *Yoatzot Halacha* is part of this process, but their role on the internet represents an important divergence as well. As mentioned earlier, the online Q&A both challenges and affirms rabbinic authority offline. This is characteristic of other iterations of religion online, and it signals the relationship between online and offline authorities in the negotiation of technology within Jewish communities. Importantly, though, this paradox is precisely what allows for the expansion of women's authority in Orthodox Judaism. Although one can understand a *Yoetzet*'s male certifiers as "gatekeepers," these gatekeepers are also those who provide her with legitimacy in Orthodox communities. With public support from prominent Orthodox rabbis, the *Yoatzot* assure all visitors to the website that their positions are accurate and within the bounds of Orthodoxy. Therefore, a *Yoetzet*'s role as a female religious authority is validated through the gatekeepers' certification of *Yoatzot Halacha*. Furthermore, as the *Yoatzot* answer questions that would not be brought to rabbis and answer them in a way that male rabbis are not qualified to do, the *Yoatzot* utilize the public display of questions and answers on the internet to carve out a space for themselves as legal advisors side by side with rabbis.

Just as the internet has allowed for the expansion of women's roles in Orthodox Judaism by creating a space for *Yoatzot Halacha* to serve as legal advisors, the internet has also softened the blow of this changed status. As mentioned earlier, in contrast to *Yeshivat Maharat*, the *Yoatzot Halacha* training program has not been questioned for their adherence to Orthodox Judaism. The internet plays a significant part in mitigating the negative responses to women's expanding roles in Orthodox Judaism. *Yoatzot Halacha*, have, until very recently, existed primarily on the internet, which I have argued is a liminal and unchallenging space for Orthodox Judaism. Furthermore, the internet, along with other new technologies, has facilitated the modernization of Orthodox Judaism, so it is a welcome arena for challenging accepted norms.

Additionally, by keeping the identities of the *Yoatzot* private, the questions and issues raised by Orthodox Jewish women maintain center stage on the website. This allows Rabbanit Henkin to stress the fact that the education of *Yoatzot Halacha* is not the ultimate goal, but rather her goal is to reinforce traditional practice of Jewish law through the *Yoatzot*'s service to women. As she emphasizes the importance of adherence to Jewish law and as the website focuses on these issues and not the *Yoatzot* themselves, the organization and the presentation of the website allow for a less threatening change in religious practice and authority. Although the hotline that *Yoatzot Halacha* initially used may have sufficiently answered women's questions, the internet provides them with a public platform to comprehensively portray the practices of *Yoatzot Halacha* as consistent with Orthodox Judaism and not a challenge to it, despite the fact that what they are doing is in fact revolutionary.

Regarding the second important innovation for women in Orthodox Judaism brought on by their use of yoetzet.org, we must return to the fact that 10 to 15 years ago, an Orthodox Jewish woman who had difficulty following the laws of *Niddah* or who discovered she had been following them incorrectly most likely avoided her rabbi and kept her secret in private. Additionally, a woman who faced a medical procedure that might affect her *Niddah* status *may* have tried explaining the laws of *Niddah* to her physician, but it is more likely that she either eschewed the medical procedure or assumed herself to be ritually impure as a result of the procedure. With the growth of *Yoatzot Halacha*, women now receive answers to their questions by professionals with empathy and broad medical knowledge, thus saving women from embarrassment, shame and the incorrect practice of Jewish law. With the creation of a website and its expanded role at Nishmat, Rabbanit Henkin and *Yoatzot Halacha* have created a space for women to inquire about topics that embarrass or possibly shame them while maintaining their anonymity. The public discussion of these topics through the internet forum emphasizes the importance of the issues. Furthermore, as female legal advisors provide answers, they augment the male-dominated nature of the legal discourse found within Orthodox Judaism. All of these factors create a way for women to practice Orthodox Judaism that adheres to Orthodox Jewish law but is informed to a great extent by women's experiences and women's applications of the laws. The internet, then, allows Orthodox Jewish women to change their roles and influence the lives of women within various sectors of both Judaism online and offline.

## NOTES

1. See, for example, Greenberg (1994), Ross (2004) and Hartman (2007).
2. By not asking one's rabbi a question about a particular stain of blood, a woman may assume she is "impure" and thus forbidden to engage in sexual intercourse with her husband.
3. See also Henkin (n.d.).
4. In fact, Henkin's fears about women not asking questions proved true in the first few months of the hotline. Zimmerman (2001) found that *Yoatzot* received calls from women who had not been to the *Mikvah* in months due to their embarrassment in asking a question of a rabbi. Others underwent medical treatments that they thought were halachically necessary because nobody could answer their medical-halakhic questions (Zimmerman, 2001, p. 19).
5. "Why a Website?" Available at http://www.yoetzet.org/article.php?id=73 [Accessed May 30, 2012].
6. *Niddah* refers to a woman's ritual status during her menstrual period and the week following the cessation of bleeding. During this time many halachically observant women will not engage in any physical contact with their husbands.
7. The conclusion of a woman's *Niddah* period each month is marked by her immersion in a *Mikvah*, a ritual bath.
8. See also Thumma (2000) and Anderson (1999).
9. In the last couple of years, Nishmat has begun to certify *Yoatzot Halacha* who are based in the United States and who have congregations or schools to which they are primarily responsible. However, the overwhelming majority of *Yoatzot* still function predominantly online.
10. See, for example, Barker (2005), Barzali-Nahon and Barzali (2005) and Cowan (2005).
11. See, for example, Campbell (2007) and Barker (2005).
12. *Sheva nikiim* literally means "seven clean" and refers to the seven days without bleeding a woman must count after her period ends before she can immerse in the *mikvah*.

13. A *Bedikah* cloth is the cotton pad a woman uses to check herself internally during her seven clean days to be sure she is not bleeding.
14. *Bedika* (sing) and *Bedikot* (pl) refer to the checks a woman performs during her seven clean days.
15. *Hefsek*: At the conclusion of a woman's period, she performs an extensive checking process in order to be sure her period ends and she can begin her seven clean days.
16. "Waiting for Rabbi's Answer." Retrieved February 7, 2012, from http://www.yoetzet.org/question.php?id=3131.
17. Rambam, also referred to as Maimonides or Rabbi Moshe ben Maimon, was a 12th-century Torah scholar, physician and philosopher. Ramban, also referred to as Nachmanides or Rabbi Moshe ben Nachman, was a 13th-century Jewish scholar, philosopher and physician.
18. *Bnot Israel*, literally, "the daughters of Israel."
19. *Humra*, "stringency."
20. *Machloket*, "disagreement."
21. "Rambam vs. Ramban."' Available at http://www.yoetzet.org/question.php?id=5033 [Accessed February 7, 2012].
22. *D'orayta* level. This refers to the fact that a particular law derives from the Torah, as opposed to from the rabbis. It is seem to have greater weight if it derives from the Torah.
23. *Temeiah*, "impure." This refers to a woman's status while she is a *Niddah*.
24. *Zavah* also refers to a woman's status as "ritually impure" because of bleeding from the vagina, but it is usually not associated with menstrual blood.
25. *Bein hashmashot* is a rabbinic term referring to twilight.
26. "Rambam vs. Ramban." Available at http://www.yoetzet.org/question.php?id=5033 [Accessed February 7, 2012].
27. This training is actually considered quite difficult and is not attained by every rabbi in the Orthodox Jewish community. If a woman wanted to go to a rabbi with one of these questions, she would need to find one with expertise in this area.
28. See, for example, Dawson and Cowan (2004) and Campbell (2005).
29. Others have argued that in Orthodox Judaism women occupy and are masters of the private realm while men maintain leadership roles in the public realm (see Leiber, 2010). Though it is not my intention to take issue with this argument here, it is important to make clear that this is not the association I am ascribing to in this chapter.
30. "Kissed and Touched While *Niddah*." Available at http://www.yoetzet.org/question.php?id=3023 [Accessed October 3, 2011].
31. "MRKH (no uterus) and *Mikveh*." Available at http://www.yoatzot.org/question.php?id=5437.
32. Ganzel and Zimmerman (2011) link the creation of a family purity hotline from Machon Puah to the success of Nishmat's hotline, thus claiming that the website has, in fact, caused a change in the practice of Judaism.

## REFERENCES

Anderson, J. (1999). The Internet and Islam's New Interpreters. In: D. Eickleman (Ed.), *New Media in the Muslim World: The Emerging Public Sphere* (pp. 45–60). Bloomington: Indiana University Press.

Barker, E. (2005). Crossing the Boundary: New Challenges to Religious Authority and Control as a Consequence of Access to the Internet. In: M. Hojsgaard and M. Warburg (Eds.), *Religion and Cyberspace* (pp. 67–85). London: Routledge.

Barzilai-Nahon, K. and Barzilai, G. (2005). Cultured Technology: The Internet and Religious Fundamentalism. *The Information Society*, 21, 25–40.

Campbell, H. (2005). *Exploring Religious Community Online: We Are One in the Network*. New York: Peter Lang Publishing.

Campbell, H. (2007). Who's Got the Power? Religious Authority on the Internet. *Journal of Computer-Mediated Communication*, 12(3), 1043–1062.

Campbell, H. (2011). Religion and the Internet in the Israeli Jewish Context. *Israel Affairs*, 17(3), 364–383.

Campbell, H. and Golan, O. (2011). Creating Digital Enclaves: Negotiation of the internet among Bounded Religious Communities. *Media, Culture, and Society*, 33(5), 709–724.

Cowan, D. (2005). *Cyberhenge: Modern pagans on the internet*. New York, NY: Routledge.

Cohen, A. (2013) Orthodox Schism Over Role of Women Widens After Ordination of Women as *Maharats*. *Jewish Daily Forward* [online]. Available at: http://forward.com/articles/178926/orthodox-schism-over-role-of-women-widens-after-gr/?p=all#ixzz2oyuvyMRJ [Accessed June 21, 2013].

Dawson, L. and Cowan, D. (2004). Introduction. In: L. Dawson and D. Cowan (Eds.), *Religion Online*. London: Routledge.

Fonrobert, C.E. and Ilan, T. (2001). Feminist Interpretations of Rabbinic Literature: Two Views. *Nashim: A Journal of Jewish Women's Studies and Gender Issues*, 4, 7–14.

Ganzel, T. and Zimmerman, D.R. (2011). Women as Halakhic Professionals: The Role of the Yo'Atzot *Halacha*. *Nashim: A Journal of Jewish Women's Studies and Gender Issues*, 22, 162–171.

Greenberg, B. (1994). *On Women and Judaism: A View from Tradition*. Philadelphia: Jewish Publication Society.

Hartman, T. (2007). *Feminism Encounters Traditional Judaism: Resistance and Accommodation*. Waltham: Brandeis University Press.

Henkin, C. (1998). Women and the Issuing of Halakhic Rulings. In: M. Halpern and C Safrai (Eds.), *Jewish Legal Writings by Women*. Jerusalem: Urim Publications.

Henkin, C. (1999). *Yoatzot Halacha*: Fortifying Tradition through Innovation. *Jewish Action, 60*(2) [online]. Available at: http://www.Nishmat.net/article.php?id=9&heading=0 [Accessed 21, 2013].

Henkin, C. (n.d.). New Conditions and New Models of Authority—The *Yoatzot Halacha*. Yoetzet.org [online]. Available at: http://www.Nishmat.net/Uploads/files/Rabbanit_Henkin_Yoatzot_Halacha1.pdf [Accessed June 21, 2013].

Leiber, A. (2010). A Virtual Veibershul: Blogging and the Blurring of Public and Private among Orthodox Jewish Women. *College English*,72(6), 621–637.

Livio, O. and Tennenboim Weinblatt, K. (2007). Discursive Legitimation of a Controversial Technology: Ultra-Orthodox Jewish Women in Israel and the Internet. *The Communication Review*, 10(1), 29–56.

Madge, C. and O'Connor, H. (2005). Mothers in the Making? Exploring Liminality in Cyber/Space. *Transactions of the Institute of British Geographers, New Series*, 30(1), 83–97.

Ross, T. (2004). *Expanding the Palace of Torah: Orthodoxy and Feminism*. Waltham: Brandeis University Press.

Steinitz, O. (2011). Responsa 2.0. Are Q&A Websites Creating a New Type of Halachic Discourse? *Modern Judaism*, 31(1), 85–102.

Thumma, S. (2000). *Religion on the Internet*. Hartford Institute for Religion Research [online]. Available at: http://hirr.hartsem.edu/bookshelf/thumma_article6.html [Accessed March 6, 2012].

Zimmerman, D. (2001). The Nishmat Taharat Hamishpacha Hotline: Women Helping Women, *Le'ela*, June, 17–20.

# 5 Sanctifying the Internet

## Aish HaTorah's Use of the Internet for Digital Outreach

*Heidi A. Campbell and Wendi Bellar*

The internet is increasingly used by different Jewish groups as a tool of outreach, especially for religious organizations committed to calling secular Jews back into a religious lifestyle. One example of using the internet to connect, educate and encourage Jews is the work of Aish.com, the digital presence of Aish HaTorah. Due to its Orthodox outlook, it functions under a set of self-imposed rules in its web work to monitor and make sure the content and images that appear on the site support its conservative values and beliefs. While it seeks to be innovative in the types of information and forums it provides (from video podcasts and blogs to online seminars and courses), it insists its work is not a whole-scale endorsement of the internet for all religious Jews. Rather, the internet is presented as a necessary tool to be used in outreach to secular Jews. Aish.com allows Aish HaTorah the means to meet and influence secular Jews wherever they are. By using the internet within a bounded approach and by carefully monitoring web content, those working for the site avoid problematic images and topics as it seeks to sanctify the internet through bringing Torah and a Torah-based lifestyle into the digital realm.

This chapter uses the religious social-shaping of technology (RSST) approach to explore how web innovation can be framed in a way that allows Orthodox Jews to justify their internet use and online presence not only as acceptable but also as essential to their religious mission. The RSST framework helps illuminate two main motivations for Jewish responses to digital technology: (a) to reach out to unaffiliated Jews and (b) to bring sanctification to the world through Torah and moral, sanctified communication. This chapter, therefore, contributes to the theoretical understanding of Jewish responses to digital technology by highlighting the highly complex negotiation process influenced by the group's history and traditions that results in framing of their engagement with the digital.

### AISH.COM AND THE WORK OF AISH HATORAH

In the winding streets of the Jewish quarter, just above the steps to the Western Wall, lie the offices of Aish HaTorah. Established in 1974 by Rabbi Noah

Weinberg, an American Jew who made *Aliyah* (i.e., immigration to the Holy Land) to Israel, the goal was to create an organization that would contribute to the revitalization of Jewish heritage and help people answer the question, "Why be Jewish?" It has 35 branches on five continents that offer a variety of programs at different *Shuls* and Torah learning centers related to Jewish faith and culture, according to Aish.com. Aish HaTorah aligns itself with Orthodox Judaism—especially the American Orthodox Community—and offers a variety of educational programs and even a rabbinical certification program. The aim of the organization is to provide resources to reach as many secular Jews as possible and demonstrate the virtues of religious life and traditions.

Aish.com was set up in 2000 as an online magazine that offered a variety of articles, audio talks, videos and blogs on subjects as diverse as dating and parenting to Jewish history and Holocaust studies. Because the site is based in Jerusalem, they also try to give a window to life in Israel by offering alternative news coverage and highlighting positive events. According to Aish.com's editor-in-chief, the website receives nearly 2.6 million visits a month and has about 270,000 e-mail subscribers, making it one of the largest religious Jewish informational sites online. It is also important to note that most of the editors for the site have also been trained as rabbis within Aish HaTorah's own Rabbinical Ordination program, giving them a certain level of offline as well as online authority. Aish.com and its parent organization are very fluent in and embracing of new media technology as they try to "use any tool available to reach as many non-religious Jews as possible" (interview, July 6, 2008). That includes actively using the internet in their quest to bring secular Jews back to the faith.

Two of the site's most unique services include the Western Wall Cam, which provides a 24-hour live video feed of the wall, and "Ask the Rabbi." The Western Wall is one of the most central places for Jews, because it is the closest physical location to where the Jewish Temple was located that Jews can still visit. Thus, a custom has emerged over time to visit the Western Wall to say and even place prayers. Through Aish.com's Western Wall Cam, Aish HaTorah seeks to provide a virtual connection point for Jews, as Aish.com's editor-in-chief explained:

> The web site gives a tangible way for Jews to connect to the *Kotel*, so that wherever you are in the world you have access, and can stand at the wall and connect your prayers in this way. It is really a way of facilitating a religious experience and tons of Jews and non-Jews come to our site to engage in this way.
>
> (interview, July 6, 2008)

Another option at the Western Wall Cam page is for users to e-mail a prayer to the site, which is printed out on their behalf and placed in the wall. These e-mail prayers are received from Jews, and even non-Jews, all over the world.

The "Ask the Rabbi" page allows users access to an extensive archive of previous questions and responses. It also allows visitors to e-mail Jewish-related questions that are received and responded to within 24 to 48 hours by one of four rabbis employed part-time by Aish.com. Each rabbi has connections with the organization and was selected for his experience and sensitivity in his responses to the diversity of issues raised by e-mail questions. According to Aish.com's editor-in-chief, the popular service provides "a good way for Jews around the world who are not connected to a Synagogue to get their questions answered" (interview, July 6, 2008). Aish.com has received as many as 2,000 questions in a month, and "Ask the Rabbi" has become an important tool in their outreach to nonreligious Jews. The editor-in-chief said, "Our hope is not just to answer their question but to help them see that Judaism has satisfying answers to their problems and issues in our world that inspire them to explore Judaism more" (interview, 6 July 2008).

In addition to "Ask the Rabbi," Aish HaTorah has an extensive social network of outreach groups located throughout North America, Canada, Israel and London that try to help educate especially secular Jews about their faith, history and culture. These offline groups become important connection points for those who contact them via the website. If online interaction piques people's interest to learn more about Judaism, Aish HaTorah actively seeks to link these individuals with one-on-one study partners to help them further explore issues. Face-to-face connection is the first option for those internet users located within a similar geographic location, but when this is not possible, Aish HaTorah also offers to pair them with study partners via phone to help people explore their questions more in-depth. The internet serves as a gateway between online questioning and offline community interaction. For Aish.com it is not just about connecting people to information but also about using the internet as a tool to connect people with a larger network of faith:

> People are often curious about their Jewish roots, but don't know what is available to them. They trust us because of what they see and read on our site. They see a relevant and balanced presentation of information and resources we offer, so the online contact helps them get over the hurdle to explore Judaism more offline.
>
> (editor-in-chief, interview, July 6, 2008)

Even with these innovative features, the editor-in-chief said that the most powerful part of Aish.com is the stories and posts it receives. He said the site has been used to facilitate amazing events in the lives of individuals as it generates not only interest in Judaism but also by soliciting prayer support for fellow Jews around the world.

This description of Aish.com illustrates several key organizational values: using the internet as a tool for outreach to unaffiliated Jews to connect with their heritage, helping people build and maintain the Jewish belief and communities and utilizing the technology for good and not for harm. These values are reflected in the website's goals as stated by the editor-in-chief: the opportunities the site provides to connect nonreligious Jews with rabbis and offline communities and the impact the articles have on everyday lives as religious practice is mediated through the internet.

## Aish.com and the Religious Social Shaping of Technology

The RSST approach (Campbell, 2010) is used in order to understand how Aish.com's values impact the way the internet is used as a tool to further its religious mission as well as to frame how the group negotiates with technology. RSST, developed by Campbell (2010), provides scholars a way to study how religious communities and individuals appropriate and to negotiate new technologies into their everyday religious lives. These complex negotiations, which are informed by the group's historical and traditional understandings as well as its core beliefs and values, can result in new uses and beliefs within given social contexts. Technology is not viewed as determinative in communities' responses; rather, communities and users are able to negotiate and shape technology to fit their unique needs. Therefore, it is important to understand the complex and involved nature of the negotiation process.

For instance, religious communities rarely reject new technologies outright. First, they determine what application the technology may have in their lives and whether those applications are problematic in relation to their values. If there is some tension between the technology and the community's values, the community must then determine what technological aspects will be resisted. Resistance can then lead to reconstruction of the technology through how the community uses the technology, how the community talks about the technology or both. Often this negotiation leads to innovation. For example, cell phones were problematic for Orthodox Jews because they provided a gateway for community members to sin through access to unacceptable content like gambling and pornography. Therefore, the group "koshered" the cell phone by removing or blocking the users' access to the problematic content (Campbell, 2010).

A holistic view of a community's negotiation with and shaping of technology requires investigation into four key areas within the RSST framework: (a) history and traditions, (b) core beliefs and patterns, (c) negotiation process and (d) communal framing and discourse (Campbell, 2010, p. 60). In the first area, *history and tradition*, it is important for researchers to have a thorough understanding of the communities' interactions with media over time and what events and decisions affected those interactions. Second, interactions and decisions lead to the development of the communities' *core beliefs and patterns*. In this area, researchers should pay close attention to how the core values of the community are actually lived out and how those values encourage patterns of use and belief. It is also important to determine who in the group has the authority to influence these beliefs and patterns. Only with a strong understanding of these first two areas can researchers begin to explore the third area, the *negotiation process*. When communities are faced with new media technologies, they must evaluate it, identify potential problem areas and negotiate with the technology before they decide whether to accept it, reject it or reshape it (Campbell, 2010, p. 168). The last area, *communal framing and discourse*, involves understanding how the adoption of the new technology changes the way the community talks about and understands the role of technology. Here attention needs to be paid to both the public and private discourse surrounding the communities' use and interaction with technology and how that discourse informs the group's identity and values. Campbell (2010) argues that all four areas must be considered if scholars wish to fully understand the motivations of a specific religious community's engagement. We apply the RSST framework to the work and mission of Aish.com in order to reflect on the grounding and implication of media motivations.

## HISTORY AND BACKGROUND: ORTHODOX JUDAISM AND ITS VIEW OF TECHNOLOGY

The religious community's history and background serve as grounding and context, which dictates how they will respond to different forms of media and new technologies. In Judaism, this requires paying attention to how the community defines itself especially in relation to religious authority, community and its holy texts.

Orthodox Judaism is a label used to describe those religious communities who seek to closely follow historic rituals, to understand Jewish law (*Halacha*) and to directly apply the interpretive codes of Torah and *Halacha* in the modern world. While Orthodox communities share common practices and beliefs they are also distinctive due to their histories, Diasporas and ethnic connections that translate into unique life practices and authority structures for different groups. Orthodox includes the Sephardim, Ashkenazi or Mitnagdim, Hassidim and National Religious (Nahshoni 2009). Aish HaTorah associates more with conservative groups in terms of social behaviors and religious practices that seek to adhere closely to traditional understandings of religious law and reject modern moral values. Aish.com's staff described themselves and the site as "broadly Orthodox," though most individually affiliate with the Ashkenazi community and Aish HaTorah synagogues.

It is important to understand that the way Orthodox groups engage media is directly related to how they view boundaries for interacting with the modern or secular world (Campbell and Golan, 2011). Many groups choose an isolated lifestyle, live in close proximity and organize around a central spiritual leader (Campbell, 2011; Friedman and Heilman, 1991). Rabbis and religious leaders are the authority when it comes to determining how the community should engage with media. This hierarchical authority structure has been in place throughout history as rabbis are the key spiritual guides that interpret holy texts (such as Torah) and documents (Campbell, 2011). Aish.com does not stray far from this authority model. For instance, whenever the production manager for Aish.com encountered issues or concerns, he said he always talked to the rabbis and asked "what is appropriate or what is inappropriate" (personal communication, July 20, 2009).

How Orthodox Jews understand and interact with media is often linked back to how they understand and interact with their holy texts. As mentioned before, rabbis and spiritual leaders are the authorities and usually are the only ones responsible for interacting with and interpreting these highly regarded historical documents (Campbell, 2011). Media, therefore, and the access the community has to it, pose a problem: Access is more readily available and may privilege the individual to make decisions for him- or herself rather than deferring to the rabbi (Campbell, 2011). We can see, therefore, how allowing the community access to create its own content may be problematic. Aish.com's director of development said that Aish.com would not allow user-created content because it needed to "stay within the Orthodox constraint in what would be considered acceptable content" (interview, July 27, 2009). Access to media may also provide a gateway to the secular world and lead the community into sinful behaviors. Therefore, rabbis and spiritual leaders are relied on to make the rules regarding media and technology use (Campbell, 2011). This relationship and response are rooted in the historical tradition and the separation between the sacred and the secular through strict control of media use.

The community's historical approach to text also provides a template for how they may respond to other technologies. While there are some differences between different Orthodox branches, historical texts and documents have traditionally been highly valued by the community and religious authorities closely control the interpretation of these texts (Campbell, 2011). Rabbis' interpretations of historical texts have broad implications for the daily life and religious practice. Study and scholarship surrounding these texts is thus held in high regard. The strict control and highly regarded scholarship surrounding texts lay the basis for how the community makes sense of and engages with new media technologies (Campbell, 2010, p. 66).

Understanding the community's historical background in the areas of community, authority and text provides a trajectory for future negotiations with technology. Orthodox groups can be expected to intensely scrutinize new technologies in terms of how they influence or interfere with the community's daily and religious lives. New technologies will be fully vetted, and instructions and guidelines for use will be driven by religious authorities.

## CORE VALUES: THE TORAH, THE COMMUNITY AND THE SACRED–PROFANE BOUNDARY

A religious community's core values and beliefs frame how its members engage with social and cultural worlds. Within Judaism, values emerge from the teachings of the Torah and help guide interactions inside and outside the community. When it comes to media, a central point of orientation and debate is how a specific group orients itself in relation to moral boundaries, or its relationship to the sacred and profane. When we look at the work of Aish.com, it draws attention to a few core values including (a) faith-based proclamation, (b) maintenance of the Jewish faith and community and (c) purity in communication. All three of these areas intermingle and are evidenced by different content and editorial decisions.

The first value, faith-based proclamation, is emphasized clearly on the "About Us" section of the website. It states that the goal of Aish.com is to "give every Jew the opportunity to connect to his or her heritage in an atmosphere of open inquiry and mutual respect," (Aish.com, 2013). The phrase "every Jew" is interesting because when asking Aish.com leaders about the goal of the website, they refer specifically to unaffiliated Jews, or Jews who are not practicing religion within the Jewish faith community. The senior editor at Aish.com explained: "Aish.com is actually unique among Orthodox sites in that it is not geared for that market. It's geared for unaffiliated Jews produced by Orthodox Jews. Geared for unaffiliated Jews, it's a unique combination" (interview, 20 July 20, 2009).

Faith-based proclamation is achieved through features of the website such as "Ask the Rabbi," "Judaism 101" and "Torah Portion," which allow leaders of the website to offer users who have questions regarding religious life the opportunity to receive information and instruction, such as guidance on proper burial rites, how to light the menorah or practical insights on the Torah readings for the week and their application to their lives. Aish.com's senior editor said that the website is a resource for people to use to get basic questions answered: "It's the how to, you know. Just tell me what to do. Now that's really the ABCs" (interview, July 20, 2009). The hope is that getting those basic questions answered in a satisfying way will lead to more questions and interaction with the faith and community.

If the user trusts the site to answer questions about burial or about how to celebrate a holiday, maybe he or she will go to the site for other issues such as parenting, marriage and dating. This points toward a second value, the maintenance of Jewish faith and community. Focusing on family and relationships from an Orthodox Jewish perspective allows the site to help unaffiliated Jews continue their understanding of how Torah is relevant in their everyday lives. Understanding and studying how Torah applies to everyday life is in fact part of the mission of Aish HaTorah. The website quotes Elie Weisel on the About Us page: "Aish HaTorah means to me the passion of teaching, the passion of learning. The study of the Torah, the source of Jewish values, is the way to Jewish survival" (Aish.com, 2013). Therefore, teaching unaffiliated Jews how the Torah applies to their lives and giving them the resources they need to interact with the community are literally a means of survival for the Orthodox Jewish faith.

Another area of concern in terms of maintaining the Jewish faith and community is assimilation. Aish.com's senior editor said that intermarriage, or assimilation, is a major reason sites such as Aish.com are need to reach out to secular Jews. He explained: "Really the step, the final step of unraveling is intermarriage. When Jews don't marry Jews . . . Intermarriage equals assimilation" (personal communication, July 20, 2009). Therefore, dating and marriage are main concerns, and a whole section of the website is devoted specifically to give advice and wisdom in this area.

Encouraging the proper maintenance of Jewish faith and community begins with providing unaffiliated Jews the information and inspiration they need to understand the Torah and how it relates to their daily lives. Once this understanding is provided in a meaningful way through Aish.com, leaders hope the unaffiliated Jew will be encouraged to dig deeper into the Torah and how it should have an impact on the personal relationships through dating and marriage within the faith.

Purity in communications, the final value, manifests itself directly through rules about what can and cannot be said or shown on the site. Aish.com's editor-in-chief explained that there is a whole world of Jewish law in the Torah that deals specifically with proper speech, which can include the messages that images convey. When content comes close to breeching the purity in communication value, Aish.com members defer to the rabbis to make a choice on whether to include or modify it. Aish HaTorah's senior editor offered a few examples of questionable material. The first involved a woman who wrote an article about her rape experience. "Though the act itself was obviously not described in graphic detail, we had to tone down much of the allusion to the act, to avoid people conjuring up the images in their mind," he said (interview, July 20, 2009). The second example focused on a "powerful" article another woman wrote about her experience fighting breast cancer. While they did not reject the entire article, they did alter it. "We deleted the part where she spoke of taking a shower for the first time after, as this would also conjure up naked imagery" (personal communication, July 20, 2009).

Stories, such as the ones mentioned earlier (videos, blogs, etc.) make up the content of the site, but another area of concern is advertisements. Aish.com is very selective when it comes to deciding which companies are appropriate for the site and which are not. These decisions often link back to all three values, as Aish.com's director of development explained: "Because of the nature of our site being an Orthodox Jewish site, the advertising has to fit into who we are and who our viewers are. Basically, it takes 99% of all the advertising in the world and eliminates them" (personal communication, July 20, 2009).

While the director of development and the other rabbis have the final say regarding who can advertise on the site, they do use a third-party company, J Media Group, which is familiar with their rules and regulations. The advertisement must be relevant. According to the director of development, this means the advertisements must be consistent with Jewish law in terms of the purity in communication value. While some advertisements are irrelevant because of lack of interest from the users, other advertisements, like the dating sites mentioned earlier, may be relevant but also improper. Therefore, Aish.com is very selective about any form of advertisement.

These three core values orient the interactions creators of the site as well as the users of the site. Negotiation with new technology is filtered through core values in that it helps proclaim the faith to secular Jews, it helps the community to maintain cultural and religious norms and it maintains content that meets the religious purification standard. These core values also guide editorial and design decisions as well as provide insight into the negotiation process that permits them to utilize an otherwise problematic technology.

## NEGOTIATION: KOSHERING THE INTERNET

In the negotiation stage, attention is paid to how the history and core values provide a framework or guidelines that direct a religious group's engagement with new forms of media. Within the negotiation process the group must consider to what extent a new medium—such as the internet—can be used or what aspect or outcomes of the technology may need to be resisted or modified. In the case of the internet, we see that it provides Aish.com with both opportunities and challenges to consider and to respond to.

Orthodox Jews have had a contentious relationship with some older media technologies, especially if they are seen to promote values that run counter to the community. Many Orthodox Jews, for example, see television, as problematic. Rabbis, especially ultra-Orthodox rabbis, often condemned TV as a "device of the devil" (Campbell 2010, p. 166). TV is seen to allow the influence of the secular world to seep into the sacred life Jews are called to live. As Cromer (1987) noted, TV is framed as a source of impurity because of immoral content, such as sexual and violent shows. Aish.com's editor-in-chief remarked that a majority of the Orthodox do not have TV, which is the best practice. For him, not having access to media in the home comes down to protecting his children from violent content. Many religious leaders' condemn of media technologies, their negotiation process with these older technologies mirrors their negotiation with the internet.

Aish.com staff, like many groups within Orthodox Judaism, note that the internet can be a problematic technology, because it offers both a valuable tool for outreach and has strong potential to become a moral threat if used incorrectly. Three core objections are often voiced by Orthodox groups regarding the internet. First, Orthodox groups highlight certain moral and ethical concerns related to the internet. Generally, they adhere to a moral code that identifies the internet with modern decadence and potential moral contamination. A key concern is the extent to which the online world may serve as a gateway to sin, providing easy access to sexually explicit materials that can lead to transgressions in thought and action. In this sense, the internet is perceived as a dangerous influence that can hamper the moral codes upheld by the enclave society (Caplan, 2003). This is comparable to other practices such as limiting interactions between the sexes (i.e., chaperoned courtships) or forbidding watching TV. The concern is over visual aspects of the internet where users may be exposed to immodest images of women or sexually explicit content. Thus, the internet is often framed as dangerous for male members of the community who may be susceptible to such temptation (Campbell, 2007).

Second, the internet is framed as violating communal behavioral controls and protocols, which leads to the disintegration of the community's social fabric. It is seen as a source dispersing disruptive or false information within communal parameters. Researchers often highlight religious leaders' concerns that the internet increases community members' exposure to secular messages that can endanger their moral codes (Horowitz, 2000), such as its ability to spread *Lashon H'ra* (gossip or slanderous information) and traditional social expectation or patterns of life (Baumel-Schwartz, 2009). Also, the internet represents a solitary activity that cannot be as easily monitored by family or community members (Neriya-Ben Shahar and Lev-On, 2009). As such, internet engagement is framed as enabling the transgression of long-established community boundaries, avenues of social control and recognized religious authorities.

Third, the internet is seen to transgress established boundaries between the sacred and secular worlds. The fear of exposure to information generated outside the community increases as the internet becomes a channel for interacting with the secular world. The internet challenges accepted foundations of the sacred, an established division between piety and profane aspects of life. In this sense the internet impinges on their basic ideals and goals and may be seen as a *moshav letsim* (a seat of scorners), a social gathering where no matters of Torah are discussed (El-Or, 1994). The fear is the internet may facilitate a transgression between sacred-secular community divides, running counter to daily rituals that seek to maintain clear distinction between sacred and secular aspects of life. Therefore, access to unmonitored, secular and sinful content online is seen as highly problematic, which individuals may easily and unintentionally access (Tsarfaty and Blais, 2002).

So how does Aish.com respond to these objections? First, they make it very clear that Aish.com is not targeting Orthodox Jews. Rather, the goal of the website is to reach the secular Jews, or those they call unaffiliated Jews.

Therefore, Aish.com frames itself as a site to reach the unaffiliated and the internet just happens to be one of the best ways to connect and engage with them. Aish.com's editor-in-chief discussed his mission in using the internet:

> My mission is to use the internet to bring, like I said before, to bring the meaning and knowledge of Judaism to as many Jews as possible. To secular Jews that couldn't care less about Judaism, or are disengaged about Judaism, who never learned that Judaism speaks to them. So we try and reach them where they are at.
>
> (interview, July 6, 2008)

Therefore, while the internet does provide a gateway to sinful behaviors, the rabbi made the point that it is where the unaffiliated are and there needs to be a site that will guide them in the right way when they face life questions. A senior editor at Aish.com reiterated this point as he discussed why he was so excited to utilize the internet. He noted the trends of people moving from watching traditional TV to watching TV online, of people reading books on an e-reader or tablet rather than a traditional book. People are living their lives through the internet, and this senior editor noted that the Orthodox community has to be online in order to reach them: "You just have to be there" (interview, July 20, 2009). This phrase is really important in Aish.com's response to the concern of using a technology that may also introduce morally objectionable behaviors. It is where the unaffiliated are; therefore, it is where Aish HaTorah should be as well.

Although the site is a place to meet the unaffiliated where they are, Aish.com's director of development does acknowledge that some of the traffic on the site comes from the Orthodox community. Although the organization is happy that affiliated Jews come to the website, the director of development maintains the real target is nonaffiliated Jews. The content on the site is geared to getting them excited about Judaism and that there is a place for them in the religion.

Along with conceptualizing the internet as the place to meet their target audience, Aish HaTorah leaders say the internet is also a tool that can be used both for good and for evil. While the internet may provide a gateway to sin, it can also provide a gateway for sanctification. The editor-in-chief explained how he conceptualizes internet technology:

> So our view of technology is that technology is neutral. It was put in the world for a reason, as a path to use for good. There's a lot of bad on the internet. No need to explain what that is. Everyone knows the negatives. But that doesn't mean it's inherently trace, it's inherently poison to use it. So we're sanctifying the internet by using it to be Torah to the world. Millions of people are learning Torah now because of the internet.
>
> (interview, July 6, 2008)

Part of this sanctification of the internet comes through Aish.com content. Content on the site must maintain modesty in order to align with the value of purity through communication. There are some very specific guidelines that Aish.com follows for specific words or phrases. For example, content will never contain immodest women, lies or falsehoods or reveal secrets. The editor-in-chief said, "These are all laws that govern our day-to-day speech. The same thing applies to the internet" (interview, July 6, 2008). Rules about pure communication are even as specific as what words should and should not be used. "Aish has its own guidelines. We must not talk dirty. We're not allowed to use the s-word (i.e. sex). Words about intimacy," a writer for Aish.com said (interview, July 23, 2009). Although she knew these words, she said that there is no document in which the guidelines are written down. Instead, rules are simply understood through to the values of the community and mission of the site and are reinforced by editors in their guidance provided to authors.

While editors and writers need to be aware of problematic words and phrases, a graphic designer for Aish.com makes sure that the visual images are modest. Although he also said that he could not think of any written rules, a few immediately come to his mind: "I remember from the onset that there were rules. Focus on the face. Don't show the elbows. Often, regularly, extend sleeves on images" (interview, July 22, 2009). All images must be approved before being displayed on the site. The editor, who oversees the technical aspects of the site, described the rules more explicitly: "The people, whatever the image is, in general the rule is that the people have to look dignified. You wouldn't mind showing any picture from Aish.com to a five year old" (interview, July 20, 2009).

It seems as though pure communication is concerned mostly with sexual, racy content and the modesty of women. However, the graphic designer did say that violence is another area that the site would not tolerate in its content: "There's no rule about this but it's obvious not to show violent pictures. Dealing with this Palestinian conflict, images and everything" (personal communication, July 22, 2009). In fact, Aish.com has a strict policy to avoid not only violence but also political content. Aish.com's graphic designer said, "Aish in general is not a political organization, so we're not deliberately taking any political stands" (personal communication, July 22, 2009). Rather than weighing in overtly on the political issues or conflicts, the organization seeks to frame contemporary issues in terms of how such event impact Jewish faith and culture. The primary goal is for people who come to the site to learn more about the Jewish faith and to have their questions about life answered by rabbis and for encouraging them to have better relationships.

Aish.com provides a safe site for both affiliated and unaffiliated Jews because, as the rabbis and leaders of the site noted, the internet is becoming a normal part of everyday life. Aish.com's editor-in-chief specifically acknowledged that religious Jews are using technologies everyday including videos, MP3 players and online resources to learn and live. He also tempered that fact with the warning that Jews should be careful when engaging with these media and should provide a safe environment in which to use them.

So what constitutes a safe environment? It is very important for those involved at Aish.com to point out they themselves do not have, or restrict internet in their own homes. The editor-in-chief explained that not having access to internet at home was a way to protect his children from the evil accessible in the online world. Another safe way to use the internet is for work purposes only. So while Orthodox Jews may be discouraged from having the internet in their home, it is deemed acceptable if used on the job.

Kosher internet filters provide another way to set up a safe environment for online engagement. These filters are software that restricts access to sites known to be problematic. Different filters work in different ways. One of Aish.com's graphic designer explained that the filter he uses at home for his family, called Moreshet, works by allowing the user to adjust the levels of control. His filter is set to the control for the religious community and restricts access to sites such as YouTube but allows access to news and general, safe sites (see Rosenthal and Ribak, this volume). Only he and his wife use the internet with filter software.

There are situations when not having internet access in the home or using the filters is not feasible. For example, one of Aish.com's writers said that her computer is kept in a room that is locked so her children do not have access to it. Because her job requires her to do a lot of online research, the traditional internet filters will not work. She explained how the locked door replaces the internet filter: "So my filter is that we lock the door when we're not here so he can't get to it. My son does not have internet access without us supervising. That's our filter. Our filter is the key to the door" (personal communication, July 23, 2009).

The graphic designer pointed out another issue that many involved in Aish.com reiterated—the internet is becoming a requirement for modern life. He acknowledged that his children will have to use it someday even though he and his wife deem it inappropriate at the moment. Aish.com's senior editor emphasized the fact that the internet is necessary:

> There's certain things that you simply cannot do. Like if you want to get an appointment to renew your passport at the American Consulate in Jerusalem you can only do that on the internet. They don't take phone calls. No faxes. No letters. No nothing. There's certain things in life that you can only do on the internet. It's phenomenal thing. There's an acceptance of that because that's just the reality.
>
> (personal communication, 20 July 2009)

We can see from the discourse framing internet use that negotiation with technology takes place in different ways. First, it is labeled as an important tool to reach unaffiliated Jews where they are—on the internet. Second, while it does pose an inherent risk of encouraging transgressions, it also poses the possibility of a tool to be used to bring Torah to the world, one of the goals of Aish HaTorah. Third, understanding the risk and benefits means that Jews need to take action to protect themselves from problematic technology. They modify the internet through filters that protect them from the bad while allowing access to the good. As the internet becomes more and more a part of life, Aish.com leaders argue that you cannot ignore it but, rather, that you have to learn how to use it in appropriate ways.

## COMMUNAL DISCOURSE: AN ORTHODOX APOLOGETIC FOR THE INTERNET

When evaluating the communal discourse of Aish.com, two types of discourse emerge in creating the framework for the use of the technology. First, prescriptive discourse is used to support the use of technology in a way that underscores a core value of the religious group (Campbell, 2010, p. 156). Second, officializing discourse provides boundaries within which the religious community should operate while using the technology (Campbell, 2010, p. 156). In this section, both types of discourses are explored in relation to the larger Orthodox Jewish community and specifically Aish HaTorah.

Prescriptive discourse from Aish HaTorah leaders begins with framing the use of the internet not for religious Jews but for engaging unaffiliated Jews. While the larger Orthodox community condemned the internet as a pathway to evil and destruction and sought to ban use of it outright, Aish HaTorah saw the potential of the technology to further its mission—bringing Torah to the world. Leaders imagined using the tool to bring unaffiliated Jews who had become entangled with the secular to reconnect with the sacred. When discussing the internet bans, leaders of Aish.com are quick to point out this distinction. The editor-in-chief said,

> I don't think any of them ever said we shouldn't use it for outreach. Everyone appreciates the importance of medium to reach secular Jews. The issue is using it for . . . the religious person himself or herself using internet. Today I think religious communities and leading rabbis recognize it's not going to go away. And instead of trying to ban it, we have to figure out how to best use it to protect ourselves.
>
> (personal communication, July 8, 2008)

The justification of using the internet to reach unaffiliated Jews is pointed to time and again by the rabbis, writers and workers of Aish.com. One of Aish.com's writers acknowledged the point of writing articles for the site: "The mission of Aish.com is to make disaffiliated Jews, unaffiliated Jews wake up to their Jewish heritage and teach them about Judaism so that they will become connected to Jewish practice and the Jewish people" (personal communication, July 23, 2009). However, gearing the site to the unaffiliated does cause problems with the Orthodox community. Also Aish.com's director of development pointed out that the site often receives complaints from the Orthodox community for being online. He noted that the way they present issues is purposefully geared to engage the non-Orthodox world, which leads to criticism from the Orthodox world. Again, the justification is that the site is geared to the non-Orthodox. This prescriptive discourse, emphasizing the use of internet technology for outreach, shows how internet use is not only appropriate for their religious community, but imperative to their mission.

For the most part, Aish HaTorah agrees that it would be best for religious Jews to distance themselves from internet technology. This is evident in the way Aish.com staff talked about internet use in the personal lives. For the most part they do not use it. Instead, their personal internet use is framed as problematic, and they relegate use of the internet for neutral tasks or work purposes only. This internet-only world forced authorities to recognize the problematic nature of an outright ban, according to the editor-in-chief: "But even within the most Ultra-Orthodox society today, they have realized its part of life right now. You can't work without it. That's why they're forced to come up with these solutions" (personal communication, July 8, 2008).

Even with filters in place a backlash in 2009 lead to renewed calls for banning internet use altogether. This time, however, the focus was geared more toward Israeli news outlets that began to include internet and mobile services. The issue was not necessarily focused on the potential to access improper material. Instead, the ban centered on publications unsanctioned by the Orthodox authorities, which were seen to be encouraging the spread of gossip, slander and impurities within communications. This is related to other discourse from Aish.com that can be seen in the rules and regulations concerning purity in communication. In the negotiation section, for example, Aish.com leaders spelled out direct words and phrases to be used, as well as specific guidelines for images on the site.

Prescriptive discourse used by Aish.com works, first, to justify use of internet technology to aid the specific goal of reaching unaffiliated Jews and, second, to set boundaries and regulations for religious Jews' internet use. It provides justification of use to target those outside the community, while also providing the framework for use within the community.

## CONCLUSION

Using the RSST framework, this case study emphasizes how Aish HaTorah frames and negotiates using new technologies within its organization to complete goals and to fulfill its mission. RSST provides historical context, insight into core values that inform negotiation with technology, and explores communal discourse that frames future interactions with technology as well as affirms the group's identity. Aish.com is used as an outreach tool to connect, educate and encourage secular Jews with their religious heritage. Internet use is framed within this context as a neutral tool that can be used for good or evil. Aish.com staff acknowledge the potential for evil and negotiates how to protect the community from possible dangers through restrictions on use and internet filters. Rather than only acknowledge the bad, Aish HaTorah is determined to use the tool for good—bringing Torah to the world. Framing their work as outreach allows them to negotiate use within the larger Orthodox community. The goal is to bring the unaffiliated Jews into the community slowly, step by step, and use the online connection to engage them with the offline community.

There are several important key concepts this case study emphasizes. First, Aish.com does not offer a wholesale endorsement of internet use. Rather, the group offers a unique insight into the negotiation with internet and the community's subsequent interactions with the technology. Aish.com is able to maintain the line that the internet is not good for Orthodox Jews to use except in the cases of work while promoting its use to bring unaffiliated Jews into the fold. Second, we show that past interactions with technology helped guiding to guide Aish.com in its approach to the internet. Orthodox leaders acknowledge its problematic nature with older media such as TV. However, they also acknowledge that the internet is different from older media and is becoming more and more a part of everyday life. Third, because using the internet is problematic, Aish.com staff reframed it as a possible tool to help fulfill an important core value—to reach unaffiliated Jews. Because the Aish.com leadership can clearly show that the internet is a concrete way to reach its key audience, it can make a concrete argument for its use. Finally, the importance of religious authority is seen throughout the history and background, core values, negotiation and communal discourse section. Throughout every process, rabbis are sought out and consulted so that Torah can be applied in the right way on every level. Aish.com always defers to the rabbis when questions or concerns arise. Therefore, we can predict that the role of authority figures will continue to be a prominent aspect of any interactions with future technologies.

The main factors and motivations that influence how Aish.com embraces digital technology include two issues: (a) reaching unaffiliated Jews and (b) sanctifying the world by providing access to the Torah and pure communication. Digital technologies, such as websites, are uniquely situated to help facilitate these motivations by allowing Aish.com to reach unaffiliated Jews where they are—online. While the internet is not sanctified yet, Aish.com uses its web site to further this goal by providing access to Torah studies online and by providing rabbi-sanctioned advice on modern life. This differs from other Jewish Orthodox groups in that access to the internet is negotiated and use of the web sites is shaped by Aish HaTorah's unique history and core values. While some Orthodox groups have sought to ban the internet outright so that the negotiation process is preempted and others still struggle with justifying their internet engagement in the face of tension with leader's beliefs, Aish.com, like the Chabad, have been able to come to terms with active online engagement. Therefore, this chapter offers a unique contribution by utilizing the RSST framework to illuminate the complex interaction of history and core values in the negotiation with digital technology within the Orthodox community.

## REFERENCES


Aish.com. (2013). About Us [online]. Available at: http://www.aish.com/about/ [Accessed February 13, 2013].

Baumel-Schwartz, J. (2009). Frum Surfing: Orthodox Jewish Women's Internet Forums as a Historical and Cultural Phenomenon. *Journal of Jewish Identities*, 29(1), 1–30.

Campbell, H. (2007). What Hath God Wrought: Considering How Religious Communities Culture (or Kosher) the Cell Phone. *Continuum: Journal of Media and Cultural Studies*, 20(2), 191–203.

Campbell, H. (2010). *When Religion Meets New Media*. London: Routledge.

Campbell, H. (2011). Religion and the Internet in the Israeli Orthodox Context. *Israel Affairs*, 17(3), 364–383.

Campbell, H. and Golan, O. (2011). Creating Digital Enclaves: Negotiation of the Internet Among Bounded Religious Communities. *Media, Culture, & Society*, 33(5), 709–724.

Caplan, K. (2003). Studying Israeli Haredi Society. In: K. Caplan and E. Sivan (eds.) *Israeli Haredim: Integration without Assimilation?* (pp. 224–278). Tel-Aviv: Van Leer Jerusalem Institute/HaQibbutz HaMe'uhad Publishing House.

Cromer, G. (1987). The Polluted Image: The Response of Ultra-Orthodox Judaism to Israel Television. *Sociology and Social Research*, 71(3), 198–199.

El-Or, T. (1994). *Educated and Ignorant: Ultra-Orthodox Jewish Women and Their World*, trans. Haim Watzman. Boulder: Lynne Rienner.

Friedman, M. and Heilman, S.C. (1991). *The Haredim in Israel*. New York: American Jewish Committee.

Horowitz, N. (2000). The Ultra-Orthodox and the Internet. *Kivumim Hadashim*, 3, 7–30 (in Hebrew).

Nahshoni, K. (11 December 2009). Rabbis Take on Haredi Websites. *Ynetnews.com* [online]. Available at: http://www.ynetnews.com/articles/0,7340,L-3818334,00.html

Neriya-Ben Shahar, R.N. and Lev-On, A. (2009). *Open spaces? Perceptions of the Internet Among Ultra-Orthodox Women Working in Computerized Environments*. Lecture at Netvision Institute, Tel-Aviv University, Tel-Aviv, Israel, June 15, submitted to *Megamot* (in Hebrew).

Sherlick, T. (2008). For First Time, Hasidic Sect Approves Limited Internet Use. *Haaretz Online*. Available at: http://www.haaretz.co.il/hasen/spages/1005913.html [Accessed June 12, 2009].

Tsarfaty, O. and Blais, D. (2002). Between "Cultural Enclave" and "Virtual Enclave": Ultra-Orthodox Society and the Digital Media. *Kesher*, 32, 47–55 (in Hebrew).

# 6 Jewish Games for Learning

## Renewing Heritage Traditions in the Digital Age

*Owen Gottlieb*[1]

## INTRODUCTION: JEWISH GAMES, PLAY, AND HERITAGE

As the mobile phone brings video games to new audiences and console game sales reach into the billions, games and game systems have become the ascendant popular medium of the 21st century. Games are also a part of Judaism's ancient heritage. This chapter argues that there is a fundamental foundation of play and game systems at the heart of Jewish literature and learning.[2] Contemporary endeavors in digital and analog Jewish Games for Learning are practices grounded in traditional, yet seldom-discussed systems of Jewish games and play for learning.

For some Jews, a shift from print to digital raises deep-seated concerns regarding cultural continuity. The notion of the Jews as "people of the book" is often tied to print media, but for at least the first hundred years after the advent of the printing press, print was not considered sacred (see Gottlieb, 2013). In the summer of 2013, *Reform Judaism Magazine*, "the world's largest circulated Jewish magazine,"[3] featured a cover article by clinical psychologist Wendy Mogel titled "Invasion of the Machines." Mogel asks and answers questions such as "How can [digital] 'immigrant' parents set digital boundaries that make sense for their 'native' children?" and "Should parents be concerned about their children becoming cyber-addicted?" (Mogel, 2013). The article argues that the answer is yes. In this article the emphasis is on fear. Technology and new media, such as video games, pose high risk to children:

> For one, video game manufacturers spend lots of money studying the neuroscience of behavior. Talking to the owner of one of these companies, I was stunned by his knowledge of children's brain development. He told me straight out that his corporate mission is to understand how to make games as addictive as possible.
>
> (Mogel, 2013)

In a marked contrast, scholars, researchers, designers, philanthropists and classroom educators are developing learning games, gathering at conferences such as Games for Change, Games Learning Society and Digital Media and Learning. These educators look to video games as models of the most rich and compelling elements with which to improve learning environments, from scaffolding to just-in-time feedback. Learners will play games for hours until they find the solution to a level (problem). How can educators and designers use the engrossing nature of games to enhance the teaching in STE(A)M,[4] history, language, civics and other subjects? It happens that traditional Jewish learning shares many parallels with games systems as well, and perhaps this is why there is a nascent movement of Jewish Games for Learning.

Rather than a discontinuity from traditional modes of learning, new explorations of digital and strategic games in Jewish learning are markedly continuous with ancient practices. An explication of the close connections between traditional modes of Jewish learning, interpretive practice, and gaming culture can help to explain how Jews of the Digital Age can adopt and are adapting modern Games for Learning practices for contemporary purposes. The chapter opens by contextualizing a notion of Jewish Games and the field of Games for Learning. Next, the chapter explains the connections between game systems and Jewish traditions. It closes with a case study of current trends in Jewish Games for Learning in progressive Judaism. How can one view Jewish holidays as heritage game systems? How are texts of the Talmud and the social practice of studying Talmud related to practices of digital and analog games and game play? The Talmud section of the chapter examines rules systems in the Talmud, the theoretical model and case generation of Talmudic *sugyot* (passages or sections), and the practice of pairs-sacred study, *hevruta*, in which study partners, sometimes overseen by a senior scholar, seek deeper understanding of the text in a collaborative delving into text and argumentation.

The purpose of this exploration is twofold: first, to demonstrate how new media are providing novel ways of viewing ancient Jewish systems for the acquisition of cultural practice. Second, this chapter shows how viewing Jewish practice, study, and inquiry through the lens of the game system can illumine seldom-explored aspects of the tradition, such as model generation in Talmudic texts and study. New Jewish Games for Learning are continuous with Jewish learning and culture over the ages, and the construct of the game, informed by contemporary Games for Learning research, can demonstrate new ways to understand both ancient and contemporary Jewish practices.

## WHAT ARE GAMES FOR LEARNING?

"Games for Learning" are often related to "Serious Games." Games for Learning refers to a class of games that is concerned with drawing on research in education, the Learning Sciences, and Media Studies regarding how to best improve learning environments. Learning Sciences comprises a number of fields including cognitive science, computer science, anthropology, design studies and educational psychology. Games for Learning are distinct from games found in "educational software," because they draw from and contribute to findings in field research. Often, they are concerned with tying a game or simulation's core mechanics (roughly, the actions that the players take during the game), to the desired learning. These games are often concerned with solving complex problems, using inquiry-based learning. Many times they involve some kind of disciplinary role playing, such as that of a scientist, a journalist or an engineer. There are two academic branches of Games for Learning, both of which are relevant to the case study later in this chapter. The first branch dates back to the 1970s (see Horn, 1980[5]; the journal *Simulation and Gaming*, 1970; and Dukes and Waller, 1976). During this period, Fred Goodman was an important teacher and game designer. He founded the Interactive Communications & Simulations Group at the University of Michigan.

A more recent branch of Games for Learning emerging in the academy and among game designers can be traced back to the literacy studies scholar, James Paul Gee and his colleagues' work in the early 2000s (see Gee, 2003). The Games, Learning, and Society Conference (GLS) is in its 10th year, and the Games for Change Festival in its 11th year. Today, funded along with Digital Media and Learning (DML) initiatives by prominent foundations such as the MacArthur Foundation and the Bill and Melinda Gates Foundation, Games for Learning labs are branching into academies around the world.

## DEFINING "JEWISH GAMES"

To understand the roles of games and play in Jewish tradition, it is important to begin with definitions. Digital systems often provide faster interfaces and feedback mechanisms than analog games (i.e., board, card games). That said, often, the underlying structures of games are common across both digital and analog games. In this chapter, simulations refer to modeled procedural systems, following Salen and Zimmerman's (2003) definition: "a procedural representation of aspects of 'reality'" (p. 243). Games are then a subset of simulations, typically, those with defined goals. This chapter refers to game play using Salen and Zimmerman's definition of play: "Play is free movement within a more rigid structure" (2003, p. 304). This more rigid structure is bounded by *rules*, one of the essential formal elements of games (see Fullerton, 2008, pp. 68–71).

Games have long been a part of Jewish culture—from table-top games played by Jews such as mahjong (see Lewis, n.d.; Luu and Cavallaro, 2005) to those played by and invented by Jews, such as *Rummikub* (Hertzano, 1978), a tile game created by Israeli game designer Ephraim Hertzano. In recent years digital games have emerged that include Jewish characters or themes, such as Shivah (Gilbert, 2006)), or references to Jewish themes or issues, as in Red Dead Redemption (Cantamessa, 2010). There are a variety of children's educational software products including games oriented toward enculturation of Orthodox or Haredi (ultra-Orthodox) children and some simple Hebrew games for progressive Jews. Wagner (2013) presents a number of these games in her presentation "Mitzvot Mash-Up: Interactivity as Transformative Interpretation."

Yet these games tend to be oriented toward either trivia or simple identification, such as learning Hebrew letters through matching or memorizing blessings. These games do not draw from the current educational research on games and learning. They seldom if ever tie game mechanics to the desired learning. For example, firing a laser beam at the correct letter Hebrew letter does not tie the action (firing a laser beam) to the learning of language. Nor do these games hint at the powerful traditions of play used in Jewish sacred texts and learning. Likewise, popular games involving Jewish trivia or symbol recognition, such as the Jewish version of the popular card game Apples to Apples (Kirby and Osterhaus, 2007), do not involve inquiry based learning or teach beyond object recognition (e.g., this is a Challah; that is a Torah scroll).

The popular conception of ancient Jewish gaming may very well be that of the *Dreidl*, the spinning top game that children play on Chanukah. But the *Dreidl* is not so ancient. Rather than dating to the time of the Maccabees and the Hasmonean Dynasty (163–142 BCE), the earliest known version of the game dates to the 16th-century English game called totem, and a later German derivative that found its way into Eastern European Jewish tradition (Golinkin, 2000, pp. 177–178). Ancient Jewish games are to be found elsewhere.

In order to understand the connection between contemporary Games for Jewish Learning and the deep roots in Jewish tradition, it is important to move beyond these commonly known children's toy-oriented conceptions of Jewish games. One must consider the simulations involved in ritual, such as those found in holidays. And it is crucial to consider the highly complex and ancient Jewish games found in both the compositional structures of rabbinic literature and in the practices surrounding the study and proliferation of those texts.

## RITUAL AND HOLIDAYS AS REENACTMENT, SIMULATION AND PLAY

By examining the relationship between play, ritual and simulation, Jewish holiday rituals can be understood as game systems. In *Godwired*, Wagner (2012b) turns to Johan Huizinga's writing on games and ritual, explaining that the formal elements of play relate closely to those of ritual. Play, like ritual, is a kind of order-making process. Ritual and play both "transport the participants to another world" (Huizinga, as cited in Wagner, 2012b, p. 2). "Ritual and play, then, both set apart a time and space in which special happenings occur, shaped by rules and in some ways different from our daily life, somehow nurturing in their predictability and in their 'other-worldliness' " (Wagner, 2012b, p. 2).

Similarly, Harlene Appleman, a Jewish educator for more than 40 years and the executive director of the Covenant Foundation, whose mission, according to its website, is "celebrating innovation and excellence in Jewish Education," argues that Jewish religious expression is directly connected to play, simulation, and games through the practice of reenactment (http://www.covenantfn.org/about/mission accessed December 8, 2013). "The core of Judaism is reenactment . . . whether you're looking at *tefilah* [prayer], which is a reenactment of what happened in the Temple, or the Passover *seder* which is a reenactment of telling the story [of Exodus] . . . Judaism isn't a stranger to play" (Appleman, interview, March 28, 2012).

One can also understand Jewish holiday rituals as simulations, because rituals, like simulations, are modeled procedural systems. The Seder not only reenacts the telling of the story of Exodus, but it simulates aspects of an Exodus experience, using all the senses. The participants are taught from a young age, they are to say that not "they" but "I" made Exodus from Egypt. They taste the bitterness of slavery by eating bitter foods and taste tears using salt water. Purim and Chanukah simulate survival from persecution. *Tu BiShvat* simulates a fruit harvest in the middle of winter. Yom Kippur simulates death; Shavuot and the Shabbat morning Torah service, the Jewish people receiving Torah at Sinai; Rosh Hashanah, the birth of the world; and *Sukkot*, the fall harvest season.

Games are simulations with goals. The goals of a ritual observance such as Passover include, achieving a connection to a sense of history, deepening ties with family and community, and the passing on of story and values associated with it. And so, these rituals function as games for the acquisition of cultural practices: heritage games. These heritage games use the same elements that contemporary Games for Learning employ: the repetition of behaviors to be learned (game mechanics) in a modeled procedural system (a simulation). While understanding holiday ritual practices as game systems requires considering simulation in the context of goals for cultural transmission, the games and play employed in Jewish sacred text study are direct and striking.

## RABBINIC LITERATURE AND GAME SYSTEMS

The structures of Jewish sacred text and the traditions of learning of those texts, this author argues, are related to and often rooted in game systems, simulations, and forms of play. In Judaism, learning from sacred text is itself a religious, spiritual, and cultural expression and practice. Jewish sacred literature includes the Hebrew Bible as well as rabbinic literature. The rabbinic literature includes but is not limited to the *halachic*, legal literature, the *aggadah* (stories), exegetical literature, and the theosophical and ecstatic mystical writings. The *halachic* literature itself is vast, including legal codes such as sections of Torah (the Five Books of Moses), the first legal code, the Mishna, legal debate and interpretative literature, most prominently, the Babylonian Talmud (the Talmud also includes *aggadic* as well as exegetical literature such as glosses); and case law, *responsa*. While some attention has been given to the *aggadic* and exegetical literature, little attention has thus far been paid to the relationship between the *halachic* literature and game systems.

Wagner (2012a, 2012b) has noted parallels between digital games, play and the rabbinic midrashic (rabbinic, interpretive) literary tradition (both exegetical and narrative). Replayability describes the multiple ways to play a game. Similarly, there are multiple ways in the Midrash to interpret a passage of Bible. Wagner also notes the narrative parallels between some video games' narrative structure and the Jewish *heichalot* mystical apocalyptic writings. Beyond Wagner's discussion of narrative, it is important to also note that at the heart of much rabbinic literature is wordplay. Midrashic exegesis often turns on the use of homophones and homographs, as meaning is derived through playing alternative meanings of words or different ways of reading words. The game of wordplay is very much at the heart of rabbinic meaning making.

Scholar of history and literature of religion, James Carse (1987), describes two classes of games in his philosophical work *Finite and Infinite Games: A Vision of Life as Play and Possibility*. He writes: "1. There are at least two kinds of games. One could be called finite, the other infinite. A finite game is played for the purpose of winning, an infinite game for the purpose of continuing the play" (p. 3). Carse (1987, p. 39) aligns evil with the end of infinite play, and by so reasoning, it appears, he places a sense of benevolence in the infinite play. Carse stated in a radio interview: "One of my favorite examples of an infinite game is the rabbinical tradition in Judaism . . . every text, every truth is open to further question . . . God himself is open to question" (Gordon, 1997). This chapter argues that not only does the play within rabbinic texts fit the model of the Carsian infinite game but that so does *hevruta*, the traditional processes of learning and studying sacred texts in pairs.

Essential contemporary understandings in economic game theory trace their earliest roots to a bankruptcy case in the Babylonian Talmud (Aumann and Maschler, 1985). With the exception of this foundational case in the field of economics, there has been little if any exploration of the *halachic* literature regarding its relationship to game systems. The examination of the Talmud (meaning learning or study) as a nexus of game systems and play is essential for understanding Jewish sacred literature's relationship to the games.

## TALMUD AND GAMES

Games can sometimes have narratives, but games always have rules; *halacha*, or Jewish religious law, is an evolving rule-based system. Examining the Talmud and Talmud study can allow for the clearest illustration of the connection between Jewish tradition and game systems. The Talmud is a primary source for legal debates. It preserves minority opinions, unresolved debates, as well as stories and tales. Traditional modes of Talmud study preserve the social practices of debate and problem solving as a means of learning.

"If the Bible is the cornerstone of Judaism, then the Talmud is the central pillar . . . In many ways the Talmud is the most important book in Jewish culture, the backbone of creativity and of national life. No other work has had a comparable influence on the theory and practice of Jewish life, shaping spiritual content and serving as a guide to conduct" (Steinsaltz, 2010, p. 3). The Babylonian Talmud (redacted roughly 600 CE—this discussion concentrates on the Babylonian as opposed to the Jerusalem Talmud) comprises the Mishnah, an early law code, (redacted 250 CE) and the Gemara, commentary, debate, and stories on and around the Mishnah. A standard printing of the Talmud also includes numerous other commentaries (such as medieval commentaries of Rashi and the *Tosafot*), indices, cross-references and glosses. The Talmud combines complex legal debate, including hypothetical case analysis, with narratives that, like the Midrash, often turn on literary wordplay. The narratives often demonstrate principles congruent with or in contrast to the legal debates that appear nearby in the text. The legal debates are sometimes resolved, sometimes left unresolved in a case of *teku*, let it stand, an essential case of Carse's infinite game.

### Players, Roles and Rules in Talmud

Players in many games take on standard roles, while in other games, there are a variety of roles that players must take in order to play (Fullerton, 2008, p. 51). Consider team sports such as soccer, or the cooperative board game *Pandemic* (Leacock, 2008), or raiding parties with varied roles in *World of Warcraft* (Pardo, Kaplan and Chilton, 2001). Professor Eliezer Diamond teaches that understanding the rhetorical game at work in a passage of the Talmud is particularly helpful for unpacking a passage (Diamond, personal communication, summer 2007). What is the "game" underlying the dialogic exchange between rabbis? What is the role each player takes and for what, often, implicit rhetorical teaching purpose? In a Talmudic debate, the surface debate often serves other implied purposes. Professor Diamond recommends the Eric Berne book *Games People Play* on transactional analysis as a means of understanding rhetorical game play and roles in the Talmud. Role taking in the Talmudic debates and stories has an important rhetorical function just as role taking in games can be an essential formal element, determining play. Once roles are determined, what are the boundaries of play? These boundaries and often the procedures that occur within the game, are determined by rules.

How are rule systems in the Talmud related to rules as an essential formal element of games? Salen and Zimmerman (2003) refer to different classes of rules in a game: operational, constituative, and implicit. Operational rules are the guidelines players follow. Constituative rules are the underlying formal, logical, and mathematical structures. In Salen and Zimmerman's example illustrating constituative rules, they remove the art from a Chutes and Ladders (Milton Bradley) board and then list out the numerical logic underlying the moves on the board: If you land on X, you move to Y. The game shifts from a board to a list of constituative numerical rules. Implicit rules are unwritten and refer to rules such as those of sportsmanship (Salen and Zimmerman, 2003, pp. 130–133). All three of these kinds of rule structures can be found in the text of the Talmud and the social practices of Talmud study. Operational rules are easily located in the Mishnah which gives extremely concise statements of law. These Mishnaic laws have constituative rules in their underlying logic, such as in the case of torts and the calculation of damages. Highly complex constituative rules also occur in the Talmud. One example is the case of distribution of debt in bankruptcy to three debtors (Ketubot 93a). Game theorists have shown that the Talmud demonstrates remarkably complex mathematical and economic understanding and that it arrives independently at conclusions today calculated with modern mathematical game theory (Aumann and Maschler, 1985). There is a wide-ranging spectrum of constituative and operational rules to be found throughout the Talmud.

Implicit rules are most easily identifiable in the social practices of Talmud study and interpretation. These rules can be found in the use of principals of exegetical hermeneutics used within Talmudic dialogues and debates. These hermeneutics are then applied in the practice of study to understand other passages of Talmud. For example, Pesachim 113b includes a *sugya*, or passage of the Talmud, that circumscribes hatred. Single witnesses cannot testify, and so in this case a single witness to a terrible act is permitted to hate his (in this case, Jewish) neighbor. The proof text given in the *sugya* is a citation of the passage of Exodus (23:5) mandating that one must raise the fallen donkey of a neighbor that one hates. The Talmud explains that the only case of permitted hatred is if one witnessed, as a lone witness, a terrible sexual transgression. Lone witnesses are not permitted to testify. One hermeneutic used in Talmudic literature and argumentation is *kal v'homer*, or "all the more so." If X is true for Y, then *kal v'homer*, all the more so, it is true for Z. An implied rule in this passage of the Talmud, which does not appear in the text is: if you must assist the neighbor that you hate, and you cannot act as a single witness against a neighbor you have witnessed committing a terrible act, and if the cases of being allowed to hate are so circumscribed (perhaps, only this one case), then *all the more so*, must you treat your neighbors with kindness, care and respect.[6] This conclusion is an implicit rule, derived from the text through the social practice of study and knowledge of hermeneutic principles elsewhere in the Talmud. Once rule systems are in place, games can allow for modeling various possible outcomes within those rule systems.

## Hypothetical Cases: Games and the Talmud as Complex Modeled Systems

Games are particularly well suited for modeling problem cases within complex, rule-based systems. Games and simulations allow theoretical cases to be visualized on a board or screen. Video games and analog strategy games demand that players learn and manage many layers of rules, resources, and strategies in the delineated conflict and/or collaboration space. Because the map is not the territory, games and simulations allow scenarios to be altered, shifted, refocused, and rerun. What if player X makes decision Y? How will the rules, other players' decision, and chance determine an outcome? Next time, a player can choose an alternative strategy and see the new results. What if a player selects these tools as opposed to those tools in approaching the problem? Similarly, learning scientists have used simulators to allow students to experiment with center of mass and center of gravity while creating digitally rendered structures. If the structures crash, those learners can quickly rerun the simulation without having to spend time manually rebuilding the structures (Shaffer, 2006, pp. 41–72). Digital simulations such as these allow for play and quick experimentation with hypothetical scenarios. Games go a step further, posing problems to be solved (make the structure stand up on its own).

Talmudic debates are often posed as problems that are framed by questions, with a variety of hypothetical cases and scenarios. These hypothetical cases range from the practical concerns to the highly theoretical and unrealistic concerns (see Steinsaltz, 2010, p. 4). These scenarios serve a variety of purposes including the exploration of a principle or the need to address previously unconsidered cases. The construction of the Talmud text often appears to be a kind of scenario generation machine. Often the redactors of Talmud generate scenarios through harmonization practices: they work to differentiate apparently contradictory rulings: ruling X does not apply to case Y but, rather, ruling X applies to case Z. Embedded within the scenarios are all the complexities of the interpretation and hypothetical application of the Mishnaic law code.

Wrestling with the problems and questions is a significant part of the process of studying and learning the Talmud. The process of working on a problem can supersede resolution, both because sometimes the debates are unresolved and also because the study of sacred texts themselves is considered a spiritual practice. The form of the writing in the Talmud is highly elliptical, requiring external sources to unpack the sparse phrases and allusions, or an experienced teacher who has learned the process of coming to an understanding with that sparse text. How do learners play out these problems and scenarios? What is the learning game? The Talmud, and Torah study in general, is embedded in the social practice of pairs' sacred study called *Hevruta.*

## The Push–Pull of Talmud Study: *Hevruta* as Infinite Game

Beyond the literary characteristics of the texts, the social practices involved in the study of rabbinic literature involve a variety of games and modes of play as demonstrated in the push and pull of *hevruta* (sacred pairs study). Torah study (the study of Jewish sacred text, not limited to the Five Books of Moses, which are also referred to as "Torah") is held in the highest regard in Jewish religious life, as it is understood to lead to the critical virtuous behaviors including peacemaking, acts of compassion, and accompanying the dead for burial (see Eilu Devarim daily prayer, Mishnah Peah 1:1, Talmud Shabbat 127a). When two people study Torah together, the Mishnah (Avot 3:2) teaches that the Divine Presence settles between them. *hevruta* study is teamwork, often competitive striving, in which study partners challenge each other and, through the challenge, reach for deeper insights and further understandings. *hevruta* can be understood as a game in which a competitively structured interaction serves both "sides" to achieve his or her goal: greater learning. The game provides an illusion of competition, for if the goal is in fact deeper learning, then the competition is a kind of ruse or rhetorical structure in which conflict or confrontation serves both parties. In *hevruta*, competition and conflict between parties *are* collaboration.

This game of sacred study is played for the purpose of continuing play, as in Carse's (1987) infinite game. *hevruta*, and sacred study in general, is for the continual learning of Torah, reaching towards greater holiness, and the application of Torah principles to life, through action (such as in the discussion in Kiddushin 40b). There are even traditions of Torah study continuing in the messianic age (Silberberg, n.d.).

*Hevruta* is learned in a social setting, not only with one's study partner, but in the case of study in a *beit midrash*, house of study, with seasoned teachers overseeing study pairs. Similarly, most games, with the exception of solitaire-style games, are played in some form of community. In the case of video games, communities of practice share strategies and video play-through on YouTube, form clubs, write fan fiction, and attend events together. Just as with *hevruta* study, what happens in the room (outside of the printed text or in the case of video games "off the screen") is critical to understanding the context in which learning occurs (Stevens, 2012).

## Reviewing the Connections between Talmud Study and Game Play

Both Talmud study and game play involve rules, roles, hypothetical cases, modeling, and learning in a community. In the case of a strategic game, the player must learn the rules and strategies for problem solving in a variety of scenarios. This occurs with other players in the moment, as well as the wider extra-textual community of players. The processes for learning Talmud, likewise, involves learning problem solving using modeled cases in rule based scenarios. The study is done in partnership with one's *Hevruta* partner and in the wider community. The next section turns to two branches of Games for Learning, both with implications for contemporary experimentation in and application of Games for Learning for Jewish communities.

## CASE STUDY: CONTEMPORARY JEWISH GAMES FOR LEARNING

> A few years ago the tide began to turn for games-based learning in formal educational settings, from cautious interest to excitement and deep engagement . . . The organized Jewish community was largely absent within that space, until 2011.
>
> —Barry Joseph, who was at the time Director, Online Leadership Program, Global Kids, Cofounder Games for Change (personal communication, February 28, 2012)[7]

Over the last 2 years there has been marked increase in publicity, action in the field and grant dollars awarded for games and game design for learning in progressive Jewish education in North America. This case study examines contemporary and nascent interventions in games and simulations for Jewish learning, centered on investment by the Covenant Foundation (see Note 1). This case study attempts to document the recent history and some of the investment activity by the Foundation in Jewish Games for Learning both in the words of members of the staff of the Foundation, and from the author's perspective. The choice of the Covenant Foundation is because thus far, it appears to be the only Foundation to fund development in Jewish Games for Learning. While both Natan (a group of young Jewish philanthropists) and the Jewish New Media Innovation Fund (a joint effort of Jim Joseph Foundation, Righteous Persons Foundation and the Schusterman Family Foundation) have funded digital projects, none of the projects include games or simulations for Jewish learning. The Avi Chai Foundation has subsidized attendees to the Games for Change Festival (including the author of this chapter), but appears to have not have invested further is Games for Learning as of the time of this writing.

This case explores the thought leadership (those taking the first steps to bring Games for Learning to Jewish education) in the current, nascent Jewish Games for Learning field and the perspectives of leadership at the Covenant Foundation regarding the foundation's investment in digital games and simulations for Jewish education. The case also draws on recent journalism, conference presentations, interviews, and correspondence with colleagues and public figures, as well as the author's own experience founding and running the organization ConverJent: Jewish Games for Learning. The chapter traces trends of acceptance and resistance in the use of games and game design in Jewish education, as well as opportunities and challenges facing a growing field.

## Jewish Games for Learning and the Covenant Foundation

In the world of Jewish education, digital media and more recently, Games for Learning, have received little attention outside of the work of individual teachers, principals, and the work of The Covenant Foundation. In recent years, Barry Joseph, a leader in secular Digital Media and Learning (DML), and a founder of the Games for Change Festival has been working with the Covenant Foundation, providing training in digital media tools and techniques, including a Serious Games intensive during the summer of 2011 (Appleman, interview, March 28, 2012; Schifrin, 2011). In January 2012, Joseph presented a workshop on Games for Learning at Covenant's annual project director's meeting. Over 2012, Joseph noted that he has seen interest and receptivity in the Jewish education community growing. During that time, Joseph conducted trainings and consultations on games-based projects for CAJE (Center for Advancement in Jewish Education) in Miami, iCenter in Chicago, the San Francisco Contemporary Jewish Museum, the Jewish Education Project, Camp Ramah, and the North American Jewish day school conference (Joseph, personal communication, July, 16, 2012).

In May of 2010, the author founded ConverJent, Jewish Games for Learning, incubated at Clal, The National Jewish Center for Learning and Leadership. Over the last 3 years, the author has run workshops, trainings, and presentations on Jewish Games for Learning at venues including Union for Reform Judaism Kutz Camp, Hebrew Union College (New York and Los Angeles) East End Temple in Manhattan, Clal's Rabbis Without Borders Program, the Jewish Outreach Institute Conference, the Jewish Education Center of Cleveland, the Games Learning Society Conference and a number of other synagogue schools. The author has also worked with organizations including the Jewish Education Project and has published articles on the subject of digital media and Games for Learning in *Contact* (Gottlieb, 2012), *Sh'ma* (Gottlieb, 2011c), the *CCAR Journal* (Gottlieb, 2011b), and *eJewish Philanthropy* (Gottlieb, 2011a). In 2013, the author piloted the digital mobile GPS Augmented Reality game/simulation and interactive story *Jewish Time Jump: New York* (Gottlieb and Ash) with Hebrew supplementary schools. The author also worked with and then observed a rabbinical student in the creation of a supplementary Hebrew school course in digital mobile game design for Jewish Learning. Following its release in May 2013, *Jewish Time Jump: New York* was nominated for Most Innovative Game of 2013 by the 10th annual Games for Change Festival.

In the summer of 2011, the Avi Chai Foundation, working in concert with PresenTense, funded nine attendees (including the author) to attend the 8th annual Games for Change Festival. The Games for Change Festival brings together professionals, academics, government, learners, and others around games for learning and social impact. In January 2012, the first funding of digital Jewish Games for Learning came to fruition. The Covenant Foundation funded two Games for Learning projects through their grants. Russel Neiss and Rabbi Charlie Schwartz of Not-A-Box Media Lab (Schwartz, interview, 23 July 2012) received an Ignition Grant to create The Aleph Bet App (Neiss and Schwartz, 2012), an early childhood game for learning the Hebrew alphabet on an iPhone and an iPad, which was released in December 2012. At the same time Covenant awarded a Signature Grant to ConverJent, for the creation of a location-based mobile GPS game/simulation and interactive story to teach Jewish History in New York City, which became *Jewish Time Jump: New York* (Gottlieb and Ash, 2013).

## Covenant's Motivations for Games in Jewish Education

Why has the Covenant Foundation taken the first step into digital Jewish Games for Learning? The foundation was established in 1990 to "significantly improve Jewish education in North America" (Isaacs, 1997, p. 9). The two major programs of the foundation are its grants and annual awards. The grants are awarded to "launch and/or replicate promising innovative educational initiatives for Jewish educational improvement" (Isaacs, 1997, p. 9). The awards are to recognize and celebrate Jewish educators.

Executive Director Harlene Appleman noted that the Covenant Foundation's interest in technology and media reaches back to its earliest moments, due in large part early on to the influence of Eli Evans:

> One of the driving forces, the chairman of our board, was the president of the Revson Foundation and was very interested in technology and saw it as an opportunity to kind of enhance and enrich the Jewish world, so you know, many things are driven by passion and information and Eli Evans really knew what that world could be. He was joined by other people on our board who were equally as passionate and informed around the area of technology—whether that was media or the internet. Whatever it was, the board, in general, there was a feeling and a thought process that evolved around technology and its potential.
>
> (Appleman, interview, March 28, 2012)

Joni Blinderman, associate director of the Covenant Foundation, discussed the foundation's interest in "serious" digital games today:

> Digital media, games, serious games, are now looked upon as a way to educate, to seriously educate. The whole society, the whole world is looking at this in a different way now than it certainly did ten years

> ago . . . then the conversation was "we can't have them [learners] play games because it's all this violent energy," right? And then suddenly there was a sophistication, from the outside [of the Jewish community], that we began to understand and learn about, and others have as well certainly, that they can be used for educational purposes. So let's dig in there and let's see who's doing what.
>
> (Blinderman, interview, March 28, 2012)

Beyond seeking to incorporate media and technology into Jewish education, some of Appleman's philosophical understandings of Judaism and education connect directly to concepts of play and simulation. Appleman described her training in secular education as an important factor in looking to games as a way to educate, dating back to the sixties. She noted that simulations have been a part of Jewish education for as long as she has been a part of Jewish education.

Appleman also spoke of the importance of her time at family camps as a factor in demonstrating to her the power of Games for Learning in the Jewish community:

> I spent a lot of time in family education at family camps . . . and I saw the power when parents and kids could play together when they had the opportunity to have a good time and good laugh and learn something. And all of that was a piece of it. It was watching the magic that it could work. In a weekend people could learn something that it would take years to learn otherwise and it was because they were engaged and having a good time.
>
> (Appleman, interview, March 28, 2012)

Beginning in 2006, Appleman had initial conversations regarding the technology-based historic simulations that were coming out of the work of the Interactive Communications & Simulations Group (ICS; the group that Fred Goodman cofounded). Covenant would go on to provide a grant to the Jewish Court of All Time (JCAT) project.

Place Out of Time (POOT), the foundation for the JCAT is an on- and offline simulation for middle and high school students (J. Stanzler and M. Fahy, interview, August 2, 2012). Users role play historical figures with guidance from university student mentors. POOT was a creation of the ICS team, including Goodman, Jeff Stanzler, Jeff Kupperman, Michael Fahy, John Miller and Gary Weisserman (Samuel Scheck Day School). It was based on a model that included elements of a virtual constitutional convention and a non-virtual transhistorical "banquet." The idea was to bring together characters from different historical periods and put them into "productive tension" for fruitful interactions. Run in concert with a university course and supporting the work of mentors, the simulation uses web-mediated interaction featuring designed-in antagonism (the court) and clearly defined scenarios drawing on current issues. Under a 3-year Signature Grant from Covenant, JCAT has been developed and run by a partnership between the University of Cincinnati's Center for Studies in Jewish Education and Culture, the RAVSAK Jewish Community Day School Network, and ICS (J. Stanzler and M. Fahy, interview, August 2, 2012.).

## The First Video Game Grants from Covenant

The 2012 Covenant Ignition Grant to Not-A-Box and Signature Grant to ConverJent appear to be the first investments from a foundation in digital Games for Learning in the Jewish community. While there are commercial digital games from Jewish educational companies, the Not-A-Box and ConverJent projects draw on the growing body of knowledge in Games for Learning. While not devoted particularly to the academic literature, Not-A-Box's rabbi Charlie Schwartz references the publications of the Joan Ganz Cooney Center and the Horizon Report, demonstrating considerations regarding contemporary research. ConverJent's work in digital, analog games, and teaching game design for Jewish learning, specifically draws from research in the Learning Sciences, Media Studies, and the broader bodies of research used in DML circles, from cognitive science to anthropology.

Will the investments in 2011–2012 signal a shift towards investment in research-based Jewish Games for Learning? As DML expands in secular schools, as young learners become more attached to their digital devices, more engrossed in secular digital games, and as pedagogies and institutions shift towards the digital, the levels of philanthropic investment in Jewish Games for Learning will likely be a determining factor. With a relatively small population and high costs of software production, Jewish Games for Learning will require support from foundations supporting Jewish education.

## Resistance and Obstacles to Jewish Games for Learning

There are a number of barriers still in place that are slowing the acceptance of Games for Learning in Jewish education. Barry Joseph writes of the secular adoption of Games for Learning: "The 'tipping point' is still a ways off—trepidation remains strong in many circles about perceived content in video game and formalizing informal learning—but there is a strong community of practices that has emerged across the country" (personal communication, February 28, 2012).

In the Jewish community, ironically, trepidation may be less of a concern while adoption of technology may be a more challenging barrier. As Jewish supplementary schools seek new ways to engage students—at what Harlene Appleman calls a "deadly time of day" (Appleman, interview, March 28, 2012) and day schools seek ways to set themselves apart from other school choices (see Mitzmacher, 2012), DML and Games for Learning are attractive options.

If one accepts Appleman's notion that reenactments are at the core of Judaism, and if as the author claims, that rabbinic literature is particularly congruent with Games for Learning, then the attraction seems obvious. The smaller school sizes and networks of schools in the Jewish community could also mean that Jewish education could more quickly adopt DML and Games for Learning than secular schools, which have larger bureaucracies.

ConverJent has often turned to paper-based game-design classes and workshops because the Jewish supplementary schools tend not to have computers or mobile devices on-site. This is likely due to both lack of funding and perhaps also the longstanding Jewish attachment to the printed page (Gottlieb, 2013). At Jewish summer camps, at least currently, digital devices are typically verboten (see Bordman, 2013).

While paper-based gaming and game design use the same kinds of pedagogies as digital games for learning (collaborative, problem-based, design-based, inquiry-based learning), the benefits of digital Jewish Games for Learning include the ability to embed assessment of learning and to gather data from each learner. Digital games are often easier to duplicate and distribute as well, eliminating the need for the manufacturing and physical distribution required for board and card games. Perhaps most important, digital games use the technology which is rapidly approaching the status of the cybernetic: Learners now use their digital apps and tools on their phones and tablet to extend their abilities to learn and create, whether in locating information or in designing new media productions as part of "participatory culture" (see Jenkins, 2006, and Squire, 2010). It may be demand in secular schools for ever-increasing digitally enhanced and informed learning opportunities that pushes further investment in digital Jewish Games for Learning.

## CONCLUSION

Some of the rhetoric in the progressive Jewish community in North America emphasizes fear and concern regarding video games and digital technology. At the same time a group of Jewish educators, exemplified by those in the case study are beginning to embrace and develop contemporary research-based Games for Learning. These educators, designers and funders seek to take advantage of the best learning attributes that video games and analog games have to offer. Games offer powerful modes of involving learners in inquiry and problem-based learning and opportunities for transmitting cultural practices and values. Although seldom discussed and analyzed, Jewish tradition itself is replete with game and simulation systems—in holiday rituals; in rabbinic word play and narrative; in the roles, rules, and modeling of Talmudic discourse and communal study practices.

By bridging Games for Learning, Jewish education, and Jewish Studies, this chapter attempts to open the door for a cross pollination of understandings and investigations. Game systems resonate through Jewish tradition and through contemporary secular society, and so Jewish culture offers a unique body of literature and tradition for Game Studies and Games for Learning. For example, Talmudic modes of model generation could lead to deeper engagement in teaching problem solving in STEM subjects. The study of Jewish ritual simulations and games could provide clues into the mechanics of one of the most enduring Games for Learning: the Passover seder. And what can Game Studies and Games for Learning contribute to Jewish education and Jewish Studies? How can research in the Learning Sciences and Media Studies help Jewish educators bring the heritage of ancient game systems into contemporary modes and media for today's learners? Such research can unlock new ways of parsing or decoding rabbinic literature. Just as economists have turned to unlocking Talmudic mathematical puzzles to push forward their field, so too can those researching Jewish civilization consider expanding their fields through the frame of the game.

## NOTES

1. The author of this chapter is a PhD candidate in Education and Jewish Studies and is a Reform rabbi. The author is also the founder and director of ConverJent, an organization dedicated to Jewish Games for Learning. The researcher stance of the author is that of both a proponent in the Jewish community of games-based learning and that of a social science researcher inquiring into the design and use of digital and analog games and game design for education and cultural heritage. In 2012, ConverJent received a Signature Grant from the Covenant Foundation (featured in the case study) to build a mobile game/simulation to teach Jewish history. As one of the only current practitioners of research-based Jewish Games for Learning the author's perspective can allow for a window into the nascent activity in the area.
2. "Jewish education" in this chapter refers to the discipline of intentionally nurturing an understanding of and an affinity for any or all of the aspects of Jewish civilization. "Jewish learning" refers to the development of such an understanding and affinity.
3. According to its website page regarding its demographics, "*Reform Judaism* has the largest circulation of any Jewish magazine in the world. We reach 310,000 Jewish families who are members of 900+ Reform synagogues in the United States and Canada"; see http://reformjudaismmag.org/adinfo/demographics/ [Accessed December 8, 2013].
4. STE(A)M stands for Science, Technology, Engineering, (sometimes Art), and Math.
5. Horn (1980, pp. 531–539) has an entire section devoted to games for learning religion with a number of Jewish games, including two created by rabbis.
6. The author learned this passage and the reapplication of this exegetical hermeneutic from Rabbi Dr. Michael Chernick.
7. As of the time of this writing, Joseph is Associate Director for Digital Learning at the American Museum of Natural History.

## REFERENCES


Apples to Apples, Jewish Edition (2007). Designed by Mathew Kirby and Mark Alan Osterhaus. Jewish Educational Toys. Out of the Box Publishing.

The Aleph Bet App (2012). Designed by Russel Neiss and Charlie Schwartz. Not-A-Box.

Aumann, R.J. and Maschler, M. (1985). Game Theoretic Analysis of a Bankruptcy Problem From the Talmud. *Journal of Economic Theory*, 36(2), 195–213.

Berne, E. (1996). *Games People Play: The Basic Handbook of Transactional Analysis*. Ballantine Books.

Bordman, L. (2013). Camp Unplugged. *Reform Judaism Magazine* [online]. Available at: http://reformjudaismmag.org/Articles/index.cfm?id=3239 [Accessed December 8, 2013].

Carse, J.P. (1987). *Finite and Infinite Games: A Vision of Life as Play and Possibility*. New York: Ballantine Books.

Dukes, R.L. and Waller, S.J. (1976). Review Essay: Toward a General Evaluation Model for Simulation Games: GEM. *Simulation & Gaming*, 7(1), 75–88.

Fullerton, T., with C. Swain and S. S. Hoffman. (2008). *Game Design Workshop Designing, Prototyping and Playtesting Games*. 2nd ed. San Francisco: CMP.

Gee, J.P. (2003). *What Video Games Have to Teach Us About Learning and Literacy*. New York: Palgrave Macmillan.

Golinkin, D. (2000). Hanukkah Exotica: On the Origin and Development of Some Hanukkah Customs. In: N. Zion and B. Spectre (Eds.), *A Different Light : The Hanukkah Book of Celebration* (pp. 177–182). New York: Devora.

Gordon, P. (1997). Infinite Games. *The Paula Gordon Show* [online]. Available at: http://www.paulagordon.com/shows/carse/ [Accessed December 8, 2013].

Gottlieb, O. (2011a). A Call for Jewish Education Through Gaming and Game Design. *eJewish Philanthropy* [online]. Available at: http://ejewishphilanthropy.com/a-call-for-jewish-education-through-gaming-and-game-design/ [Accessed December 8, 2013].

Gottlieb, O. (2011b). Moving Beyond the Limited Reach of Current "Social Media" Approaches: Why Jewish Digital Communities Require Rich and Remixable Narrative Content. *CCAR Journal: The Reform Jewish Quarterly*, Spring, 82–99.

Gottlieb, O. (2011c). Video Games, Game Design, and 21st-Century Jewish Education. *Sh'ma: A Journal of Jewish Responsibility*, 42(684), 22–24.

Gottlieb, O. (2012). An Agenda for Jewish Games for Learning. *Contact: The Journal of the Steinhardt Foundation for Jewish Life—Technology and Jewish Education*, 15(1), 9.

Gottlieb, O. (2013). You Can't Wrap Herring in an iPad: Digitization of Sacred Jewish Books, the Stripping of Embodied Ritual, and Implications for Jewish Education. *CCAR Journal: The Reform Jewish Quarterly*, Spring, 130–141.

Horn, R. E. (Ed.). (1980). *The Guide to Simulations/Games for Education and Training: 4th Edition*. Beverly Hills, CA: Cleves Sage Publications.

Isaacs, L.W. (1997). Flying Kites in the Wind: Lessons Learned by a Young Foundation. *Journal of Jewish Education*, 63(1–2), 8–19.

Jenkins, H. (2006). *Convergence Culture: Where Old and New Media Collide*. Rev. ed. New York: NYU Press.

Jewish Time Jump: New York (2013). Designed by Rabbi Owen Gottlieb and Jennifer Ash. ConverJent.

Lewis, M. (n.d.). Mah-Jongg—My Jewish Learning [online]. Available at: http://www.myjewishlearning.com/culture/2/Sports/Sports_and_Judaism/America/mah_jongg.shtml

Luu, A. & Cavallaro, C. (2005). *Mah-Jongg: From Shanghai to Miami Beach*. San Francisco: Chronicle Books.

Mitzmacher, J. (2012, July 13). Jewish Education Got Game. A Floor, But No Ceiling [online]. Available at: http://www.mjgds.org/mitzmacher/?p=1003 [Accessed December 8, 2013].
Mogel, W. (2013). Invasion of the Machines. *Reform Judaism Magazine* [online]. Available at: http://reformjudaismmag.org/Articles/index.cfm?id=3238 [Accessed December 8, 2013].
*Pandemic* (2008). Designed by Matt Leacock. Z-Man Games.
*Red Dead Dedemption* (2010). Designed by Christian Cantamessa (lead). Rockstar Games.
*Rummikub, 1930s*. Design by Ephraim Hertzano. Pressman Toy Co (1960, USA) Lemanda Light Industries Ltd. (1978, Israel.)
Salen, K. and Zimmerman, E. (2003). *Rules of Play: Game Design Fundamentals*. Cambridge, MA: MIT Press.
Schifrin, D. (2011). Playing Games with Jewish Education. *The Jewish Week* [online]. Available at: http://www.thejewishweek.com/features/culture_view/playing_games_jewish_education [Accessed December 8, 2013].
*Shivah* (2006). Designed by Dave Gilbert. Wadjet Eye Games.
Silberberg, N. (n.d.). Torah Study During the Messianic Era [online]. Available at:http://www.chabad.org/library/moshiach/article_cdo/aid/1122210/jewish/Torah-Study-During-the-Messianic-Era.htm [Accessed December 8, 2013].
Squire, K. (2010). Education for a Mobile Generation. In: *Academix Conference 2010* [online]. Available at: https://itunes.apple.com/us/itunes-u/academix-2010-conference-videos/id420557841.
Steinsaltz, A. (2010). *The Essential Talmud*. Jerusalem: Koren Publishers. Kindle Edition.
Stevens, Reed. (2012). *Keynote: Learning from Gaming and Gaming for Learning: A Dual Mission for the GLS*. Presented at the Games, Learning, and Society Conference 8.0, University of Wisconsin–Madison, June 14.
Wagner, R. (2012a). First-Person Shooter Religion: Algorithmic Culture and Inter-Religious Encounter. *Cross Currents*, 62(2), 181–203.
Wagner, R. (2012b). *Godwired: Religion, Ritual, and Virtual Reality*. Abingdon, Oxon and New York: Routledge. Kindle Edition.
Wagner, R. (2013, April). *Mitzvot Mash-Up: Interactivity as Transformative Interpretation*. Lecture at Digital Judaism: Tablet To Tablet, New York.
*World of Warcraft* (2001). Designed by Rob Pardo, Jeff Kaplan and Tom Chilton. Blizzard Entertainment.

# 7 Communicating Identity through Religious Internet Memes on the "Tweeting Orthodoxies" Facebook Page

*Aya Yadlin-Segal*

It is the well-known "bulletproof" scene from *The Matrix* movie. We see Keanu Reeves in a green hallway, wearing a black trench coat, dark sunglasses, and a *Kippah*. His hand is stretched out, holding back a stream of hovering candies, instead of machine-gun bullets. The caption above the photo states "Neo's Bar-Mitzvah." This is not a Jewish remake of *The Matrix*, it is an internet meme shared on the religious Facebook page "Tweeting Orthodoxies," that playfully presents the custom of throwing candies at the Bar-Mitzvah boy after reading the *Haphtarah* on his *Aliyah La-Thorah*. This meme, and many others like it, demonstrates how digital culture provides a group of National Religious Jews with unique opportunities to communicate about and engage in the reconstruction of their religious identity. This engagement is studied in the current chapter by investigation of the ways a specific National Religious Facebook group employs internet memes.

In recent years, studies of Jewish-religious groups' interaction with new media have focused mainly on the ultra-Orthodox sub stream (Campbell, 2011). According to Rashi (2012) this scholarly investigation has emphasized the unique enclave social structure of Jewish ultra-Orthodox communities, and their highly moderated usage of new media such as cellular phones and the internet. To gain further understanding of new media usage among Jewish groups, Campbell (2011) suggested that scholars should address additional religious and nonreligious substreams in Israel as well as additional Web 2.0 technologies such as blogs and social media. With these claims in mind, in this chapter social media usage within the National Religious Jewish community is discussed. This religious group is based in Israel and couples Jewish beliefs, principles and traditions with contemporary culture and technology in unique ways, as explored in the following.

The analysis of religious-oriented memes presented in this chapter emerges from a broader exploratory study of memes related to Christianity, Islam and Judaism (Bellar et al., 2013). That study investigated common communication styles, interpretive practices and messages about religion communicated through internet memes and found that memes both affirm and critique religious identities. Drawing on this work, the focus of this chapter is on religious-oriented Jewish internet memes shared on the Facebook page "Tweeting Orthodoxies."[1] The chapter investigates the role memes play for this online Jewish-religious group, and the religious message these memes carry about Judaism. By conducting a detailed textual analysis of twelve memes shared on this Facebook page, and eight interviews with the Facebook page's administrators and members, this study illustrates how National Religious community members reinterpret their religious identity through creating and sharing internet memes.

By producing and circulating memes via social media members of this National Religious–oriented Facebook group seek to emphasize the cultural religious aspects of their identity over the political identity markers that are usually associated with them. Such cultural religious aspects relate to experiences in educational institutions (*Yeshivot* and *Ulpanot*), National Religious youth movements (such as *Beni Akiva*), issues of fashion and style in the National Religious context (e.g., modest clothing) and social issues connected to the synagogue, Jewish religious rituals and costumes. Thus, employing and sharing memes online provide this community with a unique opportunity to negotiate and reconstruct the identity markers that are typically linked with its members.

## UNDERSTANDING INTERNET MEME CULTURE

To understand this National Religious group's engagement with religion through memes, it is important to frame this study through three main foci: First, the concept of participatory culture is introduced in order to contextualize the process of creating and circulating internet memes as engagement with the online\digital culture. Second, memes, and in specific the internet meme, are introduced as an expression of participatory culture, in which individuals engage in the production of their culture. Finally, memes are framed as an artifact reflecting lived religion, in which individuals draw on religious sources for a day-to-day practice such as participating in social media.

The study is undergirded by the understanding that new media, and specifically the internet, provide users with more control over content creation and selection than previous generations of media (Chaffee and Metzger, 2001). New media are defined by Flew (2008) as the convergence of computing and information technologies with communications networks. According to Flew, these new forms of media content gather and mix data, text, sound and image that are stored and circulated in digital formats. Jenkins (2006) conceptualized the cultural move from "old" to "new" media, by way of digital convergence, as "participatory culture." This is the shift in today's mediascape, as the distinction between media consumers and media producers blurred, inhabiting the internet with "prosumers." The prosumer represents an active audience, creating and circulating digital cultural artifacts throughout the internet. Within this realm scholars have studied how social media such as Facebook, Twitter, blogs, and YouTube enable religious meaning making processes and religious identity construction—both individual and communal (Lövheim, 2012; Mason, 2012; Miller, Mundey and Hill, 2013; Warner, 2013). The premise of the participatory culture informs not only the field of inquiry of the current chapter—internet memes that were created and shared by internet users—but also the methodological choice to conduct interviews with the creators of the memes, to fully understand the process of content creation and its relations to National Religious culture.

With the wish to address internet memes as participatory culture, a definition of a meme is needed. According to Dawkins (1976/2006) a meme is a piece of information, leaping from brain to brain through a process which "in the broad sense, can be called imitation" (p. 192). Thus, an internet meme is a cultural replicator that exists on the internet; a unit of digital or online imitation (Heylighen and Chielens, 2008), the core component of cultural transmission online (Pickerel, Jorgensen and Bennett, 2002). Internet memes contain visual and verbal images that are coupled with social norms, habits, and rituals (for example religion) which people can easily imitate and transmit to others in online environments such as social media (Dawkins, 1976/2006; Kipnis, 2012).

This study views memes as a possible manifestation of lived religion, a process in which ordinary men and women draw on religious sources to make sense of their world and the experience of the sacred in everyday practices (Maynard, Clark Moschella and Hummel, 2010; McGuire, 2008). Lived religion is manifested as ongoing, semiautonomous and dynamic relations of religion with everyday life, which traditional institutions have very little hold on (Hervieu-Leger, 1997; Orsi, 1997). Campbell (2010) argued that lived religion can be understood as an outcome of media usage, as individuals' religion is being drawn from contemporary culture. Therefore, new media should be explored as facilitator of both lived religion and contemporary culture. New media as a whole and the internet in particular provide their users with content to reformat and transmit to larger populations. Just like lived religion, the internet offers a self-interpreted cultural environment, within which user-generated cultural objects, such as the meme, circulate (Husted, 2012).

Through this brief discussion of participatory culture, internet memes, and lived religion, a few important takeaways concerning these concepts emerge. First, participatory culture in new media enables social media users with more and more control over the artifacts they construct and share online. Hence, when studying digital artifacts in online environments (i.e., internet memes) interviews must be conducted in order to understand individuals' participation. Second, internet memes are understood as lived religion. In the context of a National Religious Facebook page, the shared internet memes are viewed as Jewish lived religion, from which participants draw on the Jewish religion to make sense of and construct their world.

Thus, in this chapter the ways in which National Religious Jews negotiate, reinterpret and reconstruct their religious identity through the construction and sharing of Jewish memes are shown.

## STUDYING MEMES ON THE "TWEETING ORTHODOXIES" FACEBOOK PAGE

"Tweeting Orthodoxies" is an Israeli Jewish Facebook page, founded in July 2012, organized by "five administrators related to all ends of the [Jewish] religious sector" (Tweeting Orthodoxies, 2014), and is followed by more than 75,000 Facebook users. According to the information posted on its About page, the page aims to keep its followers "up-to-date with photos, memes, and 'hot' online statuses that relate to the Jewish-religious way of life" (Tweeting Orthodoxies, 2014). One of the page's administrators adds to that in an interview: "We created this page in order to give a glimpse into the National Religious lifestyle" (interview, March 2, 2014). The "Tweeting Orthodoxies" Facebook page is well documented in Israeli media. It is described as "the revolutionary Facebook page of the religious sector" (Rotem, 2013), "the page that makes humor kosher" (Marilos, 2013), and as "a threat to the secular-humor hegemony online" (Ferbshtein, 2012). These writers emphasize the novelty of such page, combining religion and social media in a way, according to them, never seen before in the Israeli context.

All the creators of the page self-define as National Religious Jews and see the Facebook page as an opportunity to create and share religious-related humor that is often overlooked in mainstream Israeli media. "Many times jokes about the Jewish religion seem too esoteric or too niche, so we had to create it [a Facebook page] ourselves," (interview, March 4, 2014) argued one of the page's creators. Another creator added, "It was necessary since many members of the National Religious community could not find themselves and their values in mainstream media. Most of the content on Israeli mainstream television, radio, and even newspapers are not focused on this community" (interview, March 6, 2014). So they decided to create a Facebook page focused on humoristic reading of the Jewish religion, on the National Religious subculture in Israel and on stressing that this subculture has many "shades of gray," meaning that their take on religion is not black or white, but a complex set of understandings. "We actually line-up with a long tradition of religious Jewish humor," claimed one of the creators. "It is a *Mitzvah* to always be happy [*Lihiot Besimcha Tamid*] so in that regard we are not unique or new to religion" (interview, March 4, 2014). In these quotes we see that the creators of the page not only relate the National Religious identity to an ancient Jewish identity but also view it as a flexible culture that can adopt contemporary culture, as it is shared and discussed in online environments such as Facebook.

Conceptualized also as Modern-Orthodoxy (Campbell, 2011; Guterman, 2006), the Jewish National Religious community "adhere faithfully to the beliefs, principles, and traditions of Jewish law and observance without being either remote from or untouched by life in the contemporary world" (Kaplan, 1979, p. 439). This heterogeneous religious group ranges from "Haredi Leumi" (National ultra-Orthodox) to "Liberal Religious" (A. Cohen, 2005). The identity of the National Religious community in Israel is often defined in relations to this groups' political affiliation. Until the 1980s the group was viewed as related to Mafdal, the Israeli National Religious Party (A. Cohen, 2005). Because of changes in the Israeli society (political mainly but also social and cultural), over the early 1990s and the 2000s this political affiliation was broken into various political parties that still held National Religious nature such as the National Home (Habait Haleumi) and This is Our Land (Zo Artzeinu), both identified with right-wing nationalist approach to Israeli politics (Fisher, 2008).

While many studies described the new media usage patterns of the ultra-Orthodox community, the scarcity of studies looking at the interaction of the National Religious community with such media is notable. Thus, investigating the "Tweeting Orthodoxies" Facebook page offers a unique opportunity to study media content that was explicitly produced by and for the National Religious community. This further enriches the overall understanding of how additional Jewish group (other than the ultra-Orthodox one) engage with digital and popular culture through the analysis of internet memes created and shared in Facebook.

## METHOD OF ANALYSIS

An analysis of 12 memes shared on the "Tweeting Orthodoxies" Facebook page between September 2012 and August 2013 was conducted. One meme per month was selected to reflect a range of religious themes on which the memes centered including Jewish holidays, religious events, and religious day-to-day routines. All the selected memes employ images and texts drawing on international popular culture content (i.e., images related to movies, celebrities and organizations) that were linked with Jewish commandments, rituals and sacred texts. These 12 memes were produced in Hebrew and translated into English for this chapter. Throughout the textual analysis attention was given to two main issues. The first was the relationship of the religious and the popular culture aspects of the meme. This was done to understand whether religion is presented as in conflict with or complementary to popular culture in the context of the Facebook group. Second, the issue of humor was addressed. Using Shifman's (2012) categories of humor found in internet memes, the analysis focused on the use of humor in the National Religious context. Here attention was given to the role humor has in the process of negotiating the National Religious identity. This layer of analysis sought to understand the function of humor in the presentation and possible reformulation of a religious identity.

Alongside the textual and visual analysis of memes, eight interviews were conducted with the Facebook page administrators and several participants who created or shared memes on this page. The administrators are identified on the Facebook page and were approached through it. The meme creators (i.e., participants in the Facebook page) were selected based on their relationship to the analyzed memes, thus, specific specific meme creators were approached and asked to be interviewed. Combining memes analysis with interviews enables this study to consider the ways memes may provide an outlet for the public formation and negotiation of the National Religious identity while emphasizing the centrality of users to the process of media content production and circulation.

## CONSTRUCTING AND SHARING MEMES: MEME AS A TOOL FOR CULTURAL IDENTITY FORMATION

The memes in this study show two layers of meaning: One layer relies on the ability to recognize and decode nonreligious content derived from international popular culture. The second layer draws on religious Jewish content, and requires familiarity with it. For example, in one meme the tale of Noah from the book of Genesis is combined with a reference to the quality of Ikea products, as Willy Wonka from the *Willy Wonka and the Chocolate Factory* film asks in the meme: "120 years to build an ark? Tell me more about items you have purchased in Ikea." This meme creates a sarcastic criticism about Ikea, but at the same time combines a religious story with references to contemporary culture. This is one example of the ways in which memes shared on this Facebook page mix the religious ideas and understandings of its creators with popular, contemporary culture.

Another example is the Conspiracy Keanu meme (using an image drawn from the film *Bill and Ted's Excellent Adventure*). This meme intertwines the image of the actor Keanu Reeves with a reference to a Jewish holy day Lag BaOmer in which supermarket carts are utilized for collecting bonfire wood for the celebration. The meme presents a speculation regarding the motivations of celebrating this holiday. "What if *Lag BaOmer* was invented by someone who wanted to avenge *Shufersal*?" says the meme, pointing out the possible revengeful intentions of harming a well-known chain of supermarkets in Israel (by stealing their carts for "wood hunting"). These two examples show us how group members consciously mix religious references and stories with aspects of contemporary culture. This reflects a dialog between religion and modernity, or religion and popular culture, rather than a conflict. Here the Jewish religion functions as an interpretive frame that complements contemporary popular discourses rather than excluding the religious users from modern culture.

Kipnis (2012) argues that the social functions of the meme vary: from an entertainment and humorous functions, all the way to criticism and political protest. With this in mind, it is observed that memes featured on the "Tweeting Orthodoxies" page generally avoid mockery of any kind but do share criticism. According to one of the page's administrators, users criticize some religious rituals and social structures: "memes about women's rights in the religious society, or about the treatment of animals, especially when it comes to the *Kaparot* ceremony, are presented on our page" (interview, March 4, 2014). Another administrator added, "We try to avoid political criticism, since we want to focus on the religious culture, but we will not avoid criticism about this culture if a member wishes to share it and it has a valued message. We just try to do it in a respectful way" (interview, March 2, 2014). Thus, we can see that although members use humor, it is not done only with the wish to be funny, but also with the wish to criticize, and even change, some aspects of the Jewish religion. These include, among others, the attitudes toward lesbian, gay, bisexual and transgender (LGBT) communities and women.

All of the interviewed administrators seem to view memes as a way for participants to bring their religious cultural experiences into the online conversation. Internet memes enable the participants with a safe (e.g., respecting religious modesty and religious leaders, and using clean language) and playful space to share their culture and convictions. Thus, one of an administrator stated in an interview:

> We do not share indecent visual content [i.e., nudity]. We do not share curses or harsh language in the memes, and delete such content if it appears on the comments of the memes. We do not share photos of rabbis. We, the creators of the page, do not necessarily get offended by all of these, but we learned that people do not take it easily. So if we want to create a space that is funny and culturally innovative for religious people, we have to keep the religious aspect in mind first and foremost.
>
> (interview, March 6, 2014)

In the case of "Tweeting Orthodoxies" individual Facebook users participate in a process of negotiating their own religious identity. Within this process they try to open a broader conversation about the cultural layer of this identity. One of the page administrators explained this process: "The National Religious group was perceived by the rest of the Israeli society, so far, as a political unit. We were only addressed based on the party we vote for, the political stream we follow, and the way we think about the borders of the State of Israel." Yet, as this administrator of "Tweeting Orthodoxies" claimed, things are changing:

> Our Facebook page reflects a wish to shape a new cultural identity of the National Religious group. Such identity points at the overall change

> that is happening in the National Religious society, a process of maturing and seeking for more layers of identity—other than the political layer.
>
> (interview, March 4, 2014)

The creators of the page view memes as a means to present this process of a maturing identity, because this medium allows religious users to construct and present their personal understanding of religious identity online.

## MEMES, HUMOR AND JEWISH IDENTITY

One of the earliest forms of entertainment to spread across the internet was humor, noted by the humor focused newsgroups such as alt.humor and rec.humor in the early days of the internet (Kuipers, 2006). Shifman and Lemish (2011) tie internet humor to Jenkins's (2006) concept of participatory culture and suggest that online expressions of humor are an important yet under-researched arena of participatory culture. The relationship between the Jewish people and humor dates back to the 19th century (Finkin, 2009; Ziv, 1986). Humor serves multiple functions in the Jewish context. The most prominent function is providing a way to cope with the complex Jewish identity, reconciling local culture with the global one, as well as religion and conservatism with modernity (Ziv, 1986). This relationship between religion and humor is highly evident here, as through humoristic internet memes the "Tweeting Orthodoxies" page members are able to playfully discuss the cultural negotiation of their religious identity.

Based on Shifman's (2012) categories of humor, the collected memes relate to two categories of humor, viewed in the way they express religious ideas. The first form of humor noted is the 'incongruent,' where memes feature "an unexpected cognitive encounter between two incongruent elements" (Shifman, 2012, p. 196). For example, a "Hanukkah and Santa" meme shows Santa Claus mistakenly slides down the chimney of a Jewish family kindling the Hanukkah Menorah, stating, "Oops, got the wrong house." The unexpected encounter of the religious with a secular, non-Jewish ritual and narrative is meant to be ironic yet, at the same time reinforces the practice of religious rituals.

Related to this, one of the meme creators noted in an interview: "Memes make the Jewish religion less rigid. It enables us to experience religion as less threatening; as something we can actually laugh about." He added that the way Facebook pages are built makes it easier for the members to share and comment about memes, "which makes the whole process of creating them and consuming them much more meaningful for the users" (interview, March 13, 2014). Echoing the concept of participatory culture through the emphasis on the users' involvement in constructing and circulating religious culture, this participant stresses the way religion is carried in mundane acts as sharing and posting in social media—opening the Jewish religion to new, individual meaning making.

A second category of humor found in the collection is that of "superior" memes, which feature unintentionally funny messages. Shifman (2012) claims the source of enjoyment in the case of these memes, is the "pleasant feeling of one upping the other" (p. 196). A meme shared during Passover, in which a picture of Disney's Aladdin eating a piece of bread at time in which Jews are forbidden to eat bread is presented, is an example of such superiority. The written text states, "Thank god for making me Yemeni at Passover." This meme carries a twofold representation of the Jewish religion. On one hand, this meme can be understood as playfully pointing out the diversity within the Jewish religion. On the other hand, this meme might be interpreted as containing a discriminatory perspective of Oriental Jews as religiously inferior. Still, this meme does not directly subvert traditional Jewish religious understandings and beliefs. It essentially functions as an affirmation of the religious tradition of the Passover commandments regarding *Chametz*. This illustrates how memes can include, at the same time, popular culture and the reinforcement of religious acts and religious boundaries of the community, in this case as they relate to religious practices of Passover.

The creators of the page are well aware of possible religious superiority the religious participants of the group have on secular ones. One of the administrators stated in an interview,

> The content shared through the memes is mostly religious. Outsiders [i.e., to the National Religious community] might miss the punch-line, the religious meaning that is presented. Secular members of this page sometimes get it and tell me—hey, this is so funny, and I got it even though I am not religious. I think it is really important, since humor can bridge between secular and religious people, and present the National Religious community as culturally open, something that is often missed in the mainstream media.
>
> (interview, March 6, 2014)

In this section we see that internet memes perform two additional functions in the National Religious context. First, as mentioned earlier, memes play a role in the process of identity negotiation, providing community members a less rigid (as opposed to traditional religious institutions) sphere to discuss their religion. Second, they can also provide a bridge between National Religious and secular groups in the Israeli society, as the openness of both to digital culture allows them a shared space to communicate and learn of each other's culture. In the "Tweeting Orthodoxies" page both National Religious and secular members share a cultural space that is not controlled by state or religious institutions, and thus can create and share cultural discourse that is based on their own understandings and cultural preferences.

## MEMES AS A BRIDGE BETWEEN OFFLINE AND ONLINE ENVIRONMENTS

An interesting finding stemming from the interviews is that the format of the internet meme, that is a photo combined with a pithy written punch line, have recently been incorporate into some National Religious synagogue pamphlets (*Aloney Shabbat*). These are small media produced by the community they serve (i.e., rabbis or Yeshiva schools), an important offline religious communication medium within the Jewish community. The pamphlets usually provide their audience with alternative readings of news presented in secular media (J. Cohen, 2000) and focus on issues such as education, the weekly Torah portion, and rabbis' ceremonies. Synagogue pamphlets use religious examples and analogies that are more relatable to the religious audience than mainstream secular media (Gabel, 2006). It appears that at least two National Religious synagogues' pamphlets have integrated internet memes and have featured them in a regular weekly humoristic segment. The two are "the Jewish head" (*Rosh Yehudi*, which was closed by the time this chapter was published, yet was published for seven years between 2007–2014) and *Opinions* (*Giluy Daat*, still active, published for four years). Both pamphlets have integrated meme segments in their publications called "Memes" and "the Jewish meme shelf," a playful take on "the Jewish book shelf," which symbolizes the essential Jewish readings a religious Jew should own.

The creator and editor of the meme segments in these synagogues pamphlet is a member in the "Tweeting Orthodoxies" page and usually publishes memes that were featured in the "Tweeting Orthodoxies" online platform. The editor of these segments was interviewed for this chapter and explained the use of internet memes in offline media: "Humor is wanted all week long, but as a religious person you cannot use the internet over the Sabbath. The synagogue pamphlets make the format [of internet memes] accessible even when you cannot use electricity" (interview, March 13, 2014). To the question, "Do you use memes because you want to make religion up to date?" he answered, "I do not know, I do not think so, but I do know that it keeps religion relevant. The memes I share in the synagogue pamphlets show that there is more to religion than just the *Torah*" (interview, March 13, 2014). Here we see again how popular culture is engaged with religion rather than separated from it.

The editor of these columns in the synagogue pamphlets also emphasized that the National Religious community is technologically open-minded, unlike other religious subgroups in Israel:

> Technology can actually help spread religion. As I see it, the National Religious people do not see technology as conflicting with religion, rather as complementing each other. We have a curious standpoint in regards to technology, an investigative outlook rather than a withdrawing one.

> We always ask—how can I integrate it [a technological invention] into religion, and not—why is that dangerous to my religion? When it comes to memes it is a little more complicated since religious people are not very familiar with digital culture and the meme vocabulary and structure. But they are starting to learn. That is why I use the simple structures of memes, the more obvious ones, but it is still new and interesting for them.
>
> (interview, March 13, 2014)

In this quote we see that members of the National Religious group view themselves as technologically open and ready to engage with digital culture. We also see that through memes, the group members are able to bridge between the online and the offline spheres in a way that enables them to consume content of digital culture even when online environments use is not permitted (i.e., during the Sabbath).

This innovation of taking Internet memes offline and sharing them in a traditional medium of the religious community demonstrate the unique relationship and interplay between the National Religious community and technology. While this community might not be familiar with some of the mainstream popular culture (as most of it does not relates directly to them or contains features that conflict with religious modesty), they do want to take part and use the internet and social media through which they can be a part of modern society. Memes are a medium that is highly dependent on its creator's intentions, and enable religious people to participate in online environments without jeopardizing their religious affiliations, beliefs and modesty.

Many scholars argue that religious groups transmit offline religious understandings into online environments and digital media to maintain an observant lifestyle. This is found for example in the use of internet filters, providing users with a "kosher" version of the internet that matches their religious standards (Čejka, 2009; Hack, 2007; Rashi, 2012). Such use can be understood through the religious-social shaping of technology (RSST; Campbell, 2010) approach, which views new media usage by religious groups as a negotiation between offline religious values and the features of new technologies. While the previously mentioned example of internet filters emphasizes the modification of the online media in light of offline traditions, the case of the memes in the synagogue pamphlet shows how offline religious media are changing in light of online communication formats. Here offline religious media outlets adopt online communication patterns and demonstrate how this negotiation between the offline and online works in both ways, that is, not only considering the offline in order to participate in the online but also transporting online culture (i.e., internet memes) into offline culture (i.e., the synagogue pamphlets).

## CONCLUSION

In this chapter the role memes play for an online Jewish-religious group and the kind of religious message these memes carry about Judaism was addressed. The memes shared via the "Tweeting Orthodoxies" Facebook page reflect a dialog between popular culture and religion, as well as between offline and online environments. This dialog shows that Judaism functions as an interpretive framework that does not necessarily exclude religious Jewish people from contemporary popular discourses. On the contrary, the Jewish religion as reflected in the interviews and in the analyzed internet memes, constitute a perspective for understanding popular and digital culture. This dialog is demonstrated by memes that use religion to unfold possible meanings of cultural artifact, and popular culture to demonstrate an actual millennia-old history of the Jewish religion.

This dialogue is also demonstrated by the flow of formats and information between old and new media forms. It was shown that the internet meme format is incorporated in old media format—the synagogue pamphlets. This study also reflects an RSST approach and adds to this theoretical perspective. The RSST approach stresses the need to study carefully the history and values of religious communities in order to fully understand how they negotiate their use and choices related to new media technologies. Just as this approach suggests, researchers are urged to begin their study of religious communities both offline and online by understanding the structures and beliefs that shape their negotiation processes with new media. This also shows how religious use of new media intersects with offline behaviors and cultures. In the case of memes in the synagogue pamphlets, it is notable that the use of memes led to the negotiation of offline, old medium rather than only negotiating the online sphere. Synagogue pamphlets were changed in light of new online formats, demonstrating the movement of online content to offline formats in the National Religious context. This is an example of a dialogue in which new media changes old media, rather than the other way around. Hence, by taking an RSST approach we are able to examine reciprocal relationship between online and offline spheres as demonstrated by the circulation and decoding of memes.

Finally, this chapter adds to the discussion of the National Religious group identity and their relationship to new media technology. While often defined through its leaning toward the right side of the Israeli political map, the self-definition of National Religious individuals documented in this study tends to emphasize cultural features (such as education, fashion and after-schools activities), instead of political ones. Undeniably, some members of the National Religious group do hold political affiliation with the Israeli right (i.e., supporting Jewish settlement of the West Bank and advocating for Jewish religious involvement in state matters as marital issues, for example). However, this chapter shows that the group members promote an often less discussed aspect of their religious identity. It is shown in this chapter that the National Religious community wishes to formulate a cultural identity that is not only different from the secular culture, because it stresses religious components, but also different from the ultra-Orthodox culture, because it values and underlines the benefits of technology and digital culture. The analyzed memes and interviews contribute to the understanding of Jewish religious responses to the digital media in the National Religious context. The memes and interviews show that this group's primary disposition towards technological innovations is one of embrace, rather than withdrawal. Internet memes, as an example of digital culture, enable this group with a self-constructed artifact that demonstrates their understanding of the National Religious identity. Thus, through digital media National Religious group members facilitate a discussion about and reconstruct their Jewish religious identity.

## NOTE

1. The Facebook page can be found at https://www.facebook.com/dosim.metsaitsimm?fref=ts.

## REFERENCES

Bellar, W., Campbell, H.A., Cho, J., Terry, A., Tsuria, R., Yadlin-Segal, A. and Ziemer, J. (2013). Reading Religion in Internet Memes. *Journal of Religion, Media & Digital Culture*, 2(2) [online]. Available at http://jrmdc.com/wp-content/uploads/2013/12/Studying-Religious-Internet-Memes.pdf [Accessed January 9, 2014].

Campbell, H. (2010). *When Religion Meets New Media*. London: Routledge.

Campbell, H. (2011). Religion and the Internet in the Israeli Orthodox Context. *Israel Affairs*, 17(3), 364–383.

Čejka, M. (2009). Making the Internet Kosher: Orthodox (Haredi) Jews and Their Approach to the World Wide Web. *Masaryk University Journal of Law and Technology*, 3(1), 99–109. [online]. Available at https://mujlt.law.muni.cz/storage/1267475339_sb_06-cejka.pdf [Accessed January 9, 2014].

Chaffee, S.H. and Metzger, M.J. (2001). The End of Mass Communication? *Mass Communication & Society*, 4(4), 365–379.

Cohen, A. (2005). The Crocheted Skullcap and What Lies Behind It: The Multiplicity of Identities in Religious Zionist Society. *Akdamot*, 15, 9–30.

Cohen, J. (2000). Politics, Alienation, and the Consolidation of Group Identity: The Case of Synagogue Pamphlets. *Rhetoric & Public Affairs*, 3(2), 247–275.

Dawkins, R. (2006). *The Selfish Gene*. Oxford and New York: Oxford University Press. (Original work published 1976)

Ferbshtein, R. (2012). Religious-Like. *Holes in the Net*. [online]. Available at http://old.holesinthenet.co.il/archives/54257 [Accessed May 10, 2013] (in Hebrew).

Finkin, J. (2009). Jewish Jokes, Yiddish Storytelling, and Sholem Aleichem: A Discursive Approach. *Jewish Social Studies*, 16(1), 85–110.

Fisher, S. (2008). Religious Zionism on the Brink Third Millennium. *Akdamot*, 22, 9–38.

Flew, T. (2008). *New Media: An Introduction*. Victoria: Oxford University Press.

Gabel, I. (2006). *The National Religious Public and the Media: Love and Hate Relations*. Tel Aviv: Tel Aviv University (in Hebrew).

Guterman, M.A. (2006). Identity Conflict in Modern Orthodox Judaism and the Laws of Family Purity. *Method & Theory in the Study of Religion*, 18(1), 92–100.

Hack, J. (2007). *Taming Technology: Ultra-Orthodox Jewish Families and Their Domestication of the Internet*. Masters dissertation, London School of Economics and Political Science, [online]. Available at http://www.lse.ac.uk/media@lse/research/mediaWorkingPapers/MScDissertationSeries/Past/Hack_final.pdf [Accessed January 9, 2014].

Hervieu-Leger, D. (1997). What Scripture Tells Me: Spontaneity and Regulation Within the Catholic Charismatic Renewal. In: D. Hal (Ed.) *Lived Religion in America: Toward a History of Practice* (pp. 22–40). Princeton: Princeton University Press.

Heylighen, F. and Chielens, K. (2008). Evolution of Culture, Memetics. In: *Encyclopedia of Complexity and System Science* (Vrije Universiteit Brussel) [online]. Available at http://pespmc1.vub.ac.be/Papers/Memetics-Springer.pdf [Accessed January 9, 2014].

Husted, A. (2012). *A Funny Thing Happened on the Way from the Forum: The Life and Death of Internet Memes*. Dissertation submitted to the Faculty of the Graduate School of the University of Minnesota [online]. Available at: http://conservancy.umn.edu/bitstream/137171/1/Husted_umn_0130E_13047.pdf [Accessed May 23, 2013].

Jenkins, H. (2006). *Convergence Culture: Where New and Old Media Collide*. New York: New York University Press.

Kaplan, L. (1979). The Ambiguous Modern Orthodox Jew. *Judaism New York, NY*, 28(4), 439–448.

Kipnis, J. (2012). *Internet Memes – Israel 2012. Annual Report—The Israeli Media in 2012: Agendas, Uses and Trends* [online]. Available at https://mailhost-3.tamu.edu/service/home/~/chapter7%20Israeli%20MEME.pdf?auth=co&loc=en_US&id=2092&part=2 [Accessed January 9, 2014] (in Hebrew).

Kuipers, G. (2006). The Social Construction of Digital Danger: Debating, Defusing and Inflating the Moral Dangers of Online Humor and Pornography in the Netherlands and the United States. *New Media and Society*, 8(3), 379–400.

Lövheim, M. (2012). A Voice of Their Own. Young Muslim Women, Blogs and Religion. In: S, Hjarvard and M, Lövheim (Eds.). *Mediatization and Religion: Nordic Perspectives* (pp. 129–145). Göteborg: Nordicom, Göteborgs Universitet.

Mason, P.Q. (2012). Mormon Blogs, Mormon Studies, and the Mormon Mind. *Dialogue—A Journal of Mormon Thought*, 45(3), 12–25.

Marilos, I. (2013). Moshav Leytzim of Tweeting Orthodoxies. *Ynet* [online]. Available at http://www.ynet.co.il/articles/0,7340,L-4329483,00.html [Access January 9, 2014] (in Hebrew).

Maynard, F. Moschella Clark, M., & Hummel, L. (2010) Pastoral Bearings: Lived Religion and Pastoral Theology. In: J, Maynard. L, Hummel. M, Clark Moschella (Eds.) *Pastoral Bearings Lived Religion and Pastoral Theology* (pp. 1–20). Lanham: Lexington Books.

McGuire, B. (2008). *Lived Religion: Faith and Practice in Everyday Life*. New York: Oxford University Press.

Miller, B.J., Mundey, P. and Hill, J.P. (2013). Faith in the Age of Facebook: Exploring the Links Between Religion and Social Network Site Membership and Use. *Sociology of Religion*, 74(2), 227–253.

Orsi, R. (1997). Everyday Miracles: The Study of Lived Religion. In: D. Hal (Ed.) *Lived Religion in America: Toward a History of Practice* (pp. 3–21). Princeton:

Princeton University Press.
Pickerel, W., Jorgensen, H. and Bennett, W.L. (2002) *Culture Jams and Meme Warfare: Kalle Lasn, Adbusters and Media Activism*. Center for Communication and Civic Engagement [online]. Available at http://depts.washington.edu/gcp/pdf/culturejamsandmemewarfare.pdf [Accessed May 23, 2013].
Rashi, T. (2012). The Kosher Cell Phone in Ultra-Orthodox Society. A Technological Ghetto Within the Global Village? In: H. Campbell (Ed.) *Digital Religion: Understanding Religious Practice In New Media Worlds* (pp. 173–181). London: Routledge.
Rotem, E. (2013). Tweeting Orthodoxies—the Revolutionary Facebook Page of the Religious Sector. *Mako* [online]. Available at http://www.mako.co.il/spirituality-popular_culture/Article-26015025ae92041006.htm [Accessed May 10, 2013].
Shifman, L. (2012). An Anatomy of a YouTube Meme. *New Media and Society*, 14(2), 187–203.
Shifman, L. and Lemish, D. (2011). "Mars and Venus" in Virtual Space: Post-Feminist Humor and the Internet. *Critical Studies in Media Communication*, 28(3), 253–273.
Tweeting Orthodoxies. (2014). About [online, Facebook group]. Available at: https://www.facebook.com/dosim.metsaitsimm/info [Accessed May 10, 2013].
Warner, C.D. (2013). Hope and Sorrow: Uncivil Religion, Tibetan Music Videos, and YouTube. *Ethnos*, 78(4), 543–568.
Ziv, A. (Ed.). (1986). *Jewish Humor*. New Brunswick: Transaction Publishers.

# 8 Legitimation of New Media and Community Building among Jewish Denominations in the US

*Oren Golan*[1]

Since the 18th century, Jewish communities have been faced by major transformative movements that led them to reconsider their values, social networks, practices of socialization and communication. These movements included the emergence of Hasidism, the Haskalah and the Reform movements. External forces of violence obstructing religious communities and non-religious movements have also been forces of rivalry and antagonism such as the Zionist movement (Salmon, 1998) or the usual suspects that challenge religion, namely, that of secularism and modernity at large (Asad, 1999; Casanova, 2008). Nowadays, Jewish movements and communities are threatened by new forces that can potentially rupture their way of life, with the introduction of forms of personal and mass communication, most notably the rise of new media (i.e., mobile phones, digital gaming and the internet).

With the emergence and popularity of new media since the mid-1990s, the question of boundary setting, social integration and socialization are heightened as the ubiquity and benefits of new media for everyday life are paramount in accessing knowledge, engaging entertainment and commerce. At the same time, the allure of the internet threatens the continued efforts of religious Jewish community members and its leaders to maintain a closed and protected community existence. Nevertheless, in nearly all Jewish communities a fervent use of these new media by believers can be found. This use challenges communal efforts to reproduce the social and cultural ideology, social structures and modes of power or authority, especially within certain religious communities. Thus, community leaders are faced with the dilemma of whether they should encourage believers to integrate new media into their daily lives, or rather ban it and avoid its use. In light of this development the question is raised regarding how the internet and new media are appropriated and socially legitimized among religious communities, both those that are extremely segregated and those that are more open?

Exploring modes of legitimacy used in relation to new media enables us to better understand the ways religious communities act as cultural and moral agents that shape the belief and behavior of social actors (i.e., digital entrepreneurs, devout individuals, roles of leaders and various power brokers in the community). It is argued that through exploring their process of negotiating, attainting and exercising legitimation in relation to digital technologies, it is observed that these communities often engage these technologies in ways that ultimately generate trust, and foster sociability within their communities. These communities are confronted with the allure of new technologies, and their utility for earning their livelihood, together with conflicting messages on widespread negative content that is available over the internet (e.g., pornography, adverse political/religious ideals). These conflicting notions lead to multiple modes of response, negotiation and reflection that fit different communities' moral and social life.

In this chapter it is contended that several schemes of legitimation have been developed in the Jewish world, which have validated the use of new media and enabled its use in different ways that fit in with the creed and rhythm of life of its believers. To examine the modes of legitimation, focus is placed on comparing select American Jewish communities, namely, that of the ultra-Orthodox (Haredi), Chabad (as an exception within the *Haredi* community, as it highlights Jewish information outreach, rather than segregation) and the Reform movement. By examining these denominational case studies, discussing the responses to new media that are expressed by its leaders, on one hand, and its producers, on the other, the aim of this chapter is to shed light on the balance between religious community maintenance and new media production within the Jewish world and beyond. This will be seen through observing the forms of legitimation that each group had fostered towards its engagement with modernity, with particular attention to new media, as a spearhead of modernity.

## RELIGION, NEW MEDIA AND LEGITIMACY

The process of legitimation is one where something is made acceptable or normative to a given population. Legitimacy can be seen as a perception that the actions of an entity are desirable, proper and appropriate within a socially construction of norms, values and beliefs. Furthermore, these concepts need to correspond to an overall understanding of justice, universal values or particularistic interests of a public (Kahane, 1982, p. 4; Suchman, 1995, p. 574). Within the sociological legacy, Weber's (1954) famous assertions of its sources (traditional, charismatic or legal-rational) anchored its discussion as a way to achieve a right to rule. Legitimacy is viewed, in a macroscopic framework, as an integral part of holding authority and power (Ferrero, 1942) and can be perceived as a fundamental factor in institutionalization, solidifying nations and social integration (Kahane, 1982). More recent studies have drawn the concept of legitimation from a macroscopic discussion of power and institutions in society, to a middle-range organizational level. According to these studies, organizations seek to forge congruence between the social values associated with, or implied by, their activities and the norms of acceptable behavior in their communities or larger social system of which they are a part (Ashforth and Gibbs, 1990; Markowitz, Cobb and Hedley, 2012; Mathews, 1993).

With the rise of the media, and particularly new media, the constructions of religious social institutions and organizations are challenged. Ideas and information are directly communicated to believers through cellular phones or the internet, without the mediation of religious clergy. This first-hand access to information threatens the core elements of social control, gatekeeping of information and socialization that religious institutions and leadership cultivate, particularly in enclave societies such as the Amish or the Jewish ultra-Orthodox. Under these conditions, we could expect an outright resistance and delegitimation of new media. Nevertheless, religious websites are on the rise among believers of organized (Islam, Christianity; see Bunt, 2009; Campbell, 2010) and new religious movements (i.e., Wicca, Neo-Paganism; see Cowan, 2005) and its pragmatic affordances to clergy and believers is highlighted. However, there is a dearth of research with regard to the patterns of legitimacy that facilitates the use of new media.

## METHODOLOGY

The observed communities are not always welcoming to outside researchers and are apprehensive of exposing themselves to a researcher. This concern is compounded by their overall suspicion towards outsiders and misrepresentation of their communities by journalists and academics. Given this outsider/insider challenge in the study of bounded and fundamentalist societies (as explored, e.g., in Stadler, 2009 or Davidman, 1991), it is argued that under conditions of an enclave society, such as that of the Haredi Jews, an investigation with traditional tools of social scientists (such as questioners) would be unsuccessful. Accordingly, an ethnographic approach that would be sensitive to the communities' distinctions would be useful choices for inquiry.

This research draws on a four-year study of new media engagement within religious Jewish communities in the US (2009–2013). Conversations were held with members of numerous Jewish communities in the US, including various groups among the ultra-Orthodox (Chassidic and Litvaks) as well as the modern variants of the Reform movement. The research draws on over 90 interviews from a snowball sampling and ethnographic fieldwork with a focus on the three particular groups. Among the Haredim, interviews and online observations were conducted with a selection of with avid surfers and bloggers, mobile phone marketers and internet providers as well as business web/app entrepreneurs (e.g., http://ptexgroup.com, http://jpupdates.com), entertainment webmasters (such as http://thecooljew.net), online journalists (e.g., http://www.theyeshivaworld.com, http://www.thelakewoodscoop.com) and moral agents of technology, such as the Technology Awareness Group (TAG) in the US that offers support on filtering services for the PC and smartphones. It should be noted that the selected outlets were investigated ensuing community members' recommendations. While focusing on the Chabad variant in the ultra-Orthodox world (as will be subsequently elaborated), attention has been given to avid surfers that actively use and participate in new media outlets (sharing, posting, responding and such), bloggers, community emissaries (which serve as an elite group within Chabad) and key website producers in leading and communal websites (such as http://chabad.org or http://crownheights.info) educational, spiritual and media production agencies (e.g., http://home.jemedia.org or http://meaningfullife.com).

Among the Reform movement the study examined multiple sources of religious websites and included interviews with smart phone/tablet application creators (such as I-Shofar or iMenorah), their leading Rabbinic Association that is currently producing digital applications (http://ccarnet.org), rabbinical students, rabbis and avid surfers.

Discussions with community members and web/app entrepreneurs enabled this study with an access to informants' views of their online activities in their private settings (homes, website offices, media editing rooms, etc.) as well as enabled me to collect their offline publications and reading materials (e.g., pamphlets, synagogue publications, journals). Questions were directed to address the popularity of new media technologies, the targeted audience and how (if at all) these technologies were integrated and accepted by both users and stakeholders in the community (e.g., rabbis, educators).

The data were analyzed using categorization techniques that stemmed from the fieldwork (Strauss and Corbin, 1998). The purpose of this analysis is to identify central themes in the data, to find recurrent experiences, and to link different categories to form central themes. The coding process focused on issues of authority, trust, social control and the perception of new media and was guided by principles set forth by Glaser and Strauss (1967) for comparative analyses. To ensure reliability, two independent researchers analyzed the entire data set (Strauss and Corbin, 1998). This procedure led to the identification of patterns of legitimation employed by religious communities in relation to the internet (as elaborated later: dualist, purposeful and inclusive). To further increase reliability, the analysis was reviewed by two independent readers (Marshall and Rossman, 1995). Finally, comparisons were made with the literature on legitimation of religious communities toward the internet as to increase validity (Bogdan and Biklen, 1982; Strauss and Corbin, 1998).

## FINDINGS: JEWISH COMMUNITIES, LEGITIMACY AND THE INTERNET

Findings point to the formation of three patterns of legitimacy with regard to internet use. These patterns reflect a negotiation process of accepting and integrating new technologies into respective communities while mitigating the technology's potential threat to social solidarity.

*Dualist* pattern demonstrates how users simultaneously adhere to contradictory beliefs about the internet, both rejecting and accepting its use within communal boundaries. This legitimation approach emphasizes a limited and filtered use of new media (e.g., phones, websites), and stresses the instrumental and profane nature of such technology. This strategy is most salient amongst mainstream Haredi populations in the US and Israel.

The *Purposeful* scheme is used to advance metaphysical goals through new media, and actively directing them toward community building and the fortification of communal institutions. This approach is outward oriented, strengthens their status in the public sphere and is both charismatically and traditionally legitimized as an instrumental vehicle towards religious goals. Such approach appears prominent among the Chabad movement.

Finally, an *Inclusive Adoption pattern* offers a comprehensive scheme that heralds new media's ability to educate, inform and lead social change that directly or obliquely fortifies the community's boundaries and empower its members. This approach is legitimized as a timely fit for believers' lives as well as their fluid and multifaceted identities and is most salient among the Reform movement in this study. As further elaborated, these schemes are discerned from the communal characteristics and worldviews as well as their specific discourse of technologies and new media means. Each of these processes of legitimation is explored in the following in relation to the religious communities studied.

## Dualist Legitimation

A dualist mode of legitimation refers to an acceptance of new media through the coexistence or mixture of different and even contradictory orientations (such as open to external information and closed, including user content, or rejecting public participation), within common digital realms. A dualist mode is most discernible among the US and Israeli Haredi groups. The dualist pattern of legitimation is explored here in relation to ultra-Orthodox groups. The Haredi community refers to a large segment of the Jewish world that has been socially defined, especially in the Holocaust's aftermath. Haredim dedicate their lives to the study of the Torah and to express an adherence to the strictest version of the Jewish law. However, Haredi members are not monolithic and are divided into subgroups and movements, most notably between the Hassidim and their opposers (i.e., Mitnagdim/Lithuanian, Ashkenazi Haredim of American/European descent and Sephardic Haredim of African/Asian descent), that struggle over power authority and resources. Given their inner differences, the Haredim cultivate a bounded community that is generally opposed to modern Zionism, with a segregated educational system and are symbolically identified through their strict codes of modesty, Gender separation, dress code that includes black attire for men and head covering for women (Stadler, 2009, p. 36). Nevertheless, in spite of their efforts for social segregation, these groups are mostly urban, reside in modern cities and seek to balance the demands of modern economies with their traditional lifestyles. This increased (albeit reserved) encounter with modernity serves as a background to their dualist mode of legitimacy toward new media.

### *Haredi's Dualist Legitimacy toward New Media*

Given the internet's threat of opening fields of knowledge, facilitating sources of moral pollution and undermining traditional sources of authority, the Haredi world embraces a dual scheme of legitimacy toward the internet. Cohen (2011) emphasizes this point as he discusses the Haredi ambivalence toward the internet and refers to it as a "love–hate affair." Indeed, Haredi leaders object and express their disdain for the internet and its offerings, yet do not denounce it completely (on the Haredim and the media, see also Rashi, 2011). Furthermore, all social indicators point to the Haredi public embracing the internet to a large extent, albeit with the use of filtering means (i.e., software and servers) and specialized Haredi websites (Campbell and Golan, 2011). This position offers a possibility for confusion and social anomie on the one hand, as social norms are unclear and may be perceived as inconsistent and at odds. On the other hand, their dual position offers an open approach to experiment, explore and re-affirm their communal boundaries through net surfing. To better understand this scheme, it would be useful to understand the responses of formal community leaders (e.g., prominent rabbis, Yeshiva principals), which strongly oppose the use of the internet, followed by their justifications for partially accepting its use within a bounded mundane space, which obliquely enables the Haredi world to explore the web in new, however guarded ways.

On Sunday, May 20, 2012, more than 40,000 Haredi men attended a mass rally at Citi Field stadium in Queens, New York, organized by the rabbinical group Ichud Hakehillos Letohar Hamachane (literally, the "Communities United for the Righteousness of the Camp") and prompted by Haredi "media awareness" activists from Lakewood, New Jersey, aimed to disseminate information and hold a 'prayer rally' for the success of Jews "war on the Technology which threatens the sanctity of the homes of Israel." A call to action (*kol Kore*) published in Haredi newspapers stated, "We must assemble together to protect and be protected . . . and may it be that we will be successful in encouraging the public not to stumble over this obstacle" (Shamah, 2012). The call to action is signed by some of the leaders of the ultra-Orthodox *Yeshiva* world, and is mirrored in other official decree announcements in newspapers, street posters and pamphlets (see Figure 8.1).

Accordingly, these traditional authorities (signified by the rabbis' approbation of the decree) validate the event and its content. However, further traditional informal means are also utilized to exert influence. This can be seen, for example, in the linguistic usage that was prevalent in the rally.

בס"ד

שבט תש"ע - כסלו תשע"ב

# פסק הלכה

## אודות הגדרים למניעת סכנות האינטרנט

חיים אנו בדור שבו הסכנות הרוחניות אורבות לפתחנו מהתקשורת והאינטרנט, ומאיימים לפרוץ לתוך חומות בתינו. גדולי ישראל התריעו שלא היה כלי משחית מסוכן כדוגמתו - וכבר הפיל חללים רבים, צעירים ומבוגרים

המחשב על כל צורותיו: סרטים, אינטרנט, משחקים, וכדומה - מאיימים למוטט את כל קדושת הבית היהודי ומסכנים את עתידנו ועתיד ילדנו, וכבר הכריעו גדולי ישראל בעבר שהצפייה בסרטים המופקים מכל סוג שהוא, ובמשחקים במחשב אסורים (במחשב, DVD, MP4), וחובה על המחנכים וההורים לעמוד על המשמר ולסלק לגמרי מפגעים רוחניים אלו, ולמנוע מהילדים כל גישה לדברים הללו - שסכנתם גדולה מתקופת ההשכלה שהורידה רבבות מישראל לאבדון, רח"ל.

בכלל האמור, חלילה לתת הכשר או פיקוח לאתרי אינטרנט 'חרדיים' המפרסמים חדשות כלליות וקהילתיות או פורומים, ולא להעביר להם מידע או להתראיין שם - שאתרים אלו הם מחטיאי הרבים בדברים נוראים ואיומים, ומלאים לשה"ר, הרס חינוכי, ביזוי תלמידי חכמים, מחלוקות ותועבות, וזאת מלבד שהם מביאים את הגולשים לשקוע באינטרנט ולהגיע למקומות טמאים, וחובה להוקיעם.

א. גדולי ישראל פסקו והכריעו (במכתבם תשנ"ט, תש"ס, תשס"ג, תש"ע) שהשימוש באינטרנט כרוך באיסורים חמורים. ומאחר ואין שום אינטרנט חסום לחלוטין - אסור להכניס את עצמו ומשפחתו לניסיונות ולסיכונים חמורים שכאלו.

**על-כן, יש לנתק לגמרי כל מחשב - נייח או נייד - מכל אפשרות חיבור לאינטרנט**

(ע"י רשת קווית, אלחוטית וסלולארית). וכן אין להשתמש בכל מכשיר שיש בו אפשרות חיבור לאינטרנט, כמחשבי כף-יד למיניהם, או בטלפון סלולארי שאינו מאושר.
גם מחשב שבו דואר אלקטרוני בלבד חובה לחסום מכל גישה לאינטרנט.

ב. במוסדות ובמקרה של הכרח לפרנסה שנאלצים להשתמש באינטרנט (במידת ההכרח בלבד) – אסור באיסור חמור להשתמש באינטרנט שאינו חסום כהלכה - גם מגלישה אלחוטית וסלולארית - אלא בחסימה המאושרת ע"י 'ועדת רבנים' המוסמכת לכך ע"י גדולי ישראל.

**היות וישנם חסימות שאינם חוסמות כראוי, על-כן חובה שתהיה חסימה כהלכה, ולעת עתה החסימה היחידה המאושרת היא ע"י חברת 'נתיב'.**

ועם זאת חובה למנוע גישה לאותו מחשב מכל מי שאינו מוכרח להשתמש באינטרנט, ולעשות ככל שביכולתו לא להחזיקו בבית כלל.

ג. גם המתחבר לאינטרנט חסום לצורך פרנסה הכרחית - צריך שיהיה ע"פ אישור של בי"ד או רב המוסמכים לכך מטעם גדולי ישראל.

והננו קוראים לכל רבני השכונות והקהילות, להיקהל ולעמוד על נפשם ולעשות כנסי הסברה המתריעים כנגד מחריב היהדות - האינטרנט

באעה"ח להציל רבים מעון

יוסף שלום אלישיב　שמואל הלוי ואזנר　א.י.ל שטינמן　מיכל יהודה ליפקוביץ

חיים פנחס שיינברג　נסים קרליץ　חיים קניבסקי　שמואל אויערבך　שמעון בעדני　משה צדקה

*Figure 8.1* Decree on internet use signed by leading Haredi Rabbis and halachic (practiced law and tradition) authorities (all but the last two, the Sephardic rabbis Badani and Tsadaka, are of the top Haredi/Lithuanian variant), prohibiting internet use with the exception of filtered surfing for livelihood purposes

During the event, numerous speakers lamented the spread of the internet in Jewish homes and warned against its dangers using in three languages: English, Hebrew and Yiddish.[2]

This harsh approach has been echoed in other Haredi communities in the US as well as in Israel. In January 2012 the Sephardic-Haredi newspaper *Yom L'Yom* published a letter from its rabbinical leaders, the late Ovadia Yosef and Shlomo Amar, describing the spiritual evils that the internet holds and warning that "houses and families have fallen on its account" (*Yom L'Yom*, January 25, 2012). They cited the ancient rabbinical discussions of the Gemara, saying that there is an obligation of believers to save someone who is being chased, from pillagers and from other dangers that lurk. The traditional source of the Gemara is invoked here to motivate believers to deter the use of the internet, in spite of its allures, and, implicitly, to discourage its use by their families and associates.

An extremely sensitive issue in the implementation of a ban of the internet is the case of socialization. Cultivating large families and shaping the younger generations through educational agencies is considered a major tool in the reproduction of the Haredi society. Even among secular populations the internet has been met with apprehension and occasionally with a moral panic (see Livingston, 2009), yet in a bounded community of the Haredim these sentiments are compounded and institutional pressures are accentuated. An example can be seen in a Hebrew written pamphlet handed out at Beth Medrash Govoha, a key Yeshiva (seminary) in the Haredi community of Lakewood, New Jersey. Yeshiva boys are banned from internet use as the leaflet reads (published in *Shvat*, February, 2012, unstated publisher):

1. It is forbidden to hold an internet in the home except for the purpose of livelihood
2. Whoever requires the internet for his livelihood should receive approval from a senior instructor
3. Also, whoever needs the internet for his livelihood should install on his computer excellent guards (filters) that are approved by the *Yeshiva* superiors.
4. And all this (the aforementioned) relates to the computer, but on the phone no internet is allowed, even with a filter, and even for the sake of livelihood.
5. Transgressor of these rules will lose his privilege to be part of the *Yeshiva* and has no permission to study in its halls.

The rules stated in the leaflet mirror the standing of the overall community. However, in this instance, the bureaucratic influence and indirect communal sanctions of the seminary[3] are utilized to ensure compliance to the ban of the internet, particularly among its youngsters.

All in all, we see a continued objection to the use of the internet. However the key exception that is expressed to this ban is the issue of livelihood

(*Parnasa*). Although a pious society that is occasionally at odds with the inclusion of work into their everyday lives, the Haredi world leaves much latitude when it comes to facilitating work as a means for advancing familial and religious goals, particularly in light of economic and social pressures of the modern state (in Israel, see Stadler, 2009). This form of allowance has a history of careful rabbinic acceptance and rejection (such as in the case of the Belz rabbi's allowance, see Campbell, 2010). This form of legitimation, allows the creation of a profane sphere of internet activities that are either directly acceptable or acquiescently tolerable to the Haredi elite. However, this limited legitimation of the profane has been constrained in several ways.

Both by popular demand, and encouraged by rabbinical figures (see Figure 8.1), filtered ISPs and programs are frequently used. In addition, numerous Haredi internet ventures emerged in the past decade that include filtering and monitoring web behavior companies (e.g., JNet, Rimon, guardyoureyes[4]) and Haredi websites, such as theyeshivaworld.com and vosizneias.com. According to online web analytics programs (Alexa or compare.com), as of 2012, Haredi websites such as theyeshivaworld.com yield about 60,000 to 80,000 unique users every month. These numbers may not portray an accurate measure of internet use among the Haredi population. However, it does illustrate a fervent use of these websites that are dedicated to Haredi news, lifestyles and overall community life and are certainly a far cry from a ban of the internet by community members.

To legitimate these websites, its webmasters (i.e., CEOs, content managers, design managers, web journalists and other operators within the website) constantly evaluate and negotiate their perceived notion of what is morally and politically acceptable by their community readers and balance that with external pressures of rabbinical authorities and the pressures of economic profitability and the logic of successful web performance (e.g., visibility, popularity). These webmasters have worked to create safe havens for believers to participate in communal-net culture, without the "moral pollution" offered on the net (e.g. pornography, foul language) that are viewed as a gateway to sin (see Campbell and Golan, 2011; Tsarfaty and Blais, 2002).

To conclude, as the Haredi leadership at large (with an exception of the Chabad variant) has rejected internet use, it has left some stipulations to enable its use in certain spaces that facilitate their worldly and profane activities, at the workplace or at home. This rabbinical legitimation (based on filtering and social monitoring) has been appropriated by a new class of entrepreneurs to create a Haredi "digital enclave" culture that in spite of direct rabbinical objections and decrees (particularly in 2009) has survived to become a central source of self-expression and community information for thousands of believers. This dual orientation of objection and acceptance, cultivation and prohibition can be seen as an institutionalized way of adapting to a rapidly changing world, rather than viewing it as a point of dissonance and crisis. However, this requires further observation into long-term processes.

## Purposeful Legitimation

The purposeful pattern of legitimation emphasizes a proactive approach toward new media as a way for promoting religious ideals of "reawakening every Jew" through the concept of outreach (Ehrlich, 2004, pp. 166–167) and fostering communal solidarity and growth. This is evident in use and framing of new media within the Chabad movement. Chabad is a subgroup within Haredi Judaism, and more specifically a variant within the Hassidic movement. The movement emerged in the 18th century as a charismatic religious faction that swept through Poland and the Russian Empire. With its growth, it distinguished itself with a creed that emphasized popular mysticism, reforming the use of Jewish liturgy, modifying ritual and the Jewish Eastern European dress code (Baumel, 2009; Fishkoff, 2003; Friedman, 1991). Among Hassidim it is common to be affiliated with several dynastic groups known as "courts," each headed by its own rabbi and following its respective customs. These groups differ in their conception of social boundaries and interaction with noncommunity members and may fluctuate from an extreme seclusion and separation from outsiders, such as in the case of the Satmars, to an outreach to Jews and gentiles around the world, as in the case of Chabad. Unlike other Haredi Jews, who prefer to turn inward and fortify their boundaries, the Chabad movement turns outward as well, assuming responsibility for the Jewish collective and striving to teach its ways to a broader community (Golan, 2013).

Although not the largest Hasidic court, Chabad surpasses others in its impact on the outside world, whether Jewish or non-Jewish. In fact, around the world, Chabad members periodically engage in campaigns of religious influence from street centers, university campuses, and beyond (Ehrlich, 2004, pp. 166–175; Ravitzky, 1994, p. 304). Chabad's information dissemination activities have mostly been governed from its New York center (Friedman, 1994). In the past, leaflets, newsletters, books and other means were utilized for these endeavors, and a fervent zeal for religious activism marked their approach. Most apparent perhaps is the work of the emissaries (*Shlichim*) who develop contacts with local Jewish establishments and bear a visible presence in key urban areas around the world. Since the death of its leader, the highly venerated Rabbi Schneerson (the rebbe), the Chabad community has ruptured as some have sought to affirm the rabbi's continuance and even envision his Messianic return (see Bilu, 2009; Kravel-Tovi, 2009). However, rather than the movements' deterioration and decline as a consequence of the death of its charismatic leader, with no heir in succession, Chabad has shown sustenance and growth through its institutional and media activities.

### *Chabad's Purposeful Legitimacy toward New Media*

For many Chabad members, the internet is viewed in the dualistic fashion characteristic to the aforementioned Haredi groups. However, Chabad has developed a highly rational and elaborate media operation that is backed up by a strong bureaucracy and theological creed. To understand this development, it is important to shortly focus on the history and creed of the Chabad movement, particularly with relation to new media.

Chabad's legitimacy toward new media largely stems from its creed of knowledge dissemination and its traditional allowances (focused on a constructed theology of "tools" that highlights the utilitarian aspects of media for advancing religious ideals) granted by the late Rabbi Schneerson and the core of institutions (most noted by that of emissaries as well as literary and electronic media operations) that surrounded his court.

A Chabad rabbi in Chicago described to the author the creed of the internet and the media at large:

> There is a famous discussion on the Rebbe in relation to TV. How can the Rebbe be on Cable [TV]? People used to ask. The Television is *Treif* (non-Kosher) they used to say. In the 1980's the Rebbe borrowed an explanation from the *Gemara* that referred to the Gold in the [Biblical] Tabernacle and the Temple, where is asked: how can we use something so vain in the temple? The answer is that it is not in the Gold but rather in its usage. Is it for vain usage or to enhance God's majesty in the world? So the same goes for TV and Cable. I would extrapolate this for the internet. It is not wrong but how people use it. How we educate our children. Life is very different from the *Ghetto* and *Shtetl* [old Jewish towns of Eastern Europe] to 2012 where some people are addicted to the web.
>
> (interview, May 24, 2012)

This interpretation emphasizes the "theology of tools" as a creed that legitimizes the internet as stemming from both a traditional theology (the Gemara) and the charismatic veneration that stems from the unique status that is granted to the rebbe.

In frequent visits to meet Chabad webmasters (e.g., Chabad.org, crownheights.info, http://home.jemedia.org/) in Brooklyn, one of the leaders of the Chabad.org website reported that "The technology is here for a purpose for something positive – Chabad tried to use everything we can in a positive way" (personal interview, February 10, 2010). Another mentioned a broad message: "We have a responsibility to the Jewish people . . . Many Jews know about *Yiddishkeit* [folk practices of Jews] but we can provide insights for *Hassidut*" (February 10, 2010). These webmasters words are in line with that of the Gold metaphor raised by the Chicago rabbi. All see new media as a tool to enhance goodness, and Godliness into the world and advance the arrival of the messiah.

Chabad's online presence can be traced back to the 1980s, when the internet garnered attention from mostly computer enthusiasts, students and academics (Danet, 2001). Chabad emerged online through spaces such as electronic bulletin boards (BBS) such as Keshernet, where Chabad activists, most notably the late Rabbi Kazan, initiated their religious online activism (Zaleski, 1997), with an intent to bring about a religious consciousness and promote the observance of their interpretation of Jewish law and custom. According to my interviewees, as early as 1988, the first "Ask The Rabbi" emerged over these bulletin boards, and a few years later, the entire Tanya, the 18th century central text for Chabad members, was posted online. Also, the site offered daily lessons, along with other Jewish texts and teachings (at "*Chabad* in Cyberspace"). By the end of 1993, an important source of legitimation arose with the blessing bestowed by Rabbi Schneerson and the chabad.org website was established (personal interview with a leading figure in Chabad.org, April 27, 2010). Symbolically, the websites were erected. In a building adjacent to the Rebbe's famed residence, from a few grassroots initiatives of Rabbi Kazan and others, Chabad.org emerged as a legitimized and center-based institution, rooted in the heart of the Chabad establishment.

To conclude, Chabad's scheme of legitimation corresponds with its philosophical creed of broadening the scope of religious involvement, particularly for Jews that are less committed to religious practices in their everyday life. Moreover, Chabad offers a different view of the internet as being a tool for advancing godliness into the world. Accordingly, we see how the movement legitimizes its use of the internet as a purposeful bridge to reach other populations. Mainly, but not exclusively, Jewish, as they believe that the Seven Laws of Noah (a moral code that is entrenched in the Talmud), should apply to all humankind. These legitimations draw on schemes that were established in the Chabad infrastructure and theology much before the rise of new media, yet persisted through the rebbe's promotion of televised and radio events that disseminated Chabad's perspective on Judaism, and finally his personal intervention to legitimate the early emergence of the Chabad-oriented internet.

## Inclusive Adoption Legitimation

Inclusive adoption refers to building legitimacy through framing new media as a vital part of modern times and a most fitting form to express and transmit religious knowledge and beliefs. This strategy is seen in the Jewish American Reform movements' approach to the internet.

The Modern Jewish movements stem from the 19th century and Jewish enlightenment (*Haskala*) in Germany and have been become deeply entrenched in the American and European religious landscape and, to a lesser extent, in Israel (Sheleg, 2000). First manifested through liturgy, these Jews of the 18th and 19th centuries increased contact with local Christians and embraced many practices and religious notions including prayer in the indigenous vernacular, the introduction of sermons and music, the shortening of the service and the decorum of worshipers, with an emphasis on channeling the communal prayers to Saturday morning services (De Lange, 2010). Nowadays, Reform creed incorporates an acceptance towards modernity and vis-à-vis other Jewish and non-Jewish communities, including a symmetric approach toward gender issues and an acceptance of homosexuality.

In her book, Dana Kaplan (2003) analyzes the changes in the American Reform movement during the past two generations, particularly in the US. She discusses the Reform movement's move in both directions: on one hand, embracing tradition and, on the other, promoting progressive issues and contingently changing practices to fit with current events and its Zeitgeist.

The flexibility and pragmatism of the Reform movements' theological framework can be seen as a response to its inherent challenge. On one hand, the movement seeks to fasten community alignment and strengthen its Jewish distinctiveness (vis-à-vis non-Jews and other Jewish communities), while on the other hand, it wishes to remain open to various populations, including secular and modernist inclinations amongst its followers, interfaith marriage, Christian influence in schools, media and other socializing agencies. To address these tensions, the Reform movement uses an open approach that accepts differences while highlighting their version of Jewish identity and practice. This open approach towards other groups within the Jewish world and beyond as well as the Reform movements' favorable reception of modernity fosters an inclusive adoption of new media.

### *Reform's Inclusive Adoption Legitimacy toward New Media*

The Reform movement draws its legitimation of new media chiefly from its grassroots perceptions that are well integrated with modernity, rather than drawing upon the movement's establishment, leadership or traditional authority. This is not to say that the population embraces the internet in spite of the rabbinic creed. On the contrary, the Reform Rabbinic establishment[5] embraces new media as an avenue for exporting their creed both on the overall level of the establishment, as well as among its indigenous operations and synagogues. Beyond the official Union for Reform Judaism site (urj.org) or other strongly affiliated websites, the internet is seen as a basic tool in the everyday community life of its congregants. Local synagogues have their own website that caters to its perish and advertises services and informal education activities it provides for youth; adults; Jewish lesbian, gay, bisexual and transgender (LGBT) groups; choirs; interfaith; and more (see, e.g., sholomchicago.org, chicagosinai.org or templebethor-raleigh.org). This is a growing feature in other Jewish groups, but it is much more salient for the Reform movement. Community members and rabbis interviewed discussed at length the importance of and the ways in which the internet is rooted into their lives and how Jewish features of new media are integrated into their everyday lives. For example, rabbis discussed their use of Facebook for keeping in touch and answering questions for the congregants or commented on their use of the offerings of computer apps on their smartphones and tablets.

Rabbis discussed some shortcomings of the internet given the tensions it claims between rabbis and their congregants. "When you are citing something you have to make sure that your citations are accurate because people can check you out" (personal interview, March 22, 2010) told me a rabbinical student in Manhattan, referring to an emergent form of evaluation of rabbinical knowledge by the public and a need to validate their authority through traditional sources of knowledge, such as Jewish source citations. Others discuss the lack of boundaries "everyone has a g-chat [chatting via the Gmail application OG] and my congregants keep asking me what time is services? . . . Can I get a copy of your *Dvar Torah* (sermon – OG)" (interview, October 3, 2011). The discontent expressed here relates to the easy access to clergy, the lack of boundaries and the extra workload it entails. Nevertheless, rabbis I spoke with highlighted the benefits of the internet for their work and did not report any disengagement from the medium. These interviewees discussed various applications that enhance Jewish life and religious knowledge acquisition.

For example, a New York Rabbi referred me to the Our Jewish Community reform website (OurJewishCommunity.org) and iPhone/android app as a cutting-edge Jewish site. As of July 18, 2013, un its advertisement, set within the iPhone app store, its creators pronounced its utility:

> When you are on the go. Bringing Judaism to people where they are, we're an inclusive community with a contemporary Jewish voice. Here you'll find Rabbi Barr's banter (podcasts), Rabbi Baum's Blog, Livestreaming Shabbat and High Holliday services, YouTube videos, Musings from our liturgy, and more . . . we are open 24/7 and look forward to your participation! Be part of a dynamic and evolving 21st century Jewish experience!

This application presents traditional texts such as rabbinical sermons framed within the offerings of contemporary smartphones. This amalgamation of traditional and modern means offers a legitimate pathway to religious participation through new media usage. In addition, the application demonstrates a growing practice as a world of websites/phone applications emerge that bridge between rabbis and believers. These sites facilitate Jewish practice of learning and prayer through the use of cutting edge tools such as Second Life or Tablet usage for holding standard prayers (for weddings, funerals and the like). Some synagogues facilitate free Wi-Fi and Tablets are becoming acceptable for Saturday services.

Indeed, in the past few years we see a significant growth in mobile phone and tablet applications that are geared toward Jewish practice and are both acceptable and popular among orthodox Jewry in the US as well as the Reform movement. For example, I-Shofar is an app that electronically simulates a horn sound that is incorporated on Yom Kippur and Rosh Hashanah services in synagogue, established by a California entrepreneur from a conservative movement background, yet directed to all non-Orthodox Jews, and possibly beyond, intended to "capture the essence of the Shofar" (personal interview, July 28, 2013)[6].

Another example is iMenorah, an app that simulates the lighting of Chanukah candles on the digital screen, produced in 2008 by two California-based high-tech experts and entrepreneurs (personal interview, August 26, 2013).[7]

These apps represent new ways for engaging in Jewish practice, while enjoying the fascination that accompany these technologies through their aesthetic qualities and interactive capabilities. A New York rabbi informed me of the benefits of using the *Mishkan T'filha* (iT'filah) prayer guide (established in 2011), of which liturgy is identical to customary prayer books of the Reform movement. He told me that he uses it for multiple tasks, and although not a sole source of liturgy, it is very helpful in everyday life: "I grabbed my iPad and went to a funeral, then had another event in the evening, it's all there" (interview, March 20, 2012). The immediacy and convenience of the iPad app is apparent in his rhetoric. As of July 18, 2012, the makers of Mishkan T'filah explained its use on the iPhone/iPad app store as follows:

> *Mishkan T'filah* is the siddur (prayer book) used by congregations throughout the world. Now you can carry *Mishkan T'filah* with you on your iPad and interact with the prayers in the siddur as never before. iT'filah, the *Mishkan T'filah* App, is designed to be used in services alongside the print version and as the perfect companion for quiet spiritual reflection or study. This prayer book app is versatile and engaging. Like the print version of *Mishkan T'filah*, the prayers in iT'filah are fully transliterated, and are accompanied by many inspiring readings and commentary. Move between prayers and explore additional content with the swipe of a finger. Tap to hear many of the prayers chanted or read aloud . . .
>
> This app is for all of us, and your feedback and input will help guide its direction. Please share your ideas and vision so, together, we can grow and enhance Jewish prayer.

In the application's description we see that the marketers invite its potential users with an array of novel possibilities ("as never before"). They offer a popular reading of the holy texts ("perfect companion," "versatile and engaging"), that simulate the synagogue experience ("tap to hear many of the prayers chanted or read aloud"), current with the everyday rituals (Morning Prayer) and weekly Shabbat prayers. The app's producers promise to timely update their product and adhere to users' needs and requests. They are part of the Central Conference of American Rabbis (CCAR), situated at the core of the Reform movement and are themselves pivotal players in the production of religious books for the Reform movement. In August 2013, an interview with leading developers in their Manhattan offices and was informed that the producers follow the creed of the movement and are attentive to their publics' responses. Their prayer app, Mishkan T'filah, is their most highly sold app (they market a daily blessing app, numerous religiously oriented e-books and more) and corresponds to daily services and novel activities such as slide screenings of liturgy and visual content at the synagogue (*Visual T'filah*), which has evolved recently, most prominently in California). The operators continuously evaluate their publics' response to the app through postings on the app store, from public discussion they encounter and from that app's actual sales. Commercial sales of the app, offer an opportunity for developers to constantly assess believers' affinity toward new technologies and asses the process of legitimation (or rejection) that the public bears for their religious endeavor. In this sense, it could be maintained that the app market offers an opportunity for capitalist practices (in the sales of apps) to enable the principle of inclusive adoption for legitimizing new media. This is to say, the choice-making practices of consumers allow Reform believers to actively take part in selecting their desired technologies, which in essence, legitimizing its use.

In summary, the Reform movement has cultivated an open approach toward modernity that consists of an integration of new media into the everyday practices of believers and clergy. Mobile apps, websites and social networking (e.g., Twitter, Facebook) are all embraced as legitimate tools for advancing spiritual knowledge, performing religious activities (e.g., prayer, rituals) and congregating with their communities. The Reform public, which caters to a range of Jewish and Jewish-oriented audiences legitimizes its religious praxis through the net as it validates their sense of belonging to a Jewish community albeit a fluid, diverse and pluralistic variant. Moreover, this scheme conforms to contemporary practices and enables religious entrepreneurs (on Facebook, Second Life and the like) to propagate their belief system and promote Reform ideals of *Tikun Olam* (repairing the world) in today's most ubiquitous modes of communications.

## CONCLUSION

Past research on digital religion has offered a rich discussion of the introduction of new media into everyday lives of believers and clergy. However, less is known with regard to the sources and schemes of legitimation that socially facilitate the use of these technologies. This chapter investigated the forms of legitimation that were manifest amongst three Jewish denominations and uncovered three corresponding schemes: The *Dualist* scheme discusses monitored legitimacy by Haredim; *Purposeful* draws on charismatic and traditional legitimacy entails an outward effort to disseminate Chabad–Chassidic teachings; and *Inclusive Adoption* is validated through popular-modernistic legitimacy.

For Haredi authorities, new media is viewed as a necessary evil as the Haredi ideal of having a world that is obstructed from external and polluting elements (particularly toward the young) is obstructed by the sheer reality of economic and modern life. Under these circumstances the authorities have responded with a duality in their careful allowance of new media. Accordingly, Haredim have legitimized places the internet as a part of the profane world, which has been historically rejected in its pious and monastic "society of learners." However, legitimacy is dependent on filtered and monitored use. Under these circumstances, entrepreneurs function as power brokers as they expand the limited legitimacy provided by rabbinical authorities to cultivate communal websites and expand their influence. This development can be considered part of the new forms of secondary authority that currently emerge in Haredi society (see Caplan and Stadler, 2011, p. 19), which includes new forms of leadership in medicine, education, pedagogy and other fields that draw their legitimacy from non-Haredi institutions (such as professional knowledge that is acquired from academic establishments).

Unlike Haredi's limited legitimacy toward new media, this study uncovers how Chabad embraces these modes of communication as tools for dispensing their creed. Chabad utilizes traditional-theological justifications (such as drawing selective interpretation from the Gemara or drawing on the televised practices that were encouraged in the past by their revered rebbe) to facilitate the legitimacy. This approach has helped to facilitate the creation of an institutionalized new media operation (especially in chabad.org or the JEM—Jewish Educational Media—outlet) that is positioned and supported by the core of the Chabad establishment in Crown Heights, Brooklyn.

Although in both cases of the Haredim and Chabad, traditional rabbinical authorities play an important role, in the case of the Haredim, we find a (limited) legitimation of the internet as a part of their encounter and partial acceptance of modernity, whereas among Chabad new media are legitimized as a religious tool aimed at advancing their spiritual goals. In this sense, we can find a common concept between Chabad and the Reform movement that view new media as a means to achieve Jewish education and *Tikun Olam*. However, whereas in their everyday lives, Chabad members utilize the Haredi-dualistic scheme that is cautious to embrace the internet into their homes, Reform congregants view new media as an integral part to modern life and Jewish praxis. They continuously negotiate the boundaries of legitimacy, carefully choose their technologies of choice and embrace new media in order to perform certain traditional Jewish practices such as conducting *Minyan* prayers on Second Life or use apps that function as shofars and tablets in synagogues). Hence, Reform legitimation derives from the widespread popularity of new media by both congregants and rabbinic authorities. Under these circumstances, new forms of power brokers of religion emerge as mobile app developers and website managers that often define the boundaries of accepted religious practice through media usage.

Overall this study demonstrates that a range of schemes of legitimation have been developed within the religious Jewish world to justify and validate their use of new media. Each is influenced by various religious groups' outlook toward modernity and perception of the "other," whether rivaling Jewish groups or non-Jews. Their standing toward modernity and the "other" influences how they negotiate their approach and practice of new media. Accordingly, we see a corresponding expression of their Jewish primordial boundaries (Haredi, Reform, Chabad or otherwise), within the digital world. Just as the Haredi groups are concurrently bounded, yet restrainfully accommodate modern life, their legitimation processes reflect this moral and practical paradox and ultimately shapes their utilitarian approach toward new media. In the same vein, Chabad's outward openness toward the "other" can be compared to a membrane in that they act as a selective barrier, promoting religious information to pass through and inviting new believers but not allowing outside ideals to penetrate their world. Accordingly, they view modernity as an infrastructure that can foster their outreach and new media as an instrumental means to their ends. Finally, the Reform movement's inclusive approach toward other modern communities (Jewish and otherwise) is reflected in its pluralistic assimilation of new media culture, integrating its innovations into its members' daily lives.

In the age of new media, we find a renegotiation of the legitimation toward religious authorities. Rabbis, as other religious clergy, are in need of forming policies and strategies to address these modes of communication as new media is emerging as a vibrant player in the communal, political and religious world. Indeed, it can be said that schemes of legitimacy employed reflect the spirit of the community, but at the same time renegotiate its boundaries and identity.

## NOTES

1. I wish to thank Heidi Campbell for her profound encouragement throughout this study and illuminating comments in earlier drafts of the chapter. Also, thanks are due to Ori Eyal for his most helpful comments and suggestions as well as Batia Siebzehner for her valuable comments and observations. I wish to express further gratitude to Nakhi Mishol-Shauli for his help on an early draft and bestow special thanks to Avremel Kaminetzky for assisting me in the New York–area fieldwork and for sharing his knowledge and insights. Support from the I-CORE Program of the Planning and Budgeting Committee and the Israel Science Foundation (grant No. 1716/12) is also gratefully acknowledged.
2. English being the popular language of this American rally, Hebrew as a more closed linguistic choice, representing the Israeli rabbinical perspective, as well as the Hebrew languages prominence as a holy tongue, and Yiddish, which represents a communal Haredi-Ashkenazi dialect that is perceived as an exclusive dialect of the Haredi community (on the importance of linguistic choices among Haredim, see Baumel, 2006, and on the US distinction see Benor, 2009). The code switching between different languages and dialects serve as an informal function to foster a sense of familiarity, belonging to the community and a distinction between the sacred and the profane.
3. It should be noted that Haredi seminaries play an extremely central role in community life and bear critical effect on members' life chances, mate selection and more (see Lehmann and Siebzehner, 2009; Stadler, 2012) and expulsion sanctions are extremely consequential.

4. http://www.thejnet.com/ and https://guardyoureyes.com/, and for comparison in Israel (filtering ISP), see http://www.internet-rimon.com/.
5. The Reform movement is organized through central agencies. Most notable in the US is the Central Conference of American Rabbis (CCAR), while its main institution of ordination is the Hebrew Union College.
6. https://itunes.apple.com/us/app/ishofar/id332316203.
7. https://itunes.apple.com/us/app/imenorah/id298045800.

## REFERENCES


Asad, T. (1999). Religion, Nation State, Secularism. In: P. Van Der Veer and H. Lehmann (Eds.), *Nation and Religion: Perspectives on Europe and Asia* (pp. 178–196). Princeton: Princeton University Press.

Ashforth, B.E. and Gibbs, B.W. (1990). The Double-Edge of Organizational Legitimation. *Organization Science*, 1(2), 177–94.

Baumel, S. (2009). *Sacred Speakers: Language and Culture among the Haredim in Israel*. New York: Berghahn.

Benor, S.B. (2009). Do American Jews Speak a "Jewish Language"? A Model of Jewish Linguistic Distinctiveness. *The Jewish Quarterly Review*, 99(2), 230–269.

Bilu, Y. (2009). "With Us More Than Ever": Making the Late Lubavitcher Rabbi Present in Messianic Chabad. In: K. Caplan and N. Stadler (Eds.), *Leadership and Authority in Israeli Haredi Society* (pp. 186–224). Tel Aviv: Hakibutz Hameuchad (in Hebrew).

Bogdan, R.C. and Biklen, S.K. (1982). *Qualitative Research for Education*. 2nd ed. Boston: Allyn and Bacon.

Bunt, G.R. (2009). *iMuslims: Rewiring the House of Islam*. Chapel Hill: University of North Carolina Press.

Caplan K. and Stadler, N. (2011). *Leadership and Authority in Israeli Haredi Society*. Jerusalem: Hakibbutz Hameuchad (in Hebrew).

Campbell, H. (2010). *When Religion Meets New Media*. Oxon and New York: Routledge.

Campbell, H. and Golan, O. (2011). Creating Digital Enclaves: Negotiation of the Internet Amongst Bounded Religious Communities. *Media, Culture and Society*, 33(5), 709–724.

Casanova, J. (2008). Public Religions Revisited., In: H. Vries (Ed.), *Religion: Beyond a Concept* (pp. 101–119). New York: Fordham University Press.

Cohen, Y. (2011). Haredim and the Internet: A Hate-Love Affair. In: M. Bailey and G. Redden (Eds.), *Mediating Faiths: Religion and Socio-Cultural Change in the Twenty-First Century* (pp. 63–74). Surrey: Ashgate.

Cowan, D.E. (2005). *Cyberhenge: Modern Pagans on the Internet*. New York: Routledge.

Danet, B. (2001). *Cyberplay*. London: Berg.

Davidman, L. (1991). *Tradition in a Rootless World: Women Turn to Orthodox Judaism*. Berkeley: University of California Press.

De Lange, N. (2010). *An Introduction to Judaism*. 2nd ed. Cambridge: Cambridge University Press.

Ehrlich, A.M. (2004). *The Messiah of Brooklyn: Understanding Lubavitch Hasidism Past and Present*. Jersey City: KTAV.

Ferrero, G. (1942). *The Principles of Power*. New York: Arno Press.

Fishkoff, S. (2003). *The Rebbe's Army: Inside the World of Chabad-Lubavitch*. New York: Schocken Books.

Friedman, M. (1991). *The Haredi Society*. Jerusalem: Jerusalem Institute for Israel Studies (in Hebrew).
Glaser, B.G. and Strauss, A. (1967). *The Discovery of Grounded Theory: Strategies for Qualitative Research*. Chicago: Aldine.
Golan, O. (2013). Charting Frontiers of Online Religious Communities: The Case of Chabad Jews. In: H. Campbell (Ed.), *Digital Religion: Understanding religious practice in new media worlds* (pp. 155–163). London: Routledge.
Kahane, R. (1982). *Legitimation and Integration in Developing Societies: The Case of India*. Boulder: Westview.
Kaplan, D.E. (2003). *American Reform Judaism: An Introduction*. New Brunswick: Rutgers University Press.
Kravel-Tovi, M. (2009). To See the Invisible Messiah: Messianic Socialization in the Wake of a Failed Prophecy in Chabad. *Religion*, 39, 248–260.
Lehmann, D. and Siebzehner, B. (2009). Power, Boundaries and Institutions: Marriage in Ultra-Orthodox Judaism. *European Journal of Sociology*, 50, 273–308.
Livingston, S. (2009). *Children and the Internet*. Cambridge: Polity.
Markowitz, L., Cobb, D. and Hedley, M. (2012). Framing Ambiguity: Insider/Outsiders and the Successful Legitimation Project of the Socially Responsible Mutual Fund Industry. *Organization*, 19(1), 3–23
Marshall, C. and Rossman, G. (1995). *Designing Qualitative Research*. Thousand Oaks: Sage Publications.
Mathews, M.R. (1993). *Socially Responsible Accounting*. London: Chapman and Hall.
Rashi, T. (2011). Divergent Attitudes within Orthodox Jewry toward Mass Communication. *The Review of Communication*, 11(1), 20–38.
Ravitzky, A. (1994). The Contemporary Lubavitch Hasidic Movement: Between Conservatism and Messianism. In: M.E. Marty and R.S. Appleby (Eds.), *Accounting for Fundamentalisms: The Dynamic Character of Movements Vol. 4* (pp. 303–327). Chicago: University of Chicago.
Salmon, Y. (1998). Zionism and Anti-Zionism in Traditional Judaism in Eastern Europe. In: Almog, Shmuel, Reinharz, Jehuda and Shapira, Anita (Eds.), *Zionism and Religion* (pp. 67–89). Hanover and London: Brandeis University Press.
Shamah, D. (2012). Vital, Pointless, Sexist, Hilarious? New York's Ultra-Orthodox Battle-the-Internet Gathering Goes Viral. *The Times of Israel* [online]. Available at: http://www.timesofisrael.com/42000-jews-84000-opinions-internet-asifa-gets-backers-critics-and-wise-guys-talking/ [Accessed May 31, 2012].
Sheleg, Y. (2000). *The New Religious Jews*. Jerusalem: Keter (in Hebrew).
Stadler, N. (2009). *Yeshiva Fundamentalism: Piety, Gender and Resistance in the Ultra-Orthodox World*. New York: NYU Press.
Stadler, N. (2012). *A Well-Worn Tallis for a New Ceremony: Trends in Israeli Haredi Culture*. Academic Studies Press.
Strauss, A. L. and Corbin, J. (1998). *Basics of qualitative research: Techniques and procedures for developing grounded theory*.2nd ed. Thousand Oaks: Sage.
Suchman, M. C. (1995). Managing Legitimacy: Strategic and Institutional Approaches. *Academy of Management Journal*, 20(3), 571–610.
Tsarfaty, O. and Blais, D. (2002). Between "Cultural Enclave" and "Virtual Enclave": Ultra-Orthodox Society and the Digital Media. *Kesher*, 32, 47–55 (in Hebrew).
Weber, M. (1954). *Max Weber on Law in Economy and Society*. Cambridge: Harvard University Press.
Zaleski, J.P. (1997). *The Soul of Cyberspace*. New York: HarperCollins.

# 9 On Pomegranates and Etrogs

## Internet Filters as Practices of Media Ambivalence among National Religious Jews in Israel[1]

*Michele Rosenthal and Rivka Ribak*

In the contemporary environment of media saturation, users are continually making choices about the types and kinds of media technologies to employ or avoid at different moments and places in their everyday lives. Some of these choices are based on simple technical or practical criterion (i.e., my smartphone is easy to access during my daily commute), while others are informed by a sense of decorum (i.e., one should not text during a funeral) or the idea that self-imposed limits of media use will lead to a more balanced lifestyle (i.e., no e-mail after work hours). Among such abundance, it is nearly impossible to be an early adopter or enthusiastic user of all media—users are constantly making choices (i.e., to text rather than telephone, to invest in a laptop but not in a smartphone, etc.), and through these choices they express ambivalence about certain media and enthusiasm about others. Users' deliberations and discussions about these choices and practices are increasingly employed as identity markers (Hoover, Clark and Alters, 2004; Seiter, 2003). Media consumption and avoidance of specific contents or technologies are not only practical choices but also are expressions of identification with a specific class, ethnic, religious or spiritual community.

In this chapter, users' dilemmas and deliberations concerning media practice in everyday life are reflected on by focusing on a group whose negotiations with technology are both explicitly ambivalent and ideologically informed:[2] National Religious families in Israel and their negotiation with the internet in the home. For observant Jewish families, media choices fall within the broader context of negotiation with the secular, "modern" world: Where should one draw the line? For enclave communities, such as the Haredi communities in Israel today, who regard themselves as preservers of the one and only right course of action, any media use that could possibly disturb the cultural and religious status-quo should be strenuously avoided (Deutsch, 2009). Therefore, television is explicitly banned in Haredi households by the rabbinic authorities in addition to internet and the use of "smart" phones (Campbell, 2007, 2011; Deutsch, 2009; Rashi, 2012). While the proclamations of a "ban" of these technologies or others suggests that there are users "out there" in the Haredi community that need to be corralled and pulled back into the confines of a more clearly defined territory and set of practices, the views of the leadership sound loud and clear and community boundaries are repeatedly articulated (see Barzilai-Nahon and Barzilai, 2005; Campbell and Golan, 2011; Deutsch, 2009; Livio and Tennenboim-Weinblatt, 2007; Umble, 1992).

In contrast, for the National Religious communities in Israel, whose self-definition includes full participation in civil and secular society while maintaining full religious observance, communication technologies cannot be so easily banished from the household. Rather, families discuss and decide whether to have a television screen in the home and how to negotiate the computer within the home (with or without internet, through a religiously "approved" ISP or a "regular" supplier with a home-installed filter. etc.). These discussions and deliberations take place among families and communities—in the playground, the school, the synagogue and online forums (such as Kipa, n.d.). Thus, through dinner table conversations, school regulations, rabbinical pamphlets, commercial flyers and Q&A websites, National Religious communities negotiate the challenges posed by advanced communication technologies and at the same time use them as markers of their identity (neither Haredi nor Secular). Our research focuses on understanding how these choices are conceptualized, legitimized and practiced by individuals and families.

In the following, we explore the decision to surf the internet via Rimon, an internet service provider (ISP) that offers varying degrees of filtering (visual and verbal) for its religiously observant subscribers. *Rimon* is the Hebrew word for pomegranate, which symbolizes abundance and fruitfulness and is customarily eaten at Rosh Hashanah (the Jewish New Year). By choosing to name the company with this traditional fruit, the company countered the negative discourse of certain Haredi Rabbinical authorities regarding the internet (Campbell, 2011; Campbell and Golan, 2011; Deutsch, 2009) and branded its internet services as safely within the confines of religious tradition itself. Rimon internet is Jewish internet with abundant content that safely within the boundaries of what is permissible in the domestic sphere.

We regard the decision to "domesticate" the internet into the moral economy of the household (Silverstone, Hirsch, and Morley, 1992) as emblematic of this ambivalent position, as it allows National Religious families to both surf the World Wide Web and to remain within the confines of their community. By installing the filter, National Religious individuals and especially parents, share with Rimon the moral responsibility for maintaining an observant lifestyle while surfing. In his essay "Where Are the Missing Masses?" Bruno Latour (1992) highlights the role of nonhuman actors in social life. It is only by recognizing the ways in which humans delegate authority to nonhumans and vice versa—in other words, the ways in which technology shares the burden of moral responsibility—that we can gain insight into the ways networks operate: "Depending on where we stand along this chain of delegation, we get classic moral human beings endowed with self-respect and able to speak and obey laws, or we get stubborn and efficient machines and mechanisms; halfway through we get the usual power of signs and symbols. It is the complete chain that makes up the missing masses, not either of its extremities" (p. 166). This suggests that in order to interpret internet use in National Religious households, we need to take into account Rimon—the filter to which they assign the moral responsibility of preserving the purity and piety of their homes. To appreciate the role of Rimon, as Latour has proposed, "every time you want to know what a non-human does, simply imagine what other humans or nonhumans would have to do were this character not present. This imaginary substitution exactly sizes up the role, or function of this little character" (p. 155). We draw upon interviews with users of Rimon and related cultural materials to explore how National Religious individuals and families create an internet practice that mirrors their desire to be open to the secular world while remaining halachically observant.

By focusing on users rather than producers or religious authorities, we highlight in this chapter the importance of understanding Jewish responses to the internet within the context of daily praxis. As a lived religion, Judaism is expressed through adherence to *mitzvoth* (commandments) not just in the synagogue but in the domestic sphere and everyday life as well. In the case of the National Religious community in Israel the interface between the internet and Judaism is found at what Ruth Schwartz Cowan (1987) named "the consumption junction" or "the place and time the consumer makes choices between competing technologies" (p. 263). By choosing Rimon, a religiously branded filtering system rather than simply a secular internet service, our interviewees were able to integrate the internet into their religiously inflected domestic sphere and to express their Jewish lifestyle and identity through their internet use. To frame the discussion, we briefly sketch relevant research on internet filters as well as work on Haredi approaches to digital media (Campbell and Golan, 2011; Deutsch, 2009).

## INTERNET FILTER RESEARCH

Internet filters are a type of content-control software that allows users to monitor and block access to undesired images and messages on the web. Some filters are attached to the browser (such as Chrome's safe search preferences), others to the operating system (i.e., Windows 7 parental controls), and yet others are independent programs installed on a computer (i.e., Net Nanny). These kinds of filters are connected to specific programs or computers and can therefore be modified by the user at home. One can define whether one prefers to limit only hardcore pornography, or to censor all references to sex, or simply decide to turn off the filter at a particular moment or for a period. The individualized settings allow for users to precisely define the kinds of content and times they prefer *not* to have access to from a particular computer.

In contrast, Internet service provider (ISP) filters are installed by the provider. When the internet reaches the household, the content has already been filtered. Any device that connects to the internet in the household through that ISP receives the filtered contents. ISP filters can only be modified by the provider, although users can usually request a modification by calling customer service. In this sense, the ISP filters offer a different, more holistic type of technological solution to the problem of unwanted content in the domestic sphere.

ISP filters, like other filters, offer users the opportunity to delegate moral authority. By choosing to connect to the internet through an externally filtered source, users partially remove the burden of responsibility for providing morally wholesome internet for their children or themselves. Instead, the ISP and its technological protocol share the responsibility for maintaining an environment untainted by materials that the users perceive as offensive, and even damaging, to their children and themselves (Latour, 1992). An ISP may offer different tracks with varied levels of censorship, but all of the users enrolled in the track receive the same contents. This experience of creating community that shares a similar experience of the internet can be compared to creating an imagined community (Anderson, 2006) that express their shared values through their choice to surf via a filter (or a particular level of filtering), carving out a specific niche within the broader internet landscape.

More than a decade ago, Turow (2001) proposed a framework for researching the internet and the family. Writing when only 44% of American households were connected to the World Wide Web, he noted that very little research had been conducted about the use of internet filters or content-control software in the home more generally. Since then, scholars have discussed the ethical and legal implications of filters in public venues such as libraries or work places (Allbon and Williams, 2002).

A number of studies have approached the issue from the perspective of parental mediation (Eastin, Greenberg, and Hofschire, 2006; El Batrawy, 2012; Livingstone and Helsper, 2008). Livingston and Helsper (2008), for example, examined strategies of parental mediation on the internet, and their efficacy of reducing online risk. Other researchers have examined the ways parenting style and class background (Clark, 2012; Eastin, Greenberg, and Hofschire, 2006; Livingstone, 2007; Nelson, 2010) play a role in the decision regarding the type and kind of mediation strategies parents adopt to negotiate the internet with their children, particularly the choice of technological means such as filtering. Beyond the Anglo-American context, El-Batrawy's (2012) research suggests that cultural context plays a central role in shaping parents' concerns, practices and their children's use of the internet.

In this chapter, we return to Turow's framework to examine internet filters in the moral economy of National Religious households in Israel. We ask how the filter is introduced into the domestic sphere, which practices are involved in its use, and how its use acquires symbolic value (Silverstone et al.,

1992). While we are interested in parental choices and practices, Rimon is also employed by adults who wish to monitor and censor their own internet activity, at least in the domestic realm (see, e.g., Behadrey Haredim and Kipa). In Latour's (1992) terms we are interested in understanding how people choose to share moral authority with a nonhuman actant (the internet filter), the consequences of that decision and the material practices that develop in its wake.

## JEWISH COMMUNITIES IN ISRAEL AND THE INTERNET: PREVIOUS RESEARCH

Previous research on Jewish communities in Israel and the internet has largely focused on Haredim (Barzilai-Nahon and Barzilai, 2005; Campbell, 2011; Campbell and Golan, 2011; Livio and Tenenbaum Weinblatt, 2007). Self-defined as antimodernist, Haredi communities' negotiation of technological innovations is striking and well documented in the secular and religious press, in a series of wall posters (*pashkevilim*), and even well-orchestrated rallies against media (see Nathan-Kazis, 2012; Mendelbaum, 2011). Researchers have documented the tension between the need and the value of using the internet for particular purposes, and the perception of the threat it poses to traditional lifestyle and knowledge transmission. Barzilai-Nahon and Barzilai (2005) suggested that while rabbinical authorities were weary of the potential impact of the technology on the community, users were adapting the internet for their own purposes, reinforcing the sense of community rather than only challenging its boundaries. Livio and Tenenbaum Weinblatt (2007) focused on the discursive strategies employed by ultra-Orthodox women to rationalize and explain their computer use, despite its problematic perception amongst their family and peers. Likewise, Campbell and Golan's (2011) research on websites directed to ultra-Orthodox users, and their challenge to religious authority, detailed the process of web production and the delicate balancing act required by the relevant actors (webmasters, designers, rabbis) to innovate while preserving social and cultural boundaries.

These Haredi case studies suggest that while new technologies are not always embraced quickly or adopted without hesitation (see also Deutsch 2009; Hack, 2007; Shandler, 2009), the rhetoric of prohibition often suggests a longer period of negotiation and results in restrictive use rather than complete avoidance (see Ribak and Rosenthal, 2006; Umble, 1992).

Our research on Rimon widens the discussion to include National Religious families' dilemmas regarding the internet and focuses on users and their practices rather than on producers or religious authorities. In the contemporary Israeli context, National Religious communities are less isolationist than their Haredi counterparts regarding media practices. This means they might consume secular as well as National Religious media, such as Channel 7, and the newspaper *Makor Rishon*, although recent trends regarding the decline of news consumption in general (that is, of the mainstream Israeli TV channels, newspapers and radio) might suggest that they might be consuming more community-specific media than general media. Despite the heterogeneity of the community, they share a disdain for hegemonic media; while some refrain from exposure, others do consume it in order to know what "the others" think. However, Gabel (2006) interprets this as yet another indication of their alienation from what they perceive to be the hegemonic, Tel Aviv secular culture.

## A METHODOLOGICAL NOTE

We chose to use the term *National Religious* as the closest translation to the adjective employed by our interviewees to describe their own religious identity. It is important to note, however, that this is not a homogeneous community. In the latest census, from 2009 (Central Bureau of Statistics, 2013), National Religious Jews constituted 11.7% of the total Jewish population (in contrast to the Haredim that constituted 8%). Within this population, there are diverse religious and political perspectives: right and left; more "lax" and more "pious" (Dati "light" and Hardalnikim), but nonetheless, more than 80% define themselves as right wing and more religiously inclined. The National Religious community defines itself in contrast to both the Haredi and secular communities. The Haredi communities have often been defined sociologically as enclave or bounded communities, with very clear boundaries (Heilman and Friedman, 1991; Stadler, 2002). In contrast, the National Religious community viewed integration with secular Israeli society positively, as originally had the modern Orthodox movement in the 19th century and, as a consequence, is integrated in secular higher education and economic life (in sharp distinction to its Haredi counterparts). National Religious rabbis are less likely than their Haredi counterparts to issue public statements condemning one form of technology or another as potentially problematic. Science and religion are not viewed as inherently opposed to one another, but rather, science is viewed as a resource to be harnessed—historically one of the central slogans being *Torah u'madda* (translated as Torah and science). Technology is conceptualized as a neutral tool that can be helpfully harnessed in order to remain observant in the contemporary context.[3] Yet increasingly, as portions of the community become more strictly observant (or interpret aspects of practice in what is conceived by most to be a more stringent approach to observance), they too seem more likely to practice a kind of cultural separation either by desire or default of their geographical location (Gabel, 2006; Kleinberg, 2004).

Notably, our interviewees do *not* call themselves "modern" (unlike their modern orthodox Anglo brethren) and in recent years, commentators have observed a central fracture between "Hardal" (Haredi Dati Leumi) and what Sheleg (2000) calls the "new National Religious Jew." Members of the Hardal faction are characterized by their restrictive interpretations of religious observance that were once associated only with the Haredi community. For example, women in the Hardal faction observe stricter interpretations of modesty, especially regarding head covering after marriage and longer skirt and sleeve lengths. In addition, they send their children to sex-segregated education and youth groups from as early as elementary school rather than just in high school. Recent controversies within the Israeli Defense Forces regarding *Kashrut* (dietary practices) and the role of women in public contexts, whether singing or simply appearing on stage likewise suggests a shift in approach and practice to negotiating secular Israeli society (e.g., Kordova, 2012). The "new National Religious" Jew, in contrast, can be characterized as observing more liberal interpretations of modesty, with women wearing trousers and sometimes not covering their heads after marriage. Their children attend elementary schools that are not sex segregated, and they place a far higher priority on living in harmony within secular Israeli society, particularly as regards the adoption of leisure activities (Sheleg, 2000, pp. 56–58).

The analysis is based on qualitative interviews conducted in 2012–2013 by a research assistant who defines herself as belonging to the National Religious community (although at the time of the interviews she did not subscribe to Rimon). The names cited are pseudonyms, and all identifying details were changed in order to ensure the interviewees' anonymity. Originally, we had set out to interview couples who grew up with television but had decided not to own a television in their newly established married homes. In the interviews, we noticed that as part of their observant lifestyle, our interviewees mentioned that they subscribed to Rimon. We then decided to further explore their use of Rimon and pursued additional interviews with a snowball sample of 12 couples and families who use Rimon.[4] The interviews began with a question regarding religious self-definition, particularly how they view their religious practice in relationship to their family of origin, the schools they attended and to which they sent their children, and their occupations. In addition, we draw upon related cultural texts and artifacts, including Rimon's promotional materials and website, Orthodox question-and-answer websites and information gathered through Rimon's subscriber services.

## RIMON: NETWORKED COMMUNITY

Rimon is a commercial ISP company which brands itself as catering to religious needs and is reported to have anywhere between 20,000 and 50,000 household subscribers (Ziv, 2013). It offers complete internet service (including e-mail) to home subscribers and recently began a new service, Green

Track, for smartphones. Rimon is marketed in synagogues and National Religious communities, and in some neighborhoods where the interviews were conducted, it is the normative choice for internet access. Directed at Israeli households that view themselves as traditional or observant, Rimon offers five tiers of internet filters to accommodate a variety of religious perspectives and consumer practices: (a) Protected Track, (b) Protected Track Plus, (c) Protected Track Squared, (d) Preserved Track and (e) Hermetic Track. Each track provides consumers with a different conception of the internet, its potential use, and its potential dangers. Briefly, the Protected Track provides full access to the internet with the exception of websites that contain "pornography, nudity, drugs, gambling." The Protected Track Plus provides full access to the internet within the boundaries of modesty as reflected by the current situation in the Israeli streets—that is, no websites that deal with "night life, fashion shows, swim suits, underwear websites, and similar content." The Protected Track Squared blocks all websites that are considered to be news and entertainment while allowing access to financial and commercial websites. The Preserved Track blocks all websites with visual content that is not considered appropriate from a "religious perspective," "without touching [preventing access] verbal content." Finally, the Hermetic Track allows limited access to the internet for practical tasks (i.e., bus schedules, government offices) and Torah-related content. Both visual and verbal content are controlled in the Hermetic Track.

Notably, the tracks in Rimon begin with the most open and become increasingly censored. Etrog, the sister service of Rimon directed to Haredim, operates from the opposite assumption: The tracks are listed from most restricted to the least restricted, with the first track: e-mail and list, including only personally selected websites; the Practical Track includes only banks, governments institutions, weather, transportation, Torah websites, and some of the Haredi news sites. The Expanded Track allows for those sites on the practical track as well as "economic sites," municipal and regional governments, charities and other funds, "professional websites that the chance of them being problematic is close to zero" and other industrial services such as cleaning, exterminator services, weatherproofing and so on. Etrog is endorsed on the website by a list of rabbis and rabbinical courts. The difference between Rimon and Etrog mirrors the difference in their potential consumers: National Religious of varied levels of observance (from religiously light ["Dati-light"] to Hardalnikim and Haredim from varied communities with different levels of concern about internet access).

The adoption and use of Rimon to access the internet raises several interesting questions regarding the adoption and use of digital technologies in the household. First, Rimon is a nonhuman actor (Latour, 1992) acting as a moral agent to protect the impure "secular" domain from entering and tainting the domestic realm. As Latour noted,

> In spite of the constant weeping of moralists, no human is as relentlessly moral as a machine, especially if it is (she is, he is, they are) as "user

> friendly" as my Macintosh computer. We have been able to delegate to nonhumans not only force as we have known it for centuries but also values, duties, and ethics. It is because of this morality that we, humans, behave so ethically, no matter how weak and wicked we feel we are. The sum of morality does not only remain stable but increases enormously with the population of nonhumans. It is at this time, funnily enough, that moralists who focus on isolated socialized humans despair of us—us meaning of course humans and their retinue of nonhumans.
> (1992, p. 157)

Rimon acts as the moral conscience of the household by barring potentially problematic materials on the internet from the surfers in the subscriber's home. Released from the worry of inadvertently (or purposefully) encountering immodestly dressed women or advertisements for pornography, individuals can utilize the internet without fear of transgression. As one of our interviewees noted, "open internet [connection] is very scary, not only in the homes of religious people. There is a lot of violence, perversity and explicitly pornographic contents. I do not see how anyone can install open internet today in a religious home" (Yakir family interview, April 15, 2012).

With Rimon the subscriber theoretically does not have to exercise choice to make the correct moral decision, rather he or she is shielded from encountering situations that would require an act to avoid the problematic materials (i.e., closing the pop-up or website that has offensive materials). The user has ceded moral authority to the filter. As Moriel explained, "If I pass the responsibility to something external, let's say filtering software, so what? I'm at peace with that. Some things are out of our control" (Yakir family interview, April 15, 2012).

Behind Rimon's filter, however, there are human laborers choosing which sites to block and which to leave open, and designing and adopting algorithms based on the users' responses.[5] When a user tries to access a website that has been blocked, and he or she believes it to be "safe" and mistakenly labeled, he or she can call the company, using a password, in order to "release" the website for access. One of our interviewees described this as a frustrating process, which was usually not worth the effort. While the Rimon subscriber experiences the internet in an almost seamless fashion, the labor behind the filtering process is opaque to the user. The process is not described on the website, nor is it generally well known, although it was raised in a question and answer session to a rabbi on the National Religious website, Kipa.[6] The question writer describes how he met a young man "who still doesn't keep the commandments or observe the *Torah*," who had previously worked for Rimon in the filtering department, looking at immodest content and marking them so that surfers at home could browse the internet safely. The former employee reported to the question writer that the filtering work had caused him to feel horrible about himself (presumably because of his daily exposure to such immodest content). The question writer ends his question/comment by noting that he had been convinced that the "dirty work had been done by '*goyim*' [non-Jews]," and this latest revelation had made him question whether it was appropriate to continue using Rimon. The rabbi responded by calming the writer and noting that it is not a question that is specific to Rimon but a general question of exposure to immodest contents for a broader good: "In this case, there is no question that the "dirty work" of an individual is beneficial to a multitude, and one must (and it is possible) to be rehabilitated after performing such work" (Kipa, n.d.).[7]

For most Rimon users, the service offered is accepted at face value, as a naturalized part of everyday life. When the question writer met the young man who had worked in the filter department at Rimon that creates the morally appropriate internet experience for users, the network was suddenly exposed and the moral labor involved was placed on display for all to see (Latour, 2011). There is a human judging the materials in this censorship process, yet nowhere is there an explicit articulation of the criteria (beyond the brief descriptions of the tiers of filters) used by this network. Some of our interviewees complained that websites they used and knew were "innocent" were blocked. Perhaps, this is similar to the case of the program Net Nanny supported by Focus on the Family, Christian evangelist James Dobson's organization in the United States, which not only blocked pornography, but the National Organization of Women as well, an example offered by Langdon Winner (1997) in his critique on internet filtering as censorship. In other words, although the stated purpose of the filter was moral purity, there were implicit political and social targets as well.

Second, filters create and preserve the boundaries of imagined and real communities; they signify and symbolize belonging to a certain worldview about masculinity, modesty and parenthood. In many of our interviewees' responses, they refer to their immediate neighbors who also were subscribers: "There are 70 couples here who have *Rimon*. Everybody here is like that. It is obvious for everyone, and I think that *Rimon* also has *Halachic* approval. Rabbis do not allow the use of the internet without *Rimon*" (Carmel family interview, February 14, 2012). Users usually cited their children as the reason for their choice to install Rimon at home, but young men in the forums and also in the interviews referred to their need to remove the "temptation" to surf to prohibited sites and to engage in other prohibited acts as a result. Aviad described his decision in this vein:

> When I was in 11th grade I asked my parents to install *Rimon* on our home computer. In their house, the computer is in the living room and I said that otherwise I would not be able to use the internet and I installed *Rimon* myself, based on my own opinion. It is the same problem as with television. Why should I see everything that is immodest in my face? It is enough that it is imposed on us in the street. I think that a man should see his wife all the time, not any other woman.
>
> (Carmel family interview, February 14, 2012)

Women interviewees usually discussed Rimon as an act of parenting, a decision to be part of a community of parents and children that view the world in a similar fashion. As Rebecca noted,

> There is a lot of advertising about *Rimon* in Saturday pamphlets in the synagogue, and it's pretty well known and it came up when I stopped mediating the computer for them. In the past I downloaded movies for them but once Roni has projects in school for which she needs the computer . . . then there is the concern that what they are prevented from at home they will see on the computer.
>
> (Danino family interview, October 21, 2011)

To *not* adopt Rimon for our interviewees would be a decision to remove oneself from the mainstream of the contemporary young National Religious families. Interestingly, it appears that the particular track or level of filtering is less important than simply belonging to the community of Rimon users. Interviewees occasionally did not know to which level they subscribed, and they did not usually change the track once they began. Our interviewees tended to opt for the track with the least amount of filtering. And, when one of the couples considered disconnecting, they were offered an unadvertised track that was even less restrictive:

> *R*: "We chose the lowest level of filtering, the most minimal, which is what they promised us."
>
> *Y*: "What we asked and what they promised us is that they filter only pornographic websites, and all the rest we can see like everyone else."
>
> *R*: "Which is the lowest level of filtering. And in fact what happened is that . . . for example I, because of my profession [teacher] I need a lot of colored pictures of all sorts of things, so on Google for instance they can bring me only say five results, so in effect the filtering is much more serious, a lot more massive than we imagined it would be, especially since they promised it would be the lowest and most minimal level."
>
> *Y*: "What we mean is that they filter perfectly innocent things."
>
> *R*: "Yes, really basic, so we said that we want to unplug and they said, wait wait wait, we have a filter that is more, eh, more open . . ."
>
> *R*: "That they simply don't offer it to anyone . . ."
>
> *Y*: "That we didn't tell you about, maybe you want to try it."
>
> *R*: "Now the main problem is that the internet works very slow, with *Rimon*."
>
> *Y*: "The new filter is fine, it is ok."
>
> *R*: "The new filter is reasonable, it is, I don't know, a kind of level they probably offer to people who want to unplug."

> *Y*: "Yes, it is hidden, it is not. you can't access it." (Danino family interview, October 21, 2011)

In this context, we might ask who does not install *Rimon* but is still part of the National Religious community. Among our interviewees, several referred to more liberal parents who by principal refused to use filters, or to their younger selves before they had children. One of the interviewees notably cited her liberally religious father as purposely deciding not to install Rimon, as a way of situating himself outside of the new morality of the Hardal faction. By adopting Latour's framework, it is as if he were saying that he does not need an external mode for moral accounting.

Third, Rimon can be understood as an expression of media ambivalence. National Religious Jews who are constantly trying to negotiate between the enclave nature of the Haredi community and the pluralistic, "immoral," boundaryless world of the Israeli secular community, view filtered internet as a compromise between these two extremes. Veering away from the rhetoric of prohibition and avoidance that characterizes the Haredi leadership's approach to new technologies, and the media-saturated lifestyle of the average secular Israeli consumer, National Religious Jews try to operate within the world while remaining observant. So, our interviewees adopt Rimon as a symbol of that betwixt and between status of the National Religious community, but in practice they find it frustrating that the internet is so slow and that sites that they know to be "innocent" (such as parent/child forums) are inaccessible. In forum discussion and interviews, users discuss how they "tinker" or "hack" the filter when they find it necessary, illustrating yet another insight by Latour (1992), that one technology (the filter) often breeds a problem and yet another technological solution (hacking). For example,

> *INT*: "Did you ever try to hack into a website you couldn't access?
>
> *R*: "Come on, I really have no knowledge about these things and the kids also have no knowledge yet, so the answer is no. But also, I didn't install it in order to then hack it.
>
> *Y*: "You'd be surprised that I heard colleagues at work saying they did hack websites on occasion because filtering was not justified and irrelevant. I never tried it but you know what, that's an idea."
>
> *R*: "At the bottom line, you have two options, either you call customer service or you give up. I give up." (Danino family interview, October 21, 2011)[8]

The internet is embraced, but not as the free marketplace of ideas that early entrepreneurs of the web envisioned, but rather a restrained and domesticated version that does not transverse the invisible yet clearly articulated cultural boundaries of what our interviewees believe to be appropriate media. Our interviewees express ambivalence about the media, and installing the filter is a practice that embodies this ambivalence and allows them to continue living in both worlds.

For National Religious families who choose to use Rimon (and, notably, not all do, as was hinted in several of our interviews), the internet is recognized as a part and parcel of everyday life, and Rimon is the means by which they domesticate the technology in order to signify and preserve their religious lifestyle. While self-identified secular Jewish Israelis might employ filters in order to shelter their children from unwanted contents, their motivation for such an act is not articulated in terms of their desire to be part of a specific faith community, or to keep their home "Jewish," but rather in terms of parenting style. In contrast, Haredi use of the internet is far more circumspect, reflecting a parallel approach to daily life that is more separatist in tone and practice than their National Religious counterparts. Etrog or other similar services for Haredim work differently than does Rimon because they offer a limited approved list of websites that can be accessed rather than filtering the internet for problematic materials. Rimon provides a technical solution for a community that views technology as an ally in its effort to remain in the world while being halachically observant. In that sense, Rimon is perhaps not so different than other technological "solutions" for keeping Shabbat (Sabbath), like the electric timer, the Sabbath elevator, or the Sabbath kettle (Zomet, n.d.).

In her original analysis of productivity tools, such as *Self-Control, Rescue Time* and *Freedom*, Melissa Gregg (forthcoming) highlights the religious (Protestant) ethos behind their development and use. She notes that the getting-things-done applications are based on constructions of self-discipline, self-control and productivity. The case of Rimon presents a complementary example of a technology that offers the possibility of disciplined use, but not in order to be more productive but as a marker of piety that identifies the users as observant members of the community. Adopting and using digital media in this context becomes a symbolic act of identity, a means of being and remaining a Nationally Religious Jew in contemporary Israel.

## NOTES

1. In Jewish tradition, the pomegranate is one of the seven species mentioned in the Bible and is often consumed on Rosh Hashanah as it symbolizes fruitfulness. *Etrog* is a ceremonial fruit, one of the four species that is part of the *Sukkot* festival. Notably, the internet service provider company decided to name its services using these fruit that evoke Jewish traditions practiced in the home. *Rimon* (pomegranate) and *Etrog* (yellow citrus fruit) are the names of the two different tracks offered by Rimon for National Religious Jews and Haredim, respectively.

This research was funded by the Israel Science Foundation (grant no. 536/08) and the Bi-National Science Foundation (grant no. 2010180). An earlier version of this paper was presented at the Digital Religion conference at the Center for Media, Religion, and Culture, Boulder, Colorado. We would like to also thank our research assistants, especially our interviewer and Nathan Walter for all their hard work.

2. For interesting parallels, see Ribak and Rosenthal (2006), Hijazi Omari and Ribak (2008) and Umble (1992).
3. See, for example, the Zomet Institute (n.d.), which is devoted to "integrating Torah life with the modern world," including the creation and production of new technologies that can be used on Shabbat.
4. The name of the interviewer and interviewees has been changed to aliases to protect the participants' privacy.
5. The hidden human labor behind the filter is similar to the hidden human labor in much of the web.
6. See the Kipa (2013).
7. Rimon Internet: Enjoying Something Wrong (2009). Message posted to http://www.kipa.co.il/ask/show/193663.
8. The current Rimon website (as of September 2014) now provides another technological solution to the problem encountered by the Danino family. One can log into the website and temporarily change the level of filtering for several hours or less. Thus, the user no longer needs to hack or call the provider; he or she just logs in and changes the level of filtering as needed. In addition, Rimon provides other technological solutions for surfing outside of the home, either on a smartphone or by downloading a program to your laptop, so that when a subscriber surfs on Wi-Fi in public the user can replicate his or her domestic internet environment.

## REFERENCES


Allbon, E. and Williams, P. (2002). Nasties in the Net: Children and Censorship on the Web. *New Library World*, 103(1/2), 30–38.

Anderson, B. (2006). *Imagined Communities: Reflections on the origin and spread of nationalism*. New ed. London: Verso.

Arutz Sheva (2013). *Israel News | Israel's #1 News Site* [online]. Available at: http://www.israelnationalnews.com/ [Accessed September 2013].

Barzilai-Nahon, K. and Barzilai, G. (2005). Cultured Technology: Internet and Religious Fundamentalism. *The Information Society*, 21(1), 25–40.

Behadrey Haredim (2013). The Biggest Ultra-Orthodox Portal in Israel [online]. Available at: http://www.bhol.co.il [Accessed September 2013].

Campbell, H. (2007). "What Hath God Wrought?" Considering How Religious Communities Culture (or Kosher) the Cell Phone. *Continuum: Journal of Media & Cultural Studies*, 21(2), 191–203.

Campbell, H. (2011). Religion and the Internet in the Israeli Orthodox Context. *Israel Affairs*, 17(3), 364–383.

Campbell, H.A. and Golan, O. (2011). Creating Digital Enclaves: Negotiation of the Internet among Bounded Religious Communities. *Media, Culture & Society*, 33(5), 709–724.

Central Bureau of Statistics (2013). *Israeli Population by Religion and Level of Religiosity* [online]. Available at: http://www.cbs.gov.il/reader/cw_usr_view_SHTML?ID=802 [Accessed September 2013].

Clark, L.S. (2012). *The Parent App: Understanding Families in the Digital Age*. Oxford: Oxford University Press.

Cowan, R.S. (1987). The Consumption Junction: A Proposal for Research Strategies in the Sociology of Technology. In: W, Bijker, T. Hughes and T. Pinch (Eds.), *The*

*Social Construction of Technological Systems* (pp. 253–272). Cambridge, MA: MIT Press.

Deutsch, N. (2009). The Forbidden Fork, the Cell Phone Holocaust, and Other Haredi Encounters with Technology. *Contemporary Jewry*, 29(1), 3–19.

Eastin, M. S., Greenberg, B. S. and Hofschire, L. (2006). Parenting the Internet. *Journal of Communication*, 56(3), 486–504.

El-Batrawy, S. (2012). Children and the Internet: Between Freedom and Protection. *Stirling International Journal of Postgraduate Research*, 1(1), 1–37.

Gabel, I. (2006). *The National-Religious Public and the Media: Love and Hate Relations*. Tel Aviv: Tel Aviv University (in Hebrew).

Gregg, M. (Forthcoming). "Getting Things Done"®: Productivity, Self-Management and the Order of Things." In: K. Hillis, S. Paasonen and M. Petit (Eds.), *Networked Affect*. Cambridge: MIT Press [online]. Available at: https://www.academia.edu/2403641/_Getting_Things_Done_Productivity_self-management_and_the_order_of_things [Accessed September 2013].

Hack, J. (2007). *Taming Technology: Ultra-Orthodox Jewish Families and Their Domestication of the Internet*. Masters dissertation, London School of Economics. Available at: http://www.lse.ac.uk/media@lse/research/mediaWorkingPapers/MScDissertationSeries/Past/Hack_final.pdf [Accessed September 2013].

Heilman, S. C. and Friedman, M. (1991). *The Haredim in Israel: Who Are They and What Do They Want?* [online]. Institute of American Jewish-Israeli Relations, the American Jewish Committee. Available at: http://www.bjpa.org/Publications/details.cfm?PublicationID=2577 [Accessed September 2013].

Hijazi-Omari, H. and Ribak, R. (2008) Playing With Fire: On the Domestication of the Mobile Phone among Palestinian Teenage Girls in Israel. *Information, Communication & Society*, 11(2), 149–166

Hoover, S., Clark, L. S. and Alters, F. A. (2004). *Media, Home and Family*. New York: Routledge.

Kipa. (n.d.) Believers on the Internet-Kipa [online]. Available at: http://www.kipa.co.il [Accessed September 2013].

Kleinberg, A. (2004). *Hard to Believe: Rethinking Religion and Secularism in Israel Jerusalem*. Tel Aviv: Keter and Tel Aviv University (in Hebrew).

Kordova. (2012). *Word of the Day / Hadarat Nashim—Word of the Day* [Online]. Available at: http://www.haaretz.com/news/features/word-of-the-day/word-of-the-day-hadarat-nashim-1.460930 [Accessed September 2013].

Latour, B. (1992). Where Are the Missing Masses? The Sociology of a Few Mundane Artifacts. In: W. E. Bijker and J. Law (Eds.), *Shaping Technology/Building Society: Studies in Sociotechnical Change* (pp. 225–258). Cambridge: MIT Press.

Latour, B. (2011). Networks, Societies, Spheres: Reflections of an Actor-Network Theorist. *International Journal of Communication*, 5, 796–810.

Livingstone, S. (2007). Strategies of Parental Regulation in the Media-Rich Home. *Computers in Human Behavior*, 23(2), 920–941.

Livingstone, S. and Helsper, E. J. (2008). Parental Mediation of Children's Internet Use. *Journal of Broadcasting & Electronic Media*, 52(4), 581–599.

Livio, O. and Tennenboim Weinblatt, K. (2007). Discursive Legitimation of a Controversial Technology: Ultra-Orthodox Jewish Women in Israel and the Internet. *The Communication Review*, 10(1), 29–56.

Makor Rishon. (2013). *Makor Rishon-Israeli Jewish Newspaper* [online]. Available at: http://www.makor1.co.il/ [Accessed September 2013].

Mendelbaum. (2011). *Without Plasmas-Rabbi Amnon Yitzhak Broke a Thousand Television Sets* [online]. Available at: http://www.ynet.co.il/articles/0,7340,L-4158093,00.html [Accessed September 2013].

Nathan-Kazis, J. (2012). Ultra-Orthodox Host Mega-Rally in U.S. for a More Kosher Internet. *Israel News | Haaretz Daily Newspaper* [online]. Available at: http://

www.haaretz.com/jewish-world/jewish-world-news/ultra-orthodox-host-mega-rally-in-u-s-for-a-more-kosher-internet-1.431644 [Accessed September 2013].

Nelson, M. (2010). *Parenting Out of Control: Anxious Parents in Uncertain Times.* New York: NYU Press.

Rashi, T. (2012). The Kosher Cell Phone in Ultra-Orthodox Society. In: H. A. Campbell, (Ed.) *Digital Religion: Understanding Religious Practice in New Media Worlds* (pp. 173–181). New York: Routledge.

Ribak, R. and Rosenthal, M. (2006). From the Field Phone to the Mobile Phone: A Cultural Biography of the Telephone in Kibbutz Y. *New Media and Society*, 8, 551–572.

Rimon Internet. (2013). *About Rimon* [online]. Available at: http://www.neto.net.il/ [Accessed September 2013].

Rimon Internet: Enjoying Something Wrong (2009) [online]. Available at: http://www.kipa.co.il/ask/show/193663 [Accessed September 2013].

Seiter, E. (2003). Television and the Internet. In: J. Turow and A. L. Kavanaugh (Eds.), *The Wired Homestead: An MIT Press Sourcebook on the Internet and the Family* (pp. 93–116). Cambridge: MIT Press.

Shandler, J. (2009). *Jews, God, and Videotape: Religion and Media in America.* New York: NYU Press.

Sheleg, Y. (2000). *The New Religious Jews: Recent Developments among Observant Jews in Israel.* Jerusalem: Keter (in Hebrew).

Silverstone, R., Hirsch, E. and Morley, D. (1992). Information and Communication Technologies and the Moral Economy of the Household. In: E. Hirsch and R. Silverstone (Eds.), *Consuming Technologies: Media and Information in Domestic Spaces* (pp. 15–31). London: Routledge.

Stadler, N. (2002). Is Profane Work an Obstacle to Salvation? The Case of Ultra Orthodox (Haredi) Jews in Contemporary Israel. *Sociology of Religion*, 63(4), 455–474.

Turow, J. (2001). Family Boundaries, Commercialism, and the Internet: A Framework for Research. *Applied Development Psychology*, 22(1), 73–86.

Umble, D.Z. (1992). The Amish and the Telephone: Resistance and Reconstruction. In: E. Hirsch and R. Silverstone (Eds.) *Consuming Technologies: Media and Information in Domestic Spaces* (pp.183–194). London: Routledge.

Winner, L. (1997). Electronically Implanted "Values." *Technology Review*, 100(2), 69.

Ziv. (2013). Cellcom Tries to Sell Rimon Internet for 36 Millions-TechNation [online]. *TheMarker*. Available at: http://www.themarker.com/technation/1.2106421 [Accessed September 2013].

Zomet Institute. (n.d.). *The Zomet Institute* [online]. Available at: http://www.zomet.org.il/eng/ [Accessed September 2013].

## Interviews cited

Carmel, H. and Carmel, A. (14 Feb 2012). Interviewed by M. Segal.

Danino, R. and Danino, Y. (21 Oct 2011).Interviewed by M. Segal.

Yakir, M. and Yakir T. (15 April 2012). Interviewed by M. Segal.

# 10 *Pashkevilim* in Campaigns against New Media

## What Can *Pashkevilim* Accomplish That Newspapers Cannot?

*Hananel Rosenberg and Tsuriel Rashi*

At the beginning of 2005 the leaders of Israel's ultra-Orthodox ("Haredim") community launched a massive campaign to force the replacement of commercial mobile phones with "kosher cell phones," which can be used to make and receive calls, but have no other capabilities. Much of the campaign was conducted in intra-sectoral newspapers, but the press was not the only medium exploited to wage the battle. The "war" was fought "in the streets"—on walls and notice boards—through the medium of *Pashkevilim* (wall posters), an unofficial channel of communication unique to the ultra-Orthodox community.

The kosher cell phone campaign brought two dominant media that have become integral to ultra-Orthodox daily life into opposition. The *Pashkevil* as a means of public communication dates back to the invention of the printing press; it is static and generally anonymous, and anyone can use it to send a message to a large target audience. The cellular phone, on the other hand, is a personal mobile medium that allows for readily available communication between individuals, a convenient tool for maintaining interpersonal relationships.

In the present chapter we discuss the role *Pashkevilim* played in the ultra-Orthodox community leaders' campaign against mobile phones, how their uniqueness in comparison with other means of public communication served the community's special needs and the significance of the contact point between the old medium as it was used in the struggle against the new one. This chapter contributes to our understanding of Jewish responses to digital technology in general and gives us a better understanding about religious communities' engagement with new technologies. From this campaign we can learn that extreme religious streams may engage a negative campaign to take part in the public discourse in their own religion and to fight new technologies with "primitive" media.

## THE KOSHER CELLULAR PHONE

The appearance of the cellular phone, similarly to the internet, brought an ambivalent attitude in traditional communities in its wake (Campbell,

2006a, 2007; Livio and Tenenboim-Weinblatt, 2007). On one hand, religious groups began to use the new applications for a range of religious practices, such as the use of text messages to disseminate prayers (Hindus), ideas (Christians), and verses from the holy books (Moslems). In this respect, a "redesigning" of the medium enabled expansion of religious life and the relationships between the clerics of the various communities and their followers and among the community members themselves (Campbell, 2006b; Ho, Lee and Hameed, 2008). As early as 2000, it was possible to find cellular phone companies that were providing religious content services such as *613 (the number of commandments according to Jewish tradition), which give the user access to information on religious matters, such as the times of prayer and when the Sabbath and festivals begin and end (Cohen, Lemish and Schechter, 2008). On the other hand, the cellular phone was often perceived as threatening the internal structure of groups—as in the example of the Amish community (Rheingold, 1999), or may impair the boundaries of the religious community, something that was likely to expose its members to undesirable content and to values of competing cultures.

This claim was also the basis for the opposition of ultra-Orthodox leaders to the mobile phone, opposition that developed into an aggressive public campaign the likes of which had never before been seen in that community.

At the outset, the central claims that were emphasized in the ultra-Orthodox newspapers were "time and money," in other words, "*Bitul torah*" (time spent—wasted—on anything other than Torah learning) on the part of the users and a waste of money, which most of the community could ill afford. However with the development of the commercial content services and the cellular internet, the focus of the discussion shifted to the threat imposed by the content: the cellular phone provides access to soul-destroying secular entertainment and culture and blurs and endangers the boundaries that the ultra-Orthodox community built for itself (Campbell, 2007). During the discussion of the rabbinical committee that convened to assess the threat of the cellular phone, the rabbis stressed that the struggle was not against the technology per se, but rather against the problematic content: "We are not against technology as a matter . . . but the fear that the latest feature-packed telephones would provide the opportunity to access corrupting influences" (MacKinnon, 2005).

However, unlike some critiques of television (Cromer, 1987) and the internet (Rashi, 2011) as being wholly unacceptable, the cellular phone challenged the religious leadership in a new way, as its basic function—a spoken conversation—is not categorized as a threat. A few years after the cellular phone had been introduced into the community and had become a common and necessary medium, the attempt to prohibit its use altogether was perceived as an edict that the public would not accept. This situation forced the leaders of the community to begin a complex negotiation process to adapt the new medium to the communal ideology so that it would be possible to continue to make use of its benign functions but to neutralize the perceived threats to the views and values of the users.

The process of adapting the mobile phone began in 2005, when the Committee of Rabbis for Media Matters convened in an attempt to propose a solution that would allow the ultra-Orthodox community to continue to use the medium (Rashi, 2012). The Committee of Rabbis for Media Matters was set up initially as a group to negotiate the establishment of a cell phone device fitting the requirements of the ultra-Orthodox community but later went on to become an important vetting and oversight structure of a wide range of technologies used and allowed within these groups. The committee's recommendations concluded with a demand that the mobile phone companies produce a "kosher phone" adapted to the needs of the ultra-Orthodox community. The first company to respond that same year was Mirs, which produced a "sterile" phone that did not allow internet surfing, texting, the taking of pictures or the viewing videos and was devoid of content. All the other companies, understanding the market potential of this modified instrument, eventually followed suit. Cohen, Lemish and Schechter (2008) defined the kosher telephone as "a slim phone" that had been divested of all the content services and was designed as a partial communication channel intended solely for vocal interpersonal contact. This description was emphasized in the ultra-Orthodox daily *Yated Ne'eman*, one of the leading newspapers in the campaign for kosher cell phones, in an article from March 15, 2005: "Our demand was a simple request from the client: we want vocal communication, and nothing else" (p. 1). The acceptable instrument bears an external kosher seal from the committee, as well as a prefix of three numbers, identifying it as a kosher telephone, so that the respondent can tell whether the incoming call is from an ultra-Orthodox phone or not.

At first it seemed as though the struggle for the acceptance of kosher telephones was a great success. The acquiescence of the ultra-Orthodox community was touted as a great victory and as proof of the adherence of the members of the community to its conservative values and their obedience to the dictates of "the great rabbis of the generation." Those who refused to go along were portrayed as "the stragglers who had not switched to kosher cellular phones, the fringe elements of the camp" (Bar-Yosef, 2006, p. 11) or "marginal rebel elements" in contrast to the rest of the community who had happily exchanged their phones (Levor, 2005). However, it would seem that the reality was more complex, and many members of the ultra-Orthodox public owned—and still have—a nonkosher cellular phone, often in addition to the kosher phone. The cell phone companies refused to provide any information about the number of ultra-Orthodox subscribers on their books and the types of phones they own, but the estimate is that in 2007, immediately after the public campaign on the issue and some two years after the launching of the kosher cell phone, a high percentage of the community still owned a non-kosher instrument (Ettinger, 2007).

## ULTRA-ORTHODOX RHETORIC IN THE STRUGGLE AGAINST CELLULAR PHONES

According to Campbell (2006b), initial opposition to a new medium and subsequent technological adaptation are the two of three stages that are necessary for the acculturation of a new technology. The process of localization and the adaptation of the instrument to the needs of the community are accompanied by cultural modification and rhetorical justification of the acceptance of the medium. In fact, the innovations that the committee instituted involved not only practical negotiation with the cellular phone companies, but also a change in the community leaders' rhetoric regarding this medium. When the mobile phones first appeared, the intra communal rhetoric included rules and instructions regarding the way the phone was to be used and the permitted frequency of usage. After the problematic functions for the phone were developed, the rhetoric changed and totally rejected the use of cell phones, stressing the dangers of the medium. As part of the discussion around the rejection, the committee was portrayed as being at the forefront of a life and death battle: "a battle for our very existence, a battle for the soul which we must make every effort to win" (Kahn, 2005).

After the work of the committee and along with the launching of the kosher cell phone, the rhetoric of the community's representatives focused on the features of the acceptable instrument, justifying certain applications that the phone made possible while rejecting others, together with a demand for a commitment from the members of the community to adopt the modified instrument. The intra-communal rhetoric that accompanied the technological acculturation reveals the value system as it interfaces with the new medium, as Silverstone, Hirsch and Morley (1992) define it: "the moral economy" from which the attitudinal patterns and possibilities of inclusion of technology are derived. Campbell's (2006b) and Rashi's (2012) studies on cellular phones followed the work of the Committee of Rabbis on Media Matters, the way it was presented to the public, and the public struggle that accompanied the efforts to force acceptance of the kosher phone among the entire ultra-Orthodox community. Both researchers focused on the media campaign as it appeared in the ultra-Orthodox establishment newspapers and in official publications of the committee.

Rashi (2012), who surveyed the ultra-Orthodox daily newspapers throughout the whole campaign (from the end of 2004 to the beginning of 2007), contends that the newspaper campaign not only accompanied the public struggle from its inception but also advanced it, defined its aims and helped accomplish them. He noted that the main strategy was a consistent attempt to keep the cellular phone issue at the top of the media agenda by inserting regular news items about what was happening at the meetings of the committee, by frequent newspaper reports about public incidents dealing with the subject (including front-page pictures) and by publishing readers' letters and *Halachic* (Jewish Law) rulings from rabbis representing different groups in the ultra-Orthodox world rejecting the use of nonkosher cell phones. The subject was kept in the public eye even when there were stormy events on the local or international scene.

## THE *PASHKEVIL*

The newspapers that were published by the Haredi political parties were not the only platform—and perhaps not even the primary one—through which the ultra-Orthodox waged the battle to get rid of the mobile phone. In tandem with the editors, commentators and reporters who acted as their spokesmen through the official newspaper channels, community leaders made extensive use of *Pashkevilim* .

*Pashkevilim*, which are usually written in mocking language, are an inseparable part of the urban scenery in ultra-Orthodox neighborhoods: "*Pashkevilim* are not only stuck on the walls of the neighborhood, but they hold the walls up so that they will not fall" (Friedman, 2005, p. 15). The Yiddish word *Pashkevil* derives from the name of a citizen of Rome by the name of Pasquino, who used to hang satires and critical comments about the pope on the pedestal of a headless Roman statue. His name was eventually given to the statue and then to the square where the statue stood (Piazza Pasquinate); the initiative taken by one individual became a phenomenon whereby citizens used to hang anonymous vilifying signs around the city. The phenomenon was very common all over Western Europe throughout the 16th century when this channel accompanied religious and social struggles; the original name was adopted into the various languages with slight changes. The German term *Pasquill* entered the Yiddish language, and from there, the word and the phenomenon came to the old Ashkenazi settlement in Jerusalem.

Over the centuries, *Pashkevil* literature, which avails itself of the cheap and accessible method of dissemination through the printing press, became important socioreligiously and politically. This was and is especially true in societies or subgroups that are beholden to a central authority, which precludes criticism for nationalistic or religious reasons. One of the most important features of the *Pashkevil* is its anonymity, which allows the authors to challenge the controlling leadership or the religious establishment (especially in Europe) without fear of condemnation, ostracism, or punishment.

Similarly to the European context, today *Pashkevilim* function as an unofficial channel for ideological stands, for the expression of intra-sectorial criticism and slander, comments on social phenomena and competing worldviews. Parallel to this—but to a lesser extent—the *Pashkevil* is a means of passing on information vital to the ultra-Orthodox community as well as a source of tidings about deaths, conferences and demonstrations and is a venue for the publication of rabbinic opinions on a range of current affairs (*Da'at Torah*; Friedman, 2005). Most of the research that deals with the *Pashkevil* culture focuses on a survey of the sociological aspect of the phenomenon (Friedman, 2005; Kaplan, 2007). A few studies concentrate on the sociolinguistic aspects: gender (Mutchnik and Kantor, 2000), linguistics (Schlezinger, 1992) and syntax (Kantor and Mutchnik, 2004; Shapira, 2005). Harlap (2010) is concerned with the syntactical aspect as well as the genre of the discourse. He delineates the various kinds of rhetoric writers of *Pashkevilim* use to achieve their aims, such as contradiction patterns, rhetorical questions, repetition of expressions and many punctuation marks and emphases. Harlap contends that extensive use of these features is a sign of rhetorical sophistication, and although it is characteristic of *Pashkevilim*, it is not unique to that culture and can be found in other persuasive genres. On the other hand, elements such as an extensive use of initials and imitation of accepted literary patterns of the ultra-Orthodox culture are unique to this specific genre and reflect an attempt to create an exclusive discourse space, shutting out those who are not familiar with the lingual culture.

## The Role of *Pashkevilim* in the Campaign against Cellular Phones

The current study deals with the role of *Pashkevilim* in the intra-ultra-Orthodox struggle against the use of mobile led by the Committee of Rabbis on Media Matters and the way the struggle was presented to the public, ending with the campaign for the adoption of the kosher cell phone in the community. Anyone going through Israel's ultra-Orthodox neighborhoods between 2005 and 2007 could not help but be impressed by the sheer number of *Pashkevilim* on the subject. In light of this, the questions that we examine are: What did the use of *Pashkevilim* contribute to the battle as compared the widespread exploitation of the official newspapers? How did the unique character of this medium express itself in the battle? Did the features of the *Pashkevilim* shape the nature of the negotiation during the cultural modification process?

We surveyed some 100 *Pashkevilim* from two main sources. First, we studied *Pashkevilim* found in the database of the National Library. In September 2011, the National Library of Israel finished scanning approximately 15,000 *Pashkevilim* that had been donated by Yoel Kraus, a private collector, who belongs to the Toldot Aharon sect—a splinter group that is perceived as extreme, even within the secluded ultra-Orthodox community. The public can access the site through the virtual database of the National Library (http://dlib.nli.org.il/new-site/collection_pashkevils_heb.html). Some 248 of the *Pashkevilim* from the last decade on the site were identified as dealing with a range of media issues (television, computer games, printed magazines, and surfing the internet); of those, 70 dealt with cellular phones.

Second, we looked at *Pashkevilim* that had been photographed and downloaded onto the news portals and ultra-Orthodox forums such as Bhadrei Haredim (http://www.bhol.co.il/) by internet surfers. This site, set up in 2002, was the first ultra-Orthodox forum on the internet and was considered groundbreaking because, for the first time, it enabled critical intra–ultra-Orthodox discourse that was not supervised by the rabbinical hierarchy (Rose, 2007). Many intra-communal matters were discussed: clarification of painful historical events, inter-party conflicts, distressing social problems that were not covered in their official newspapers, such as racism and sexual harassment. At the close of 2007, Behadrei Haredim, along with the other ultra-Orthodox internet sites, were banned by most of the community's prominent rabbis. The ultra-Orthodox owners sold the website to a nonreligious customer, who let the website to continue working. Today it is still a very popular site among ultra-Orthodox surfers as well as among non-Orthodox surfers who wish to learn more about the ultra-Orthodox community.

Because Behadrei Haredim is a central platform for intra-communal discussions on current issues in the ultra-Orthodox domain, it was only natural that a subject as loaded as the battle against cell phones became a forum for lively debate. In fact, dozens of relevant discussion clusters were uploaded onto a range of forums on the site; on some of them, surfers shared news items, notices and pictures of *Pashkevilim* with their friends. An examination of 20 such discussions (some of them very brief and some that included concatenation with dozens of responses) turned up some 30 *Pashkevilim* that were photographed by surfers (some of whom said they had taken them close to their homes), and these were added to the body of material of the current study. Using the Behadrei Haredim forum as a source of information revealed another layer: The publication of *Pashkevilim* on the site was usually within the context of the discussion (usually critical) about the content of a *Pashkevil* or remarks about the campaign against cell phones in general. Thus, we get a glimpse of the dimension of acceptability, even if it is not the main thesis of this study, and where appropriate, we relate to it briefly to reinforce the themes noted earlier.

We analyzed the *Pashkevilim* in line with the theory of Critical Discourse Analysis (CDA); according to CDA, following rhetorical means and their analysis in a given text makes it possible to discern the connection between the text and its cultural context, as well as identify the underlying social and political messages (Petrina, 2002). The rhetorical analysis includes relating to the three components of the text: the content, the structure and the language; the integration of the three offers some understanding of the cultural world that lies behind the texts (Bakhtin, 1986). By association with the earlier studies that dealt with *Pashkevilim*, we also focused on the author of the appeal, the intended addressees, the nature of the appeal and major linguistic features.

## THE SPEAKER (WRITER) AND THE AUDIENCE (READERS)

The first step in the analysis of the rhetoric mandates explicating the strategy of the message, that is, the way the message is designed through its "appeal" to the addressee: what the speaker says to the addressee and how he says it.

However, when we analyze *Pashkevilim*, owing to the nature of the medium, there is an additional stage during which we address earlier questions concerning the active and passive participants in the media act: Who wrote the *Pashkevil*, and how does he present himself? Who are the addressees of the *Pashkevil*, and how are they related to in the *Pashkevil* itself?

Anonymity has characterized the *Pashkevil* ever since the phenomenon appeared in Rome. It is true that on the ultra-Orthodox street, the *Pashkevilim* are occasionally signed by rabbinical courts or rabbis who are members of the extreme religious stream Eda Haharedit; nevertheless, many are published anonymously. This feature allows the writer to express himself in very strong language, to slander individuals (even rabbis) or to harshly criticize phenomena that he regards as unacceptable without having to deal with the consequences of what he has written. That being said, as we noted earlier, many of the *Pashkevilim* do bear a signature at the end—not of an individual but of an organized group. The writer's choice to sign in the name of a fictitious organization is an indication of his motivation, his self-perception, and his perceived mission as he hung the *Pashkevil* on the wall.

The *Pashkevilim* we studied can be divided into three groups:

1. "Official" *Pashkevilim* that were signed by the Committee of Rabbis on Media Matters, the secretariat of the committee, or the public relations department of the committee. Most of these *Pashkevilim* are just copies of the opinions expressed in the official ultra-Orthodox press. In this respect, the *Pashkevilim* are an *extension* of the official channel in an effort to reach as wide an audience as possible. This type of *Pashkevil* targets groups such as women, ultra-Orthodox youth and Yeshiva students, who do not usually read newspapers; in part, they are nothing more than informative, verbose bulletins that report on the work of the committee.
2. *Pashkevilim* signed by the rabbis of the Eda Haharedit, who also joined in the struggle against cellular phones. These rabbis are not members of the central leadership of the ultra-Orthodox community, so they were not part of the Committee of Rabbis on Media Matters; nevertheless, they also wrote many *Pashkevilim* condemning cellular phones. These *Pashkevilim* are an *alternative* to the official channel to which this group has no access.
3. Anonymous *Pashkevilim* : unsigned *Pashkevilim* or signed in the name of an unofficial organization, such as the Committee to Save the Youth in the Holy Land, the Actions Committee or the Committee for Protection from the Dangers of the Telephone. What power does an anonymous *Pashkevil* have compared to the other two?

Unlike editorials and newspaper articles, *Pashkevilim* facilitate an awareness of "an all-out struggle" in the eyes of the readership. The anonymous "speakers," who present themselves in various guises of official groups, create the impression of widespread support, a kind of loud cry coming from all the elements of the society—in this case, against the dangers inherent in the use of the cellular phone. A continuous stream of articles by journalists who are identified by name or the Committee of Rabbis on Media Matters is likely to suggest the campaign as one set up and developed by a small group at the forefront of the whole community. A prerequisite for the success of such a campaign is raising awareness in the community; herein is the role of the *Pashkevilim*, which reflect the many groups who have joined in the struggle, even if there is only one person behind each of these "groups."

The authors of *Pashkevilim* use several rhetorical strategies to intensify the sense of widespread support. The first, which is very common in this genre (as in many publication formats), is the use of the verb in the plural masculine form, usually as a participle: "Oy, who will heal us?" Who will stop the penetration of the phone depravity?" (Figure 10.1). Writing in the first-person plural reinforces the reader's identification with the writer's words and creates the impression of an absolute truth; moreover, it

בע"ה
אוי! מי ירפא לנו?
אוי! מי יעצור את חדירת זוהמת הפלאפונים אשר הפכו
את חמד בחורי הישיבות ל"בוחרנט"? רח"ל
אוי! מי ירפא את תחלואי הנפש של עוללי טיפוחינו
אשר הולכים שבי לפני צר האופנה? רח"ל
אוי! מי ישמור על גחלת בחורי הישיבות שעדיין לא
הצטרפו ל"נושרים"? רח"ל
אוי! מי יערב לנו ליום מחר על קדושת צאצאינו,
ואפילו רק להמשך לימודם בישיבה? רח"ל
הביטו וראו אם יש מכאוב כמכאוב תקופתינו
דור העתיד מתדרדר לתהום בדהירה שטרם היתה כמוה,
הריקנות אכלתה כל חלקה טובה, לדאבונם הקשה גם אין
כנגדם תוחכה מכל סוג שהיא, וזו היא שבעכרם להמשיך
להמשיך בנפילתם ואין חומל ואין מרחם.
למי אבכה, וכף אכה ומי הוא זה עלי הדור יגונן???
עורו ישנים מתרדמתכם
הוועד להצלת הנוער

*Figure 10.1* "Oy! Who will heal us?"

carries the suggestion that everyone agrees: "It is *our* obligation to fight the man-eating bacteria: the internet on the phone and the internet on the computer!" "The concern of parents: *We* must protect ourselves from the Web of the enemy."[1] Occasionally, this strategy appears as an appeal in the name of the whole community against the owner of the smartphone in a *Pashkevil* that demands: "iPhone owner—get out of our camps!" or a direct appeal in the name of the community to educational institutions to act: "To the heads of the *Yeshivot* and educators in the seminaries—to war!!!" This rhetoric pulls the public to the side in favor of the struggle for change; in all these cases, the *Pashkevil* is unsigned.

In some of the *Pashkevilim* we are relating to here the "speaker" was presented in the first-person singular: "I also do not read any weekly magazine that advertises non-kosher cellular phones." This terminology has the writer present in the text and creates a certain sense of intimacy. It suggests that the author is "the man on the street," who does not belong to a committee or organized group. Thus, his protest is perceived as an individual, spontaneous act designed to convince readers to adopt the same practice. In all of these cases, the *Pashkevil* complements the official channel by creating an impression of popular support, something that cannot be achieved by the official press.

Another strategy to complement "the show of public support" is to define the audience. Writers of *Pashkevilim* appealed directly to users who still owned regular cell phones, labeling them "deviants," "felons," "strays," or "rebels." Branding them as outcasts created a sharp contrast between the holdouts and the rest of the public, who has already obeyed the dictates of the rabbis: "All the great rabbis of Israel absolutely forbid non-kosher cellular phones and you cannot hear?? You are cruel!! Stop causing harm to the people of Israel."[2] This rhetoric conceals a dual appeal: the direct object of the *Pashkevil* is attacked for his disobedience and should be ostracized by the whole community; the indirect object, the readership, is strengthened by the picture of widespread support that draws attention to the owners of regular cellular phones, depicting them as loners and deviants. Occasionally, the separation between the deviant and the rest of the public is more explicit: Impure one! Owner of an iPhone who is enveloped by depravity 24 hours a day . . . Get out of our camp[3]." The writer of this *Pashkevil* formulated his appeal as a command from the whole camp to the owner of the iPhone to leave the bounds of the society. Sometimes a writer used the opposite strategy of expressing pity (explicitly) and patronizing (implicitly) the owner of the iPhone, as in the following case: "All iPhone owners *the whole nation of Israel* is praying for you" (Figure 10.2).

Unlike most *Pashkevilim* that address the nameless believer as a member of the community (and, actually, the whole community), in this campaign we found many *Pashkevilim* that targeted specific audiences, such as "To heads of *Yeshivot*, educators and teachers in seminars—start the war to save the younger generation! We have to fight against the predator germ!"[4]

*Figure 10.2* "iPhone owners and the like! The whole of the nation of Israel is praying for you: 'Bring him back to the faith of his fathers!' "

Here there is also evidence of the technique of "grassroots power"—the public is perceived as calling to the leaders to act, as if to say that the campaign was not forced on the public but developed from popular demand. As the campaign progressed, *Pashkevilim* appeared that presented a picture of its widespread success, using similar rhetorical and linguistic strategies: "Indeed they have all returned home. Thousands of people have taken upon themselves . . . not to give their sons and daughters any kind of cellular phone for any purpose whatsoever and they will make every effort to ensure that the telephone and the cellular instrument will be locked and cleansed of every undesirable line or program and *to stand behind the activists to build a clean kosher system*."[5]

## THE ISSUE OF CONTEXT AND OWNERSHIP

There are two other areas in which the difference between the press and *Pashkevilim* is apparent: context and ownership. One feature that characterizes the *Pashkevil* is connected to the fact that its range is limited. Unlike an ultra-Orthodox newspaper, which is distributed right across the country and even abroad, the exposure to the *Pashkevil* is restricted to a confined area: sometimes just the length of a street, usually in the ultra-Orthodox neighborhoods of Jerusalem and B'nei B'rak; only rarely is a *Pashkevil* seen in other ultra-Orthodox areas in the country. It is this feature that gives the *Pashkevil* channel contextual immediacy as well as its ability to relate to a specific context. Hence, it is not unusual to find *Pashkevilim* distributed in the neighborhood of a rabbinic figure that the writers want to slander or in the vicinity of a targeted firm. Within our context, we identified *Pashkevilim* that attacked sales and service centers that operate in ultra-Orthodox areas and continued to sell regular cellular instruments despite the rabbis' orders: "And you will eradicate the evil from within you: the Orange communication store—get out of our neighborhood—stop distributing contaminated cellular phones that make people descend to Hell and have been forbidden by all the great rabbis of Israel—get out of our neighborhood. Enough of the ruination!!!" (Figure 10.3). Here also the *Pashkevil* singled out the cellular phone store and anyone connected with that enterprise for attack, and the assumption was that the rest of the public agreed with the sentiments expressed.

*Figure 10.3* "And you will eradicate the evil from within you . . ."

These examples represent one of the traditional uses of *Pashkevilim* : a targeted attack on an institution, a business or even a social phenomenon that is perceived as dangerous. Very often, as in the present case, the attack is more personal, directed at a person in or outside the ultra-Orthodox camp, who is "targeted" by the *Pashkevil*, which lists his sins. One interesting example is the *Pashkevil* that addresses the ultra-Orthodox (former) minister of communication: "Attias—you failed!!" (Figure 10.4), and an even more extreme case is the *Pashkevil* that shows pictures of the directors of cell phone companies, accusing, "White collar crime! These people are not members of Hamas or Hezbollah. They are respected members of the community . . . who are poisoning the future generation of our nation with active poisonous nerve gas that turns a person into a wild animal chasing the most depraved abominations" (Figure 10.5). The *Pashkevil* went on: "All the educators and social activists who must be concerned that the future generation is of sound body and mind . . . take no notice." This *Pashkevil* also attacked the (former) minister of communication again: "And also the ultra-Orthodox Minister of Communication who, more than any other, is authorized to stop the crime and prevent the backsliding of our youth, does not act nor do his job properly . . . we will not sleep nor slumber until the phenomenon is eradicated. Wake up. Wake up!!!"[6]

*Figure 10.4* "Attias [the ultra-Orthodox (former) minister of communications]—you failed!!! Rabbis and educators are howling with pain. We are going downhill fast and there is a serious holocaust in all the media and the cellular phone business in Israel."

*Figure 10.5* A wall poster against the heads of the cellular phone companies in Israel before the "kosher cellular" line was introduced: "White collar crime: these people are not members of Hamas or Hizballa. They are respected members of the community . . . who are poisoning the future generation of our nation with active poisonous nerve gas that turns a person into a wild animal chasing the most depraved abominations."

These bitter attacks also tend to create a sense of "an all-out war" and complement the official press channel. Apart from the clear stand taken by the press and the pressure on the users, these *Pashkevilim* directly and scathingly attack other powers that be in both the political and the financial systems, in an attempt to create pressure upward. Clearly the official press cannot allow itself to publish similar attacks using the same style, tone, and target material.

Another difference between the *Pashkevilim* and the press has to do with the question of ownership. The fact that a newspaper has editors and owners that have political and financial interests that are known to the public reduces its ability to act in contexts that the public perceives as arising from vested interests. In our context, we can see it in the boycott on advertisements (by order of the rabbis) for cellular phone companies that initially refused to meet the demands of the committee to develop and supply kosher cell phones. In contrast to the ultra-Orthodox political party newspapers, several labeled "more modern" weekly ultra-Orthodox magazines refused to cooperate with this ban. An attempt by the committee to exploit the official press to gain public support for a boycott of the "recalcitrant" magazines would have aroused suspicion, as the press would have been regarded as having a vested interest in the matter; moreover, the party newspapers and weekly magazines have a long history of ideological and financial disagreements. It is not surprising, therefore, that the *Pashkevilim* were enlisted (Friedman, 2005) to encourage such a boycott and to present it as an authentic public protest: "I also do not read any weekly magazine that advertises non-kosher cellular phones."

## "SHOUTING WALLS": *PASHKEVIL* VERSUS GRAFFITI

The function of the *Pashkevil* presented earlier suggests a comparison with a similar genre: protest graffiti (Kohn and Rosenberg, 2013). They are both media models that are written anonymously and displayed publicly to appeal to the addressee directly and to the readers indirectly; both function in a confined geographical area and are perceived as public but unofficial media channels (Blume, 1985). The act of disseminating both the *Pashkevil* and graffiti is considered subversive—almost anarchistic—since many of the *Pashkevilim*, like the graffiti, are posted on the walls of houses, fences, and places that are not intended for that purpose (Barozi-Baroz, 2005). These channels have similar rhetorical characteristics, but whereas the graffiti is, in fact, considered "a short text," the *Pashkevil* is often extremely verbose. Nevertheless, they both have dramatic headlines with a very prominent graphic visual element using many exclamation marks and question marks. Both have intercontextual features that relate to previous writings as well as linguistic characteristics adopted from familiar cultures; they also both have a tendency to use strong language and invective that include warnings and even threats to catch the eye of the passerby (Shapira, 2005).

The comparison is also relevant to the ideological motive behind the use of *Pashkevilim*, as Friedman (2005) notes, "[The *Pashkevil*] serves as means for individuals and groups to mock figures who are considered authoritative and to challenge the current leadership . . . as well as those who want to protest against wrongdoings and corruption" (p. 10). The idea that the genre is anti-establishment in its substance is relevant with regard to graffiti as well. Friedman also discusses the psychological aspects of the phenomenon: the point is not only "to strike the opponent but also to give the writer a feeling of satisfaction" (p. 11). This is similar to the conclusions reached in the psychological studies focusing on the motives of writers of graffiti.

Writing graffiti is perceived as a spontaneous, personal, momentary act. The *Pashkevil*, on the other hand, is a product of printing, necessitating financial investment, advanced organization, and a production and distribution system (even if the original *Pashkevil* in the Roman square did not involve financial investment, distributing one *Pashkevil* in the Jerusalem neighborhoods today requires skilled workers).

This comparison is relevant to our context since the difference between the genres is largely in their degree of acceptability: *Pashkevilim* will always engender more suspicion than graffiti. This is apparent in the discussions on Behadrei Haredim that developed after pictures of *Pashkevilim* were uploaded to the site. Every single one of the *Pashkevilim* "was suspected" of being planted by one of the forces in favor of the campaign or against it, such as the cellular phone companies or rabbis who were not invited to join the committee. It is also possible that the anonymous *Pashkevilim* aroused more suspicion than the others as in the absence of a signature it was less clear who was leading the fight—the rabbis or the leaders of the community.

There is another interesting perspective in the comparison between graffiti and *Pashkevilim* . Whereas graffiti often combines pictures and writing (Kohn and Rosenberg, 2013), and sometimes has only drawings, the *Pashkevil* is generally perceived as a text-only medium, its visual features being functions of a variety of writing styles, variable text size or exaggerated use of punctuation marks. However, in the campaign against the use of cellular phones, there was a new element, which has appeared only in the last few years and has not yet been researched: *Pashkevilim* that combine text, photos and drawings. There are many such examples in the *Pashkevilim* that were examined for this study; one such example is the *Pashkevil* with the pictures of the heads of the five largest cellular phone companies (Figure 10.5) alongside the text; another shows a picture of a young man talking on a smartphone and appeals to him: "iPhone owners and the like! The whole of the nation of Israel is praying for you: Bring him back to the faith of his fathers!" (Figure 10.2). The best example is the *Pashkevil* that has a picture with very little text to explain what is happening. It shows an ultra-Orthodox young man secluded in his home next to a bookcase keeping the threats of the secular culture—in the form of animals of prey—from entering the home: television, internet, singers, videos and so on. Simultaneously, the phone (nonkosher, of course) in his pocket, which brings all these problems into the home, is ringing (Figure 10.6).

It is possible that this phenomenon is the harbinger of change in the traditional nature of *Pashkevilim*; for hundreds of years they were only textual. It may be connected to the discovery by Kantor and Muchnik (2004) and by Harlap (2010), that today one can find *Pashkevilim* that are cast in the mode of contemporary speech and even modern slang. According to Harlap (2010) this is a hint of a group of young people called "the new ultra-Orthodox," an ever-growing stratum in the community who are more modern in their outlook and less conservative. In fact, the young man who appears in the picture in Figure 10.2 looks as though he belongs to this group.

Many researchers have discussed the relationship between the visual and the verbal in advertising texts and have characterized the use of the visual component as a rhetorical complement designed, in most cases, to attract attention and highlight the message within the congestion of texts

*Figure 10.6* The mobile phone brings home the secular street culture.

that appear in the public space (Berger, 1972; Penn, 2000). It would seem that, whereas this element also exists here, the visual and verbal components have another point in common. The campaign against mobile phones is a battle waged against modernizing processes in the ultra-Orthodox community. Perhaps the combination of an old medium—the *Pashkevil*—and new rhetorical methods that are different than the genre's traditional nature but more appropriate to the advertising genre, such as pictures and photographs, is really no more than adapting the veteran *Pashkevil* to modernity and current issues that symbolize that modernity. Thus here, too, the *Pashkevil* acts as "complementary rhetoric" to the official ultra-Orthodox press, which, even today, does not publish such announcements. The proclamations that appeared in the press in the name of the Committee of Rabbis were mostly textual except for informative items that included pictures of the kosher cellular phones with the committee's seal. Moreover, this picture of the kosher phone appeared in many places both in the press and on the notice boards in the streets of the city.

## CONCLUSION

The battle to acculturate the kosher cellular phone was different from any other battle against a medium waged within the ultra-Orthodox community. The secular radio stations, television and the Israeli daily press were intuitively perceived by the whole community as constituting dangerous exposure to the values of Western society and as a threat to its cultural boundaries, which is why the battles against those media were completely successful.

The attempt to prevent the personal computer from being adopted in the society (before the age of cell phones) was largely unsuccessful because the arguments regarding the possible dangers of the medium (CDs, computer games, etc.) were countered by the claim that these were technologies that could be controlled. Moreover, some stressed the potential advantages offered by the computer, word processing and CDs that have databases of Torah literature and so were framed as a technological opportunity that could make daily life easier and even advanced important religious practices such as Torah study and the dissemination of religious ideology.

Yet a few years later, a widespread public campaign against the internet led by ultra-Orthodox leader also proved quite successful. The slow spread of the new medium into the homes of the ultra-Orthodox gave public leaders time to mount a broad offensive against the dangers of the internet. Most of the ultra-Orthodox community that had not yet connected to the web began to see its destructive potential and did not allow it into their homes. However, the internet did find a niche among certain sector of the community, and rabbis eventually permitted connecting to limited networks that strictly filtered the content that was perceived as pernicious. Today, the vast majority of lively intra-communal discourse on the internet takes place on "kosher" connections (Neriya-Ben Shahar and Lev-On, 2011).

In the campaign against the cellular phones, the public leaders faced a serious problem. When the phones first appeared, the ultra-Orthodox community perceived them as an effective inter-personal channel and a "clean," nonthreatening medium. At the beginning, those who disapproved on the grounds of wasting time and the cost were barely heard and did not succeed in preventing the community from enthusiastically adopting the new medium. Hence, by the time the leaders began the campaign, a considerable percentage of the ultra-Orthodox community already owned mobile phones. Moreover, in a survey conducted at the beginning of the campaign (April 2005), it transpired that in connection with certain functions, the ultra-Orthodox were among the leading users in Israel; for example, 49% of the ultra-Orthodox users said that they sent text messages on a regular basis as opposed to 41% of the general population (Klein, 2005). This reality made the campaign more complex than the earlier ones. It forced the leaders not to be content with just demonstrating the potential threat and publishing rabbis' opinions on the issue but demanded that they also make use of a range of strategies to show how the public was responding to their pleas. Their agenda also had to include the creation of a picture of unqualified support for the campaign to get rid of the cellular phone and adopt the kosher phone. The *Pashkevilim* were more appropriate for accomplishing this latter goal than the official ultra-Orthodox press because, apart from all the features we discussed previously and their anonymity, they are folksy.

In response to the questions we asked earlier, we found that in this campaign there were definite purposes behind the extensive use of *Pashkevilim* that were adapted to the features of the medium: (a) the presentation of the battle waged by the Committee of Rabbis in the service of the community leaders as a popular struggle that (b) was made to appear as though the leaders did not initiate the campaign by themselves but, rather, that the struggle was a response to public demand and (c) a perception that suggested that the whole public was in favor of adopting the committee's recommendations, is working to apply them on the street, enforce them and condemn all those who do not comply. In these respects, the *Pashkevil* complements the official channels, contrary to the popular view that it is an alternate and antiestablishment medium. The battle against the nonkosher cellular phone, the struggle to get the cell phone companies to adapt the technology to develop the kosher cell phone and the campaign to enforce the latter's use by the entire ultra-Orthodox community required the support of all the media, and the utilization of all possible measures. Whereas the press concentrated on the "downward flow" in its reports on the committee's work, the publication of rabbis' *Halachic* opinions, editorials and advertising bans against the cellular phone companies, the *Pashkevilim* were enlisted to create a public climate of total support and of pressure "from below" on the leaders and on those who refused to go along. The simultaneous use of these two channels, together with mass demonstrations and public addresses by rabbis, created the ambience for a complex, intransigent battle over the character of the community.

This study gives a better understanding of the responses by the ultra-Orthodox leadership as well as the sartorial media to digital media. Any kind of media which may be considered as a threat on the tradition of cultural closure and hiding behind the community walls would be attacked in the public sphere by using a militant rhetoric. Sometimes the means would be very simple such as using wallpapers and sometimes by declaring a costumers' boycott. It seems to be that the fear of bad influences from the secular world, which may leak through the media and the new media, was the factor that deeply influenced on the decision makers to embrace of digital technology.

This is different from other Jewish sectors who responded to new media mainly because that after the hedgehog's instinct, there was a general recruitment of the printed media to reject the new media, such as the 3G cellular phones. In this sense, this case study taught us a lesson about responses of the ultra-Orthodox Jewry in Israel: They will not tolerate a technological improvement if it may jeopardize their traditional education. A new technology that improves people lives will be accepted only if it does not put at risk any communal value.

This chapter uniquely contributes theoretically and methodologically as well as from a particular disciplinary perspective to our understanding of the Jewish experience with digital media. It tried to draw the lines of the religious–secular clash of civilizations between the leadership of ultra-Orthodox Jewry in Israel and its cultural neighbors by analyzing the most common media in the ultra-Orthodox sector, the *Pashkevilim* . Although people may disregard it since it is not a daily newspaper, yet it considered to be an influential media in the ultra-Orthodox public sphere. If someone would think to bring into the ultra-Orthodox communities a new media in the coming years, and he would like to feel its pulse, he would not be able to ignore the *Pashkevilim*: Even though they are simple, they are significant.

## NOTES

1. *Pashkevil* from Me'a She'arim, Jerusalem, March 2005.
2. *Pashkevil* from Giv'at Sha'ul, Jerusalem, February 2006.
3. *Pashkevil* from Giv'at Sha'ul, Jerusalem, March 2008.
4. *Pashkevil* from Benei-Brak, August 2005.
5. *Pashkevil* from Benei-Brak, December 2005.
6. *Pashkevil* from Ge'ula, Jerusalem, August 2005.

## REFERENCES


Bakhtin, M.M. (1986). The Problem of the Text in Linguistics, Philology, and the Human Sciences: An Experiment in Philosophical Analysis. In: C. Emerson and M. Holquist (Eds.), *Speech Genres and Other Late Essays* (pp. 103–131). Austin: University of Texas Press.

Bar-Yosef, N. (2006). The First Anniversary of the Kosher Cellular Phone Revolution. *Yated Ne'eman*, February 7, p. 11 (in Hebrew).

Barozi-Baroz, N. (2005). *Pashkevilim, Posters and Polemic Placards in the Ultra-Orthodox Street*. Tel-Aviv: Ertz-Israel Museum.

Berger, J. (1972). *Ways of Seeing*. Harmondsworth: Penguin Books and BBC.

Blume, R. (1985). Graffiti. In: T. A. van Dijk (Ed.), *Discourse and Literature*, vol. 3, *Critical Theory* (pp. 137–148). Amsterdam and Philadelphia: John Benjamins Publishing Company.

Campbell, H. (2006a). Religion and the Internet *Communication Research Trends*, 26, 3–24.

Campbell, H. (2006b). Texting the Faith: Religious Users and Cell Phone Culture. In: A. Kavoori and N. Archeaux (Eds.), *The Cell Phone Reader: Essays in Social Transformation* (pp. 139–54). New York: Peter Lang.

Campbell, H. (2007). What Hath God Wrought? Considering How Religious Communities Culture (or Kosher) the Cell Phone. *Continuum: Journal of Media & Cultural Studies*, 21, 191–203.

Cohen, A., Lemish, D. and Schejter, A.M. (2008). *The Wonder Telephone in the Land of Miracles: Mobile Telephony in Israel*. Cresskill: Hampton Press.

Cromer, G. (1987). The Polluted Image: The Response of Ultra-Orthodox Judaism to Israeli Television. *Sociology and Social Research*, 71, 198–199.

Ettinger, Y. (2007). Rabbi Elyashiv: Ultra-Orthodox Schools Will Not Accept Pupils Whose Parents Do Not Own a Kosher Cellular Phone. *Ha'aretz*, February 4, p.11 (in Hebrew).

Friedman, M. (2005). *The Pashqevil (Pasquinade) and Public Wall Poster/Bulletin Board Announcements in Haredi (Ultra-Orthodox) Society: The Exhibition Catalog in the Eretz-Israel Museum (June-July 2005)*. Tel-Aviv-Jerusalem: The Eretz-Israel Museum and Yad Ben-Zvi (in Hebrew).

Harlap, L.R. (2010). The *Pashkevilim* Culture through the Mirror of Language: Studies in Phenomena of Text Syntax and Discourse Style. *Iyunim Besafah Vehevra*, 3, 104–121 (in Hebrew).

Ho, S.S., Lee, W. and Hameed, S.S. (2008). Muslim Surfers on the Internet: Using the Theory of Planned Behavior to Examine the Factors Influencing Engagement in Online Religious Activities. *New Media and Society*, 10, 93–113.

Kahn, B. (2005). New "Kosher" Cell Phones Free of Content Services. *Dei'ah veDibur: Information & Insight*, March 25, 15–17.

Kantor, H. and Muchnik, M. (2004). Unique Linguistic Usages in ultra-Orthodox Announcements. *Mehkarei Morashteinu* b–c, 239–249 (in Hebrew).

Kaplan, K. (2007). *The Secret of the Ultra-Orthodox Discourse*. Jerusalem: Mercaz Zalman Shazar leToldot Israel (in Hebrew).

Klein, G. (2005). Survey: Women Are the SMS Champions. *Yediot Aharonot*, 20 April [online]. Available at: www.ynet.co.il/articles/0,7340,L-3075184,00.html [Accessed March 17, 2012].

Kohn, A. and Rosenberg, H. (2013). Collapsing Walls and the Question of Commemoration: Graffiti in the Israeli Withdrawal. *Social Semiotics*, 23, 606–631.

Levor, A. (2005). Cellular—A Battle for the Soul. *Hamodi'a*, September 27, 16–18 (in Hebrew).

Livio, O. and Tenenboim-Weinblatt, K. (2007). Discursive Legitimation of a Controversial Technology: Ultra-Orthodox Jewish Women in Israel and the Internet. *The Communication Review*, 10(1), 29–56.

MacKinnon, I. (2005). Kosher Phone Taps into New Market for Mobiles. *Times Online* [online]. Available at: www.timesonline.co.uk/article0,251–1508115,00.html [Accessed April 12, 2012].

Mutchnik, M. and Kantor, H. (2000). Language and Gender: Differences between Males and Females in ultra-Orthodox Announcements. *Balshanut Ivrit*, 45, 49–56 (in Hebrew).

Neriya-Ben Shahar, R. and Lev-On, A. (2011). Gender, Religion, and New Media: Attitudes and Behaviors Related to the Internet Among Ultra-Orthodox Women Employed in Computerized Environments. *International Journal of Communication*, 5, 875–95.

Penn, G. (2000). Semiotic Analysis of Still Images. In: M. Bauer and G. Gaskell (Eds.), *Qualitative Researching With Text, Image & Sound* (pp. 227–245). London: Sage.

Petrina, S. (2002). The Politics of Research in Technology Education: A Critical Content and Discourse Analysis of the *Journal of Technology Education*. *Journal of Technology Education*, 10 [online]. Available at: scholar.lib.vt.edu/ejournals/JTE/v10n1/petrina.html [Accessed January 20, 2013].

Rashi, T. (2011). Divergent Attitudes within Orthodox Jewry toward Mass Communication. *The Review of Communication*, 11, 20–38.

Rashi, T. (2012). The Kosher Cell Phone in Ultra-Orthodox Society: A Technological Ghetto Within the Global Village? In: H. Campbell (Ed.), *Digital Religion: Understanding Religious Practice in New Media Worlds* (pp. 173–181). London: Routledge.

Rheingold, H. (1999). Look Who's Talking. *Wired*, 7 [online]. Available at: http://www.wired.com/wired/archieve7.01/amish_pr.html [Accessed January 20, 2013].

Rose, A. (2007). The Ultra-Orthodox and the Internet: Enemies: A Love Story. *Eretz Aheret* [online]. Available at: acheret.co.il/?cmd=articles.124&act=read&id=356 [Accessed September 7, 2009].

Shapira, Z. (2005). The Language of the *Pashkevilim* . In: N. Barozi-Baroz (curator): Pashkevilim: *Wall Posters and Polemic Announcements in the Ultra-Orthodox*

*Street*. Tel Aviv and Jerusalem: The Eretz Israel Museum and Yad Ben-Zvi (in Hebrew).
Schlesinger, Y. (1992). The Language Components of the Language of the Learned. *Bikoret Uparshanut*, 28, 141–147 (in Hebrew).
Silverstone, R., Hirsch, E. and Morley, D. (1992). Information and Communication Technology and the Moral Economy of the Household. In: R. Silverstone and E. Hirsch (Eds.), *Consuming Technologies: Media and Information in Domestic Spaces* (pp. 15–31). London: Routledge.

# 11 The Israeli Rabbi and the Internet

*Yoel Cohen*

Orthodox rabbis often find themselves in conflict with mass media, because they perceive mass media as threatening the Jewish value system, by catering to popular tastes in the search for the ratings, rather than encouraging or supporting religious ideology (Cohen, 2012a). Portrayal of sex and permissiveness, and the publication of political and social gossip thus become areas of conflict between rabbis and the media. These concerns are raised not only in relation to traditional mass media but increasingly also in relation to newer forms of media technology. This chapter examines the attitudes of rabbis in Israel to media technology such as computers and the internet. Based on survey data in this chapter, questions such as whether rabbis believe that the internet damages religious values, the extent to which rabbis use internet filters and whether they believe that internet use by children should be limited are explored. These questions were part of a larger survey carried out by the author with rabbis in Israel regarding a range of media-related issues. The intent of this chapter is to provide an overview of Israeli rabbis' perceptions of and negotiation with new media in order to illuminate how these religious community leaders, an influential social group generally not open to scholarly research, relates to new media and seeks to respond to the challenges of modernity they represent.

## AN OVERVIEW OF ISRAELI JUDAISM

The religious community in Israel comprises the Modern Orthodox (Dati Leumi) and the ultra-Orthodox/Haredim accounting for 17% and 8%, respectively, of the Israeli Jewish population (Central Bureau of Statistics [CBS], 2009). The Modern Orthodox seek to reconcile religion with modernity and perceive the contemporary state as a clue to Jewish redemption (Cohen, 2001). A substream of the Modern Orthodox is the Hardal, which while identifying with the mainstream Modern Orthodox on matters relating to Zionism—unlike the Haredim—are nevertheless characterized by an inclination toward cultural withdrawal, including exposure to mass media. The Haredi (Hebrew for "fearful ones") community is characterized by social withdrawal from what the Haredi Jews see as the dangers of modern society. Haredim do not identify with the modern state of Israel, believing that Jewish statehood requires awaiting the coming of the Jewish Messiah. In contrast, Conservative Judaism, while also favoring the emancipation of the Jews and opposing ghettoization, adhere to key tenets of Judaism, for example, the observance of *Kashrut* (*dietary laws*) and the Sabbath (Ringler, 1989). Furthermore, Reform Judaism, which originated in Germany in the 19th century, legitimizes change in Judaism and denies the eternal validity to Jewish law.

Reflecting its philosophy of withdrawal from modernity, and seeking to maintain religious values in a cultural ghetto framework, the Haredi rabbis have issued over the years religious decrees (*Pesukey Din*) against mass media as being threat to Torah family values. From the appearance of newspapers in the 19th century, through the development of radio and television, and latterly video, computers, the internet and portable phones, Haredi rabbis have enacted such decrees against media, with different levels of success.

By contrast, rabbis from the Modern Orthodox (*Dati Leumi*) stream have not issued official Jewish legal rulings regarding media use, but instead have offered a thoughtful yet critical response towards the internet by advocating the need for media literacy in order to create a balanced and acceptable relationship between Torah world and world of modern media. The Haredi–Dati Leumi diversity may appear similar to the different Protestant and Roman Catholic views of media. Whereas the Roman Catholic Church are strongly critical of the media, and for hundreds of years maintained an Index of Forbidden Books and latterly an Index of Forbidden Films, and placed an embargo on Hollywood and Disney, mainline Protestants are characterized by a more liberal attitude which includes that each individual possesses self-discipline to self-censor—him- or herself (Buddenbaum, 2001). Some of the Modern Orthodox rabbis, particularly those identified with the Hardal substream, encourage controlling exposure particularly of children to the general media. The Hardal or Haredi Leumi combine a Haredi separatist view towards modern culture with a strong nationalist or Leumi view supporting notions of Zionism and the Israeli state. While the mainstream Modern Orthodox community are less restrictive in their exposure to media and in the main watch television as well, the Hardal have constructed "cultural walls" to distant themselves from perceived dangerous influences. These range from fewer secular studies in their schools to avoiding exposure to television and the internet.

Orthodox Jews—Haredi—and Modern Orthodox (including the Hardal) account, according to the government's CBS (2009), for 25% of Israeli Jews. Few of the remainder which according to the CBS compose 40% traditional and 35% secular Israeli Jews, are formally members of the two non-Orthodox streams, the Conservative and Reform movements.

It is important to note that the synagogue in Israel has a limited impact on the majority lives of Israeli Jews both in functional terms and in audience terms. Its functions are narrower than synagogues in Jewish communities abroad and mostly comprise the holding of religious services and educational activities such as religious lessons (*Shiurim*) and lectures. Apart from the strictly religious—whether defined in terms of Haredi and Modern Orthodox terms or whether including also the small Conservative and Reform communities in Israel—the Jewish state itself, its official organs and other non-official institutions, have replaced the synagogue to a considerable extent as foci of Jewish identity. The rest of the Israeli Jewish population have no regular daily or weekly interaction with the synagogue in Israel. Nevertheless, the traditional, as distinct from the Orthodox Jewish communities—which account for 40% of the Israeli Jewish population—also have varying degrees of selective contact with the synagogue, comprising attendance at the Jewish holydays including the New Year and participation in holidays such as Passover, Sukkoth, Hanuka, and Purim, and life-cycle events including the Bar-Mitzvah, circumcision or funeral. Moreover, religion enjoys a centrality in Israeli public life, which does not exist in many other countries. This includes responsibility by the state rabbinical religious courts (*Batei Din*) for certain aspects of legislation concerning personal status such as determining who is a Jew, conversion, marriage and divorce. Rabbis play important roles in the state education system notably in the Modern Orthodox (Dati Leumi) stream and Haredi stream, but also Conservative rabbis also play an important role in the newer Conservative-affiliated Tali school network.

## RABBIS' RESPONSES TO MASS MEDIA

The rabbinical profession may be broken down into three groupings: community rabbis, rabbis teaching in schools or at higher institutes of religious study (*Yeshivot*) and religious court judges (*Dayanim*) who are authorized by the state to adjudicate in personal status matters (Stern and Friedman, 2011). In Israel, the rabbi and the synagogue do not enjoy a monopoly in being a single focus of Jewish identity, as they do in the Diaspora.

The interaction between rabbis of different streams and mass media may be broken down into five responses. First, some rabbis serve as moral leaders that legitimize—and delegitimize—mass media. For example, the non-exposure of Haredi Jews to mass media has been heavily influenced by their spiritual leaders. The influence of religious hierarchies—notably rabbis—is paramount in the Haredi communities—whether in the Lithuanian Haredi stream, where the rabbi's role is to interpret *Halacha* (Jewish religious law), or in the hassidic Haredi, stream in which the *admor* fulfills a father figure role in the community and his influence is wider ranging; he is also consulted on a range of social and other matters. The rabbi-teacher in the school system in the Haredi and Modern Orthodox communities has an important pedagogic function in influencing the outlook of religious children and youth toward the wider society, including toward the media and regarding such values as freedom of speech and tolerance. These include taking positions on whether adults or children should be exposed to the media, particularly to television and the internet.

Second, rabbis of all streams often use the media to stay updated both about events in the news and about current religion-related developments. To be effective, rabbi-teachers and synagogue rabbis require to be exposed to the media to which their own audiences, children or synagogue congregants are exposed. Rabbinical court judges (*Dayanim*) of all streams, for example, in determining decisions (*Pesukey Din*) require not only mastery of Jewish religious law (*Halacha*) but also awareness of contemporary affairs because a religious law decision also requires taking into account the specific circumstances of the inquirer.

Third, rabbis—particularly synagogue community rabbis—increasingly recognize the opportunities which mass media channels offer as alternative "pulpits." For example, rabbis appear on television programs about Jewish tradition on the eve and at the termination of the Sabbath. Also, they write columns in the general media on the Friday Sabbath eve issue about the weekly Bible reading. The rabbi's influence is felt within the religious population such as through the Sabbath sermon from the pulpit to congregants, but the media are an additional channel to spreading the rabbi's religious message even if this tends to occur much more in the religious media than in the secular Israeli media. Apart from rabbis in the Haredi stream, other rabbis and communal leaders in other streams are discovering the value of the internet in circumventing the mainstream media and in building community websites.

Fourth, the media play an important role in building mutual perceptions between religious and secular communities. The media of one sector—secular, Haredi or Modern Orthodox—is a prism through which the respective community perceives the other communities. For example, the Haredi press often portrays secular Israelis, painting an image of them as "lesser Jews" because they fail to observe religious law. In turn, secular news media present the religious political parties, which often form part of Israel's coalition government in Israel, as focused on making deals related to their own interest such as issues of government funding for *Yeshivot*, and the question of recruitment of Haredim to national military service. Fifth, in addition to the broader question of rabbis' attitudes toward new media, the internet has also become subject of Jewish religious legal discussion concerning specific questions such as internet copyright, Sabbath observance and the computer and virtual prayer services (Cohen, 2012b; Dickovsky, 2002). While Orthodox rabbis (Haredi and Modern Orthodox) have begun considering the question of whether copying texts from the computer, the question is not new and had been raised earlier in the context of books, newspapers and broadcasting (Bar-Ilan, 1987; Batzri, 1986; Goldberg, 1986). copyright has received renewed rabbinical attention in the computer age. Given that downloading and copying texts are regarded by many as acceptable practices, why, it is asked, should religious Jews be deterred? True, there is a basic principle in Jewish law that once an owner has given up possession of an object that has gone missing and that somebody in whose possession it falls does not have to return to him. But some rabbis have ruled that since some people do pay for downloaded texts, the owner has not "given up hope of receiving it back" and that the unauthorized copying of texts is, therefore, forbidden.

The prohibition of work on the Sabbath Day, as enjoined by the fourth of the Ten Commandments (Exod. 20:8), has implications for the functioning of the internet on the Sabbath and Jewish holydays (Schwartz, 2005). Given the prohibition on activating electricity on the Sabbath, the computer and the internet may not be switched on, according to Orthodox as well as Conservative Judaism. But Reform Judaism, which does not oppose the use of electricity, have fewer objections for the use of computers and the internet. The prohibition of work on the Sabbath day has implications given both that the internet operates simultaneously across time zones and that the Sabbath—the period commencing at sunset on Friday and continuing for 24 hours to Saturday eve—falls at different times in different parts of the globe. Rabbis have discussed—and divided over—whether it is permitted for an observant Jew to open up a website situated in a country where it is the Sabbath (Cardon, 2006; Cohen, 2005, 2012b; Eretz Hemdah, 2003).

Little applied research has been carried out concerning the interplay of media and religion in the Israeli Jewish context, especially when it comes to investigating the role Israel rabbis play in media choices and religious community response to media. Most research about media and religion in Israel has focused on the Haredim. The Haredi sector is estranged from the general population, with their own separatist media, raising important anthropological and sociopsychological questions (Baumel, 2002, 2005). Baumel (2005) examined the Haredi press through linguistic tools in order to generate a picture of the Haredi outlook on the social role of media. Religion content in different Israeli news media forms, religious and secular, was examined (Cohen, 2005). Other questions addressed concerns related to Jewish theological attitudes to mass media (Cohen, 2006). Gabel examined the relationship of the modern religious community and the media (2006). Regarding new media, Horowitz (2000) described early Haredi rabbinical attitudes about the internet; and Cohen (2011) updated the picture. Barzilai-Nahon and Barzilai (2005) examines how the internet has been adapted to Haredi community needs, and Tydor Baumel-Schwartz (2009) analyzed Orthodox Jewish women's internet forums. Among questions yet to yield academic research is the exposure of children in religious communities in Israel to the internet. Therefore, this study seeks to add to and extend this previous research by providing comparative insights about Jewish response to media from rabbis in a range of sectors within Judaism.

## SURVEYING RABBIS ABOUT MEDIA TECHNOLOGY

Given their central role as community builders, it is relevant to examine rabbis' evaluations of media performance and their usage of the media in community work and rabbis' exposure to mass media. To draw a picture of rabbis' attitudes to computers and the internet, a survey of Israeli rabbis was carried out by the author.[1]

The survey polled rabbis of four main branches of Judaism (Haredi or ultra-Orthodox, Modern Orthodox, Reform, and Conservative). In addition, members of the Hardal stricter substream of Israeli Modern Orthodoxy were polled. Rabbis polled included those on the mailing list of the chief rabbinate of Israel and rabbis on the mailing lists of the Conservative and Reform movements in Israel. Other listings of rabbis included those in the telephone book and such groups within the Modern Orthodox like the rabbis serving on a kibbutz or agricultural settlement. In the questionnaire rabbis were asked to define their identification—Reform, Conservative, mainstream Modern Orthodox, Hardal and Haredi. The vast majority of rabbis in Israel and their synagogue communities belong to the Orthodox—Haredi or ultra-Orthodox, mainstream Modern Orthodox and Hardal. In contrast to their communities in the US (the second-biggest center of Jews in the world after Israel) which account for 80% of the American Jewish community, the Conservative and Reform communities in Israel are very small. Because of pressure from the Orthodox streams, they have not been recognized by the Israeli state. But given the latter's more enlightened views on the wider culture including mass media, it seems important to examine also these.

Questions examined in the survey are (a) rabbis' evaluations of the internet and whether they think that some internet content, such as access to porn sites, damage religious values; (b) if so, whether a filter should be used with the internet connection, and whether access to the internet for children should be limited; and (c) rabbinical usage of Torah databases (online and computer DVD). The survey was based on a detailed questionnaires survey sent to 1,800 rabbis in Israel.

In total, 302 questionnaires were returned. The study also sought to examine differences between rabbis from different religious streams: Haredi, mainline Modern Orthodox, the Hardal subgroup of Modern Orthodox, Conservative and Reform. Each group was also broken down according to different places of birth, age differences and whether they had children at home. Places of birth were divided between those born in Israel, Western countries (North America, West Europe, South America), East European–born rabbis and Sephardi rabbis born in Arab or Middle Eastern countries. As an immigrant society, it is instructive to consider whether the place of the birth of the rabbi influences his or her attitude to computer media. Rabbis were also broken down according to age groupings of rabbis, born between 1961 and 1980, between 1941 and 1960, between 1921 and

1940 and between 1901 and 1920 to see whether there were any differences by age. It is postulated that rabbis who grew up in the computer age might have different attitudes toward the media than will older rabbis.

## FINDINGS: ISRAELI RABBIS' RESPONSE TO THE INTERNET

Survey data from this study revealed a broad range of interesting findings, related to rabbis' negotiation with computers and the internet. Specifically the following issues are discussed: (a) rabbis' evaluations of computers and the internet, (b) computer and internet usage by rabbis, (c) limiting the exposure of children to computers and the internet and (d) computers as a modern tool for Jewish education.

### Rabbis' Evaluations of Computers and the Internet

Rabbis of all religious streams claimed that internet sites, by providing access to certain sites such as those sex and porn related, damage religious values. In contrast to leaders of some other faiths, rabbis over the years have been less concerned about media portrayal of violence. Yet, a distinction was found between the Orthodox (Haredim, mainline Modern Orthodox, and Hardal), on one hand, and the non-Orthodox (Reform and Conservative) rabbis, on the other hand, regarding the damage to religious values. Eighty-seven percent of Haredi rabbis, 75% of Modern Orthodox, and 92% of Hardal rabbis said that the internet damaged religious values to a "very great extent," a "great extent," or a "considerable extent"—with the mainstream Modern Orthodox more inclined than the other two to perceive the internet as damaging religious values to a considerable extent rather than "to a great extent" or a "very great extent" (Table 11.2).

By contrast, 33% of Reform rabbis and 59% of Conservative rabbis surveyed said that the internet, by providing access to sex and porn sites, damaged religious values to a "very great extent," "a great extent" or "to a considerable extent." Of all the forms of media—press, radio, television, cinema, theater and the internet—rabbis identified with the non-Orthodox streams (Conservative and Reform) were most critical of the internet. There were wide gaps between rabbi-respondents of all streams (Haredi, mainline Modern Orthodox, Hardal substream, Conservative, Reform). For example, Israeli- and Middle Eastern–born rabbis were more inclined than Western- and East European–born rabbis to view the internet as damaging religious values.

The difference between the Orthodox and non-Orthodox is less in outlook about internet dangers and more in the practical measures to be taken to deal with the perceived danger. The mainstream Modern Orthodox, as well as non-Orthodox, disagree with the Haredi worldview of cutting oneself off from the wider society. The mainstream Modern Orthodox and

*Table 11.1* Are you connected to the internet?

| | |
|---|---|
| **Stream** | |
| Haredi | 22% |
| Hardal | 37% |
| Modern Orthodox (mainstream) | 68% |
| Conservative | 97% |
| Reform | 96% |
| **Place of birth** | |
| Israel | 49% |
| Western countries | 81% |
| Eastern Europe | 45% |
| Arab countries | 10% |
| **Year of birth** | |
| 1901–1920 | 67% |
| 1921–1940 | 60% |
| 1941–1960 | 52% |
| 1961–1980 | 62% |

non-Orthodox seek to be fully integrated into modern society, including the use of advanced media technology and oppose the construction of cultural barriers. Haredim have nevertheless found in the growing subsection of Hardal natural allies in limiting exposure to these various websites.

## Computer and Internet Usage by Rabbis

Rabbis were surveyed regarding their usage of computers and the internet. Most rabbis in this study possess a computer. Of the respondents 74% of all Haredi rabbis possess a computer. It was noted that many Haredi rabbis who own a computer come from a Sephardi (or oriental) background. Within the Modern Orthodox (including mainstream Modern Orthodox and Hardal) 87% of rabbis have computers (Table 11.3).

Of rabbis without a computer at home 73% of all Haredi rabbis cited religious reasons as opposed to 51% of all Modern Orthodox (combined Modern Orthodox mainstream and Hardal) rabbis. Israeli-born (86%) and Western-born (92%) rabbis were more inclined to have computers than East European born (65%) rabbis or rabbis born in Arab countries (72%). There was no significant difference accord to age groups.

There was a major difference between Hardal and mainstream Modern Orthodox regarding being linked to the internet; for example, 68% of mainstream Modern Orthodox respondents are linked to the internet in contrast to only 37% of all Hardal respondents (Table 11.1).

Also, 73% of all Haredi rabbi respondents who are not linked to the internet cited religion as the reason for not being linked to it. There was

*Table 11.2* Does the internet damage religious values?

| | | | | | |
|---|---|---|---|---|---|
| **Stream** | | | | | |
| Haredim | 5% | 8% | 13% | 15% | 59% |
| hardal | 2% | 6% | 19% | 28% | 45% |
| Modern Orthodox—mainline | 3% | 22% | 23% | 21% | 31% |
| Conservative | 22% | 19% | 33% | 16% | 10% |
| Reform | 45% | 22% | 22% | 7% | 4% |
| **Place of Birth** | | | | | |
| Israel | 7% | 13% | 22% | 20% | 38% |
| Western countries | 15% | 24% | 22% | 21% | 18% |
| Eastern Europe | 30% | 8% | 15% | 8% | 39% |
| Arab countries | – | – | 13% | 25% | 62% |
| **Born** | | | | | |
| 1901–1920 | 33% | 33% | – | 34% | – |
| 1921–1940 | 12% | 21% | 21% | 18% | 28% |
| 1941–1960 | 7% | 15% | 23% | 19% | 36% |
| 1961–1980 | 13% | 14% | 22% | 18% | 33% |

*Table 11.3* Do you possess a computer?

| | |
|---|---|
| **Stream** | |
| Haredi | 74% |
| Hardal | 85% |
| Modern Orthodox (mainstream) | 89% |
| Conservative | 94% |
| Reform | 96% |
| **Place of birth** | |
| Israel | 86% |
| Western countries | 92% |
| Eastern Europe | 65% |
| Arab countries | 72% |
| **Year of birth** | |
| 1901–1920 | 75% |
| 1921–1940 | 81% |
| 1941–1960 | 87% |
| 1961–1980 | 88% |

only a marginal difference between rabbis linked to the internet who had children at home (55%) and those who did not have children at home (63%). Yet, of those who did not have the internet and cited religion as the factor, 78% had children at home in contrast to 22% who did not. Of those who did not have the internet, Israeli-born and Middle Eastern–born rabbis were more inclined to cite religious reasons. In the age breakdown, older rabbis, born between 1921 and 1940, were much less inclined to cite religion (25%) in contrast to middle-aged and younger rabbis: 73% of those born between 1941 and 1960 and between 1961 and 1980. The major difference, therefore, both between Haredi rabbis and Modern Orthodox rabbis and between the mainline Modern Orthodox and the Hardal substream was less in possessing the computer but rather in using the internet.

## Limiting the Exposure of Children to Computers and the Internet

In building an ideal Jewish life, Orthodox rabbis favor limiting the exposure of children to the media. In part the ban was directed at children whose religious studies had been distracted with computers, both by the internet and by databases.

In the survey 56% of all Haredi rabbi respondents with the internet said that they had computer-filtering devices. Of the Modern Orthodox broken down, there was a greater inclination for Hardal (36%) to use computer-filtering devices than for mainstream Modern Orthodox (17%). Of the non-Orthodox, 12% of Reform rabbis and 7% of Conservative rabbis used a filter. There was a greater inclination for rabbis with children at home to have a computer-filtering device (24%) than those without them at home (16%). There were no significant difference in terms of national backgrounds between those born in Israel, Western countries (North America, West Europe, South America), East European-born rabbis and Sephardi rabbis born in Arab countries (Table 11.4).

The responses of the Modern Orthodox were particularly important given that they seek to synthesize between the world of Torah and modernity. Goodman (2010) surveyed the exposure of Modern Orthodox youth to the internet. Exposure of children to mass media (according to the Modern Orthodox approach) ought to be handled by inculcating the child towards media literacy rather than withdrawal to a Haredi ghetto-like existence. But 78% of mainline Modern Orthodox rabbis in the author's study believe "to a great degree" or "to a very great degree" that children's exposure to the internet should be limited (Table 11.5).

By contrast, 57% of Modern Orthodox rabbis "very much agree" and 32% of modern Orthodox rabbis "much agree" to the need to control children's exposure to radio broadcasting. The lesser need to control children's exposure to television was also found; 37% and 29% of Modern Orthodox rabbis "very much agreed" or "much agreed," respectively, to the need to control children's exposure to television. A leading rabbi of the Modern

*Table 11.4* If you are connected to the internet, do you use a filter?

| | |
|---|---|
| **Stream** | |
| Haredi | 56% |
| Hardal | 36% |
| Modern Orthodox (mainstream) | 17% |
| Conservative | 7% |
| Reform | 12% |
| **Place of birth** | |
| Israel | 29% |
| Western countries | 8% |
| Eastern Europe | 40% |
| Arab countries | 67% |
| **Year of birth** | |
| 1901–1920 | 25% |
| 1921–1940 | 11% |
| 1941–1960 | 27% |
| 1961–1980 | 19% |

*Table 11.5* I think that internet access for children should be limited.

| | Not at all | To a little extent | To a considerable extent | To a great extent | To a very great extent |
|---|---|---|---|---|---|
| **Stream** | | | | | |
| Haredim | 5% | – | 14% | 5% | 76% |
| Hardal | 3% | 3% | 6% | 19% | 69% |
| Modern Orthodox—mainline | 2% | 8% | 12% | 27% | 51% |
| Conservative | 8% | 15% | 42% | 27% | 8% |
| Reform | 13% | 13% | 29% | 42% | 3% |
| **Place of Birth** | | | | | |
| Israel | 4% | 9% | 14% | 17% | 56% |
| Western countries | 10% | 5% | 26% | 34% | 25% |
| Eastern Europe | – | 11% | 33% | 45% | 11% |
| Arab countries | – | 17% | – | – | 83% |
| **Born** | | | | | |
| 1901–1920 | 33% | – | 33% | 34% | – |
| 1921–1940 | 4% | 12% | 24% | 26% | 34% |
| 1941–1960 | 7% | 10% | 15% | 15% | 53% |
| 1961–1980 | 3% | 5% | 23% | 29% | 40% |

Orthodox sector, Yaacov Ariel, rabbi of the city of Ramat Gan, was unwilling to rely merely on self-discipline. Quoting the biblical edict, "do not put a stumbling block before the blind," Ariel favored computer-filtering devices.[2] As we can see, while Modern Orthodox rabbis were more inclined in the case of internet than traditional media forms such as press, radio and television to control children's access to computers, only one sixth did so—which reflects the Modern Orthodox outlook of the modern world being an integral part of their identity.

## Computers as a Modern Tool for Jewish Education

Against the background of rabbinical qualifications regarding computers and the internet, there is an increasing recognition that the computer is a positive tool for religious study. Since the eighties there have been a proliferation of attempts to apply different technologies to Jewish religious study. These include Torah databases comprise comprehensive collections of traditional texts from the Bible, biblical commentaries, Mishnah, the Babylonian and Jerusalem Talmuds and later Jewish codes, covering 3,300 years of Jewish written scholarship. While these attempts did not replaced traditional frameworks for Jewish education, such as the *Shiur*—a frontal lecture by the rabbi to students—they were a new dimension to *Limud Torah* (or the study of Judaism).

Non-Orthodox rabbis surveyed in the current research were most inclined to use *Torani* religious websites about Judaism and Haredi rabbis least; 40%, 22% and 15% of non-Orthodox, Modern Orthodox and Haredi, respectively, use these websites a lot or even "all the time"; for instance, 67%, 49% and 30% of Haredim, all Modern Orthodox and non-Orthodox, respectively, said that they do not use them at all. Reform rabbis were marginally more inclined than Conservative rabbis to make use of it. Middle East– and East European–born rabbis were less inclined than Western- and Israeli-born rabbis to use it. Younger rabbis, born between 1961 and 1980, were more inclined than older ones to use it. Thus, whereas 50% and 56% of rabbis born between 1921 and 1940 and between 1941 and 1960, respectively, did not at all or infrequently used such websites, only 36% of rabbis born between 1971 and 1980 said so.

The discussions within the Haredi rabbinical leadership about the threat of the internet occurred at the same time as the proliferation of Jewish-related websites emerged, many of which were educational and made it more difficult for rabbis to impose their anti-internet line. The Torah data base revolution in Israel has been most felt in the non-Orthodox and Modern Orthodox sectors. All Hesder Yeshivot (Yeshivot of the Modern Orthodox sector that combine yeshiva study with army service) have incorporated computers into the study hall—enabling students to open database sources as the rabbi refers to additional sources. In one, Yeshivat Har Etzion, students can receive *Shiurim* on their e-mail; the Yeshiva's archive numbers more than 2,000 *Shiurim*. In 2007 the Web Yeshiva, which is identified with the Modern Orthodox stream, was established.[3] Students study in a live online *Shiur*—as well as learning online with a *Chavruta* (a study partner). Transcending geographical limitations, classes are available from 4 a.m. to midnight in Hebrew, English and Russian.

Parallel to other faith groups, a large range of Jewish websites provides a myriad number of services. These include such listings as synagogues, community websites, Jewish schools, burial societies, kosher restaurants, Jewish bookstores and Jewish dating (Romm, 1998). The Israel government's Ministry of Religious Affairs' and the chief rabbinate's websites [4] list rabbinical courts for matters of marriage, divorce and religious conversion (all of which in Israel are the responsibility of the rabbinical courts) and circumcisers (*Mohel*).

## REFLECTING ON FINDINGS CONCERNING ISRAELI RABBIS AND THE INTERNET

In discussing rabbinical attitudes to the internet, this chapter has shown variegated positions among different religious streams in Judaism. In the case of the Haredim, for example, the survey found widespread criticism of Haredi rabbis toward the computer and their rejection of the internet. While there are gaps between the mainstream Modern Orthodox and the stricter Hardal substream in the different questions discussed, overall even the mainstream Modern Orthodox rabbinate, as distinct from their community members who are as active on the internet as secular Israelis, are victims of their soul-searching in reconciling Orthodoxy and modernity. The moral dilemmas about the internet were seen even among the non-Orthodox rabbis.

This survey found that in terms of place of birth, rabbis born in Western countries were least critical of computers and the internet and rabbis born in Arab lands were most critical. Interestingly, older rabbis were inclined to be less critical than were younger rabbis, many of whom have children at home. But in terms of computer savviness, younger rabbis were leaps and bounds ahead of their older colleagues, which was reflected in part in the wide use of Torah databases. And the grave concerns that rabbis may have about internet content have not stopped either Modern Orthodox rabbis or their non-Orthodox rabbinical colleagues from making full use of such databases. Indeed, Haredi rabbis, it is argued, may also be expected in the longer term to recognize the revolutionary value of databases for their single-minded objective of Torah study.

Given the campaign by Haredi rabbis over the years against the internet it is instructive to view the findings of the author's survey of the rabbis against the background of the campaign. In 1998 Haredi rabbis imposed a ban on computers. But there is a recognition by Haredi rabbis that computers are an integral part of modern life. Following the development of the internet in the mid-1990s a special *Bet Din* (rabbinical law court) of Haredi rabbis was established to examine how to react (Cohen, 2012a). Haredi rabbis in general regarded the internet as a far worse moral threat than television: Whereas Israeli public television was supervised, the internet enabled access to pornographic sites. The internet had other dangers; it enabled the Haredi surfer to get information beyond his religious stream or indeed his Jewish faith. In 2000, the Haredi rabbinical leadership imposed a prohibition on the internet "as a moral threat to the sanctity of Israel" (Barzilai-Nahon and Barzilai 2005). The internet threatened the high walls that Haredi rabbis had set up to resist secular cultural influences.

Not all Haredi rabbis have been as intense and uncompromising in the ban. A distinction within the Haredi world could be delineated between the so-called European Lithuanian branch and the European Hassidic branch of Haredim and the Sephardic or oriental branch of Haredim. The stricter Lithuanian school placed a ban not only on the internet but also on computers as a whole, calling on its members to get rid of them from the house. Haredi rabbis from a Sephardi background were inclined to be more lenient. Notwithstanding this, there are also a few Haredi groupings with a different view. Certain Haredi groups take a more neutral view about computers and the internet. For example, the Chabad, or Lubavitch, view new media technologies as a neutral means for distributing Torah and other religious materials. For example, the Chabad website or its use of radio and television stations to broadcast programs of Jewish religious content. Indeed, the information highway is part of the divine plan. For example, under the title '"The Computer in the Service of God," a Chabad publication, it is written "that the computer does not innovate things. Man is able to think without a computer, but it makes calculations much faster" (Ginzberg and Branover, n.d.).

Overall, internet proved to be the major anti-media battle that Haredi rabbis lost. Haredi rabbis have been faced with the realization that the ban on computers and the internet has not been entirely accepted, and given the realization of the centrality of the internet in modern life, rabbis have allowed the internet for businesses. Drawing on the standard in Jewish law-making (*Halacha*) of not legalizing something which would not be acceptable by the community (and that would therefore raise questions about the legitimacy of their rabbis and the Torah itself) Haredi rabbis recognize that the internet is an integral factor of business life today.

The compromise by Haredi rabbis from an outright ban on the internet to allowing the internet at businesses was the culmination of a series of attempts by the rabbis to provide their followers with a filtered internet. One early attempt, Torahnet, undertook to process requests for access to websites within 24 hours. Another program, Nativ, comprised software blocking everything but e-mail or access to a limited number of websites operated by business-related and official institutions. In later years, an agreement was reached with the Israeli telephone company, Bezek, to provide access for businesses to a small number of websites.[5] The Belze Hassidic court became in 2008 the first Hassidic branch of Haredim to allow its community a special package of some 150 websites both in businesses as well as at home. The Belze court reached what would be a short-lived agreement with one religious internet server, Rimon. This was the creation of a special package of 150 sites—comprising both sites of general interest, including some quality Israeli newspapers, and business-related websites. But the system was not foolproof. Seemingly clean sites led to other sites that were problematic, such as through links, or to sites that were originally deemed OK but were updated subsequently with problematic material, or to sites which carried problematic advertising. For example, an innocuous site dealing with health might have a link to AIDS—regarded as taboo in Haredi circles. One body of Haredi rabbis, the rabbinical committee for communication affairs, recommended an alternative system of "white" sites: Access would be allowed to only those sites relevant to a specific profession. But this had an inbuilt contradiction in which some Haredi customers would be prohibited access to websites that were allowed to other Haredi customers whose businesses needed those sites. Haredi entrepreneurs created computer-filtering programs.

In assessing the extent to which rulings by Haredi rabbis regarding computers and the internet have been accepted it is noteworthy that while many Haredi households today possess computers, Haredim still have lower exposure to computers and to the internet than the rest of the Israeli Jewish population. In 2007, 55% of Haredi households possessed a computer, and some 57% of these households were linked to the internet (CBS, 2007). True, this was higher than the same survey two years earlier by the CBS (2005), which found that only 10% of Haredi families were linked to the internet (in contrast to 61% of the total Israeli Jewish population). But, surveying those without computer or the internet, the CBS found that Haredim were the largest sector reporting no computer: 42% of Haredim had no computer at home—in contrast to 29% of the general Israeli population. As part of its attempt to impose the Haredi ban, since Haredi schools did not accept children from homes that failed to sign an undertaking that they were not linked to the internet, or in some cases, schools even banned computers. Schools in the Haredi city of Betar—which regards itself as an internet-free area—were instructed not to accept children who had unlimited access to the internet.[6] Elsewhere, there have been instances of so-called modesty squads demonstrating outside internet cafes used by Haredim to surf.

By 2008 a notable increase in Haredi usage of the internet had occurred: Of those who possessed computers but were not linked to the internet, 27% were Haredi Jews. Another measure of the non-usage of the internet was that in the Haredi town of Benei Beraq (situated near Tel Aviv) only 53% possessed personal computers, while in mixed neighborhoods and cities such as Ramat Gan and Ashkelon, 73% and 71%, respectively, of households did. And, while 66% and 61% of households in Ramat Gan and

Ashkelon respectively used the internet, only 29.5% of Benei Beraq households did (CBS, 2008). Haredim were also less inclined to be heavy internet users. Broken down according to "light users" of the internet (less than once a day), 1 to 3 times daily and "heavy users" (at least 4 times daily), 58% of light users were Haredim (CBS, 2008). In the Haredi case, as Campbell (2011) argued, religious engagement and perception of the internet is primarily a question of identity management, information control, and community boundary maintenance.

A further breach of Haredi rabbinical hegemony came in the form of Haredi news websites. These include Behadrei Haredim, Kikar Ha-Shabbat and LaDaat. They were aware of the acceptable social limits within the Haredi religio-culturo ghetto, such as no pictures of women. But the sites did not subject themselves to the rabbinical censors, and some Haredi rabbis refused to be interviewed by the sites. The names of those sponsoring the sites, and editing them, were hidden from public light. The rabbinical leadership had already been challenged with the independent commercial Haredi weekly magazine press that has been a feature of Haredi media patterns since the 1980s. These magazines are not subject to rabbinical control, but the Haredi websites went a stage further and challenged the ban on the internet itself. If the independent weekly magazines looked over their shoulders not to offend rabbis, this was passe for the Haredi news sites, which by virtue of their online nature were intrinsically *Treifa*ʿ (or "ritually unclean"). Moreover, internet sites such as Behadrei Haredim became a platform for the Haredim to speak out against rabbis and institutions.

In the case of Haredim, for example, their leaders faced a new challenge with the creation of Facebook. While Facebook did not pose the direct threat as internet sites with sexual content, social networking did breach the Haredi rules of conduct notably by building relationships between men and women. This was seen as problematic by Haredi leaders who have emphasized the importance of interpersonal relations both in terms of family and community. It also resulted in the free passage of information and gossip in a society in which social gossip is frowned upon by Jewish religious law. Yet Haredi Facebook users themselves responded to concerns about the problematic nature of social media by developing their own Haredi Facebook code of networking—not dissimilar from the strict code that is encouraged in the community and characterizes offline Haredi interpersonal behavior.

For the Modern Orthodox, the question of the internet went ideologically even deeper because by definition, the Modern Orthodox sought to reconcile modernity with Jewish values. Fifty-one percent of Modern Orthodox Jews, 54% of Jews defining themselves as traditional-cum-religious and 62% of traditional Jews had access to the internet. By 2009, 95% of Modern Orthodox were linked to internet, according to the CBS. The number of Modern Orthodox using the internet is no less than the general population. There was also a higher percentage of Modern Orthodox (combined academic and nonacademic) internet users, 95%, than the other sectors.

The survey further illuminated the essence of Hardal Judaism. A clue to what the Hardal outlook is all about—a Zionist cultural ghetto—was evident in that only 37% of Hardal rabbis were linked to the internet in contrast to 68% of the mainstream Modern Orthodox—this is despite the shared outlook on Zionism between the Hardal and the mainstream Modern Orthodox—and that Hardal is broadly seen as a subdivision of the Modern Orthodox or Dati Leumi. Moreover, only 45% of Hardal said that the internet damaged religious values "to a very great extent" compared to 59% of Haredi rabbis, but when "to a very extent" and "to a great extent" are combined, the same figure between the Hardal and the Haredim is almost the same: 73%. In this sense there is no difference between the Hardal and Haredim regarding the internet.

The more positive response to the internet within Modern Orthodox communities is reflected in trends toward online rabbinic counseling, particular responding to Jewish law questions. Websites such as Kipa, Moreshet, Moriah, Jewish Answers, and Project Genesis often have a panel of 10 to 20 rabbis whom they engage as advisors and who serve in counseling roles on their sites.

One rabbi, Yuval Churlow, who provides online rabbinic counseling, receives between 20 to 40 questions per week, answering an estimated 5,000 questions a year, and estimated that 30% to 40% of questions are male–female related, such as marriage, relationships and sexuality. According to a survey by the website Kipa, which asked to whom site visitors turn if they have a religious question, 33% and 8% of women replied an internet rabbi and an internet forum, respectively, in contrast to 16% and 4% of men, respectively.[7]

Online rabbinical counseling has generated debate among Modern Orthodox rabbis about its pluses and minuses. Supporters of the new trend argue that nonaffiliated Jews now have access to rabbis that they would not otherwise have. Online counseling offers anonymity, which a local community rabbi does not; it also enables people to raise questions they would not otherwise feel comfortable doing. Critics of online rabbinical counseling argue that online answers offered by rabbis are too short. Second, that personal circumstances cannot be taken into consideration by the rabbi who is unacquainted with the questioner, even though sometimes the personal circumstances can be crucial in a particular instance. Third, quoting "Make/Find a Rabbi for yourself," a dictum of the Mishnaic tome *Ethics of the Fathers*, then Ashkenazi chief rabbi Yonah Metzger characterized the rabbi not only as being a functionary but also being a role model to emulate and identify with. One would not "make oneself a rabbi" if one already has a virtual rabbi. Fourth, instead of accepting the decision of the rabbi, people would be inclined to "shop around," to different online rabbis to find the reply that is most agreeable to them. Fifth, the ease of online counseling discourages the Jew from studying the original sources in the *Halachic* literature (Jewish religious law). With a few exceptions like Chabad rabbis, Haredi rabbis do not engage in online counseling.

In evaluating the overall impact of the internet on Judaism, it is important to note that few questions about media-related matters, including computers and the internet, directly impinge upon Jewish religious law in a fundamental manner (Cohen, 2012b). Rather, media technologies raise more direct questions related to education and religious identity. What this study shows is that notwithstanding the inherent differences between Haredim, Modern Orthodox, Conservative and Reform groups response to *Halacha* itself, the variation in response between the Modern Orthodox and non-Orthodox groups on computer and internet-related matters, as reflected in the data presented here, are somewhat surprising. These findings shed light on the attitudes of the different streams—Haredi, Modern Orthodox, its Hardal substream, Conservative and Reform—not only to computers and the internet but also how these response reflect difference in attitudes toward religion and modernity in general.

Overall, in examining rabbinical attitudes toward computers and the internet, two distinct groupings among the various streams surveyed could be identified, namely, similarities in response from Modern Orthodox and Haredim rabbis and from Reform and Conservative. Like the non-Orthodox, the Modern Orthodox believe that there is no inherent conflict between Judaism and modern life. Yet given the theological and social similarities in outlook between the Modern Orthodox and Conservative—both recognizing the laws in the Bible as valid and both being committed to reconciling Torah with modern society—the gap itself of those rabbis linked to the internet between the 68% of Modern Orthodox rabbis and 97% of Conservative rabbis was surprising. Another area in which their response aligned was in relation to beliefs about exposure of children to the internet. Modern Orthodox rabbis stress that children should be schooled in media literacy to help them discern their response to the internet, rather than withdrawal to a Haredi ghetto-like existence. Yet, as noted by the fact the majority (81%) of Modern Orthodox rabbis surveyed agreed with Haredi rabbis that children's exposure to the internet should be limited (Table 11.5). Even Modern Orthodox rabbis seem to agree about the need to control children's exposure to the internet more than they stressed the need to limit television, as shown by 66% of Modern Orthodox rabbis agreeing to the need to control exposure of children to the internet. The similarities between Modern Orthodox and Haredim regarding computers and internet matters, and the difference between the Modern Orthodox and the non-Orthodox, as reflected in the author's survey of rabbis, raise the broader question of to what extent the Modern Orthodox view of media illustrate a particular leaning towards or resistance to aspects of modern society. Modern Orthodox rabbis aligned closely with Reform and Conservative rabbis on whether or not they use computer filters or not; only 17% of Modern Orthodox, 12% of Reform and 7% of Conservative admitted to using filters while 36% of Hardal and 56% of Haredi rabbis with the internet did.

Democracy and the free flow of information appear irreconcilable to their beliefs. Antagonism toward modern media and popular culture suggests that the Hardal Jew does not belong to the Modern Orthodox camp beyond questions concerning territorial matters and national redemption.

One of the most illuminating patterns among the religious streams and the internet shown in the survey was the distinction between Reform and Conservative. The theological differences in outlook between the two came to expression in terms of whether the internet damaged religious values. While 26% of rabbis of Conservative Judaism said that the internet damaged religious values to a "very great extent" or to a "great extent," and a further 33% said it damaged religious values "to some extent"—a total of 59%—this contrasted with only 11% and 22% of Reform rabbis responded that the internet damaged religious values to a "very great extent" and "a great extent," respectively. Only 22% of Conservative rabbis thought "not at all" in contrast to 45% of Reform rabbis—a clue to how enlightened the Reform rabbis were.

## CONCLUSION

The data presented here confirm the main hypotheses about rabbis in Israel and the internet. There was a clear gap noted between rabbis of different streams regarding whether they were linked to the internet or not. The views of Orthodox—Haredi, Modern Orthodox and the Hardal subsystem—that the internet damages religious values—was predictable.

The more Orthodox the rabbi is, the more he was inclined to be critical of the internet and its damage to religious values. While rabbis of all streams possessed computers, including the ultra-Orthodox, and Haredim, the more Orthodox the rabbi is, the less he is inclined to be linked to the internet and if he is, he has a filter. Moreover, the research showed that even the non-Orthodox streams, Reform and Conservative—who were generally uncritical of traditional media such as the printed press, radio and television—were critical regarding the internet.

The research confirmed that the Hardal substream, which is stricter than the mainstream Modern Orthodox on the broader question of exposure to the wider cultural environment, also use internet filters and supporting the controlling of children's access to the internet.

The research confirmed that Rabbis make certain use of Torah educational websites. But surprisingly, the Modern Orthodox were only about half the percentage amount of non-Orthodox rabbis using Torah websites—despite the high priority that Orthodox rabbis give to studying Jewish law sources such as the Talmud.

The tension depicted in this chapter is not surprising given that the rabbi emerges from a conservative culture having grown up against a background of established religious traditions and is confronted with accelerated cultural change exemplified by the media. Not only was the religious stream a factor in rabbis attitudes to the internet, but so, too, was the country in which the rabbi was born and grew up. In terms of a rabbi's country background, there was little difference between rabbis born in Israel and those born in Western countries in terms of computer ownership—86% and 92%, respectively. But in terms of internet access, and whether the internet damaged religious values, the research found that the distance between rabbis born in Arab countries and other groups is clear. Only 10% of rabbis born in Arab countries had internet access—as opposed to 84% rabbis born in Western countries, 49% born in Israel and 45% born in East European countries. There was also a wide difference between the four country groups regarding whether the internet damaged religious values: Israel was closer to East Europe than to Western Europe. Of Israeli rabbis and East European rabbis, 38% and 39%, respectively, said it damaged religious values to a "very great extent" in contrast to those born in Western countries. This suggests that rabbis from Western European backgrounds appear to be more open to engagement with new media technologies than those from Eastern descent, a hypothesis worthy of further exploration.

Age was much less a factor than either the religious stream of the rabbi or the rabbi's country background in determining Israeli rabbis' attitudes to the internet. True, younger rabbis are computer media savvy, but the responses of all rabbis about the internet—in terms of the rabbi's evaluation of the influence of the internet on religious values, and in terms of rabbis' usage of the internet—showed little significant difference between age groupings.

While religion in traditional societies is often based on authority vested in religious bodies and leader, in complex, industrial societies there is an increased emphasis on personal choice in moral and religious matters. Against this background Jewish religious leaders exist within a context where religious hierarchical authority is frequently challenged, and it can be argued that media culture, including the internet, contributes to this. Increasingly within Israeli society, as seen also in other parts of the world, organized religion is undermined—people find alternative—perhaps more deeply spiritually meaningful means—to give religious expression. This is a reality with which rabbis must come to terms. To the extent that computer-mediated communication is not formally under the control of the rabbis, such leaders may appear to have lost the battle for influencing how technologies shape society. Instead, they must focus their attention of their sphere of influence, the Jewish religious community. The religious life of both the Haredi and Modern Orthodox still centers today on the Jewish home and Torah study, and the synagogue remains the center of Jewish spiritual life. So is the Jewish home, which functions in accordance with a Jewish code of life as expressed in the 613 positive and negative commandments in the Bible regulating humanity's relationship with God and with others. These include kosher food, Sabbath observance and marital life. Notwithstanding the monumental impact the internet is having throughout contemporary society, religious study characterized by the offline rabbi's *Shiur* (religious lesson), and offline Yeshiva study, remain paramount in both the Haredi and Modern Orthodox communities.

## NOTES

1. The author is grateful to the Research Unit, The Lifshitz College of Education, Jerusalem, for providing financial support to undertake the survey of rabbis.
2. "Schools Face Internet Dilemma," *Hatzofe*, December 6. 2007 (in Hebrew).
3. www.webyeshiva.org [Accessed December 6, 2012].
4. Ministry of Religious Affairs website, www.religions.gov.il [Accessed November 21, 2012].
5. "Bezeq provides Internet to Belze," *Haaretz* December 18, 2007 (in Hebrew).
6. "No Internet in Betar," *Yerushalayim*, September 25, 2009 (in Hebrew).
7. Kipa survey, private communication by website management to author, April 3, 2006.

## REFERENCES

Bar-Ilan, N. (1987). Copying Books and Tapes. *Alon Shevut: Tehumin,* 7, 360–367 (in Hebrew).

Barzilai-Nahon, K. and Barzilai, G. (2005). Cultured Technology: The Internet and Religious Fundamentalism. *The Information Society*, 21, 25–40.

Batzri, E. (1986). Copyright. *Alon Shevut: Tehumin*, 6, 169–184 (in Hebrew).

Baumel, S. (2002). Communication and Change: Newspapers, Periodicals and Acculturation Among Israeli Haredim. *Jewish History*, 16(2), 161–187.

Baumel, S. (2005). *Sacred Speakers: Language & Culture among the Haredim in Israel.* Oxford and New York: Berghahn.

Baumel-Schwartz, J. (2009). Frum Surfing: Orthodox Jewish Women's Internet Forums as a Historical and Cultural Phenomenon. *Journal of Jewish Identities*, 2(1), 1–30.

Buddenbaum, J. (2001). Christian Perspectives on Mass Media. In: D. Stout and J. Buddenbaum (Eds.), *Religion and Popular Culture* (pp. 81–94). Ames: Iowa State University Press.

Campbell, H. (2011). Religion and the Internet in the Israeli Orthodox Context. *Israel Affairs*, 17(3), 364–383.

Cardon, D. (2006). Electronic Mail on the Sabbath Eve. Alon Shevut: *Tehumin*, 27, 84–89 (in Hebrew).

Central Bureau of Statistics (2005). *Social Survey*. Jerusalem (in Hebrew).

Central Bureau of Statistics (2007). *Social Survey*. Jerusalem (in Hebrew).

Central Bureau of Statistics (2008). *Social Survey*. Jerusalem (in Hebrew).

Central Bureau of Statistics (2009). *Social Survey*. Jerusalem (in Hebrew).

Cohen, Y. (2001). *Mass Media in the Jewish Tradition*. In: D. Stout and J. Buddenbaum (Eds.), *Religion & Popular Culture: Studies on the Interaction of Worldviews* (pp. 95–108). Ames: Iowa State University Press.

Cohen, Y. (2005). Religion News in Israel. *Journal of Media and Religion*, 4(3), 179–198.

Cohen, Y. (2006). Judaism—Entry. In: S. Daniel (Ed.), *Encyclopaedia of Religion, Communication and Media* (pp. 206–212). New York and London: Routledge.
Cohen, Y. (2011). Haredim and the Internet: A Hate-Love Affair. In: M. Bailey and G. Redden (Eds.), *Mediating Faiths: Religion and Socio-Cultural Change in the Twenty-First Century* (pp. 63–71). Farnham and Burlington: Ashgate.
Cohen, Y. (2012a). *God, Jews & the Media: Religion & Israel's Media*. New York and London: Routledge.
Cohen, Y. (2012b). Jewish Cybertheology. *Communication Research Trends*, 31(1), 4–14.
Dickovsky, S. (2002). Internet and Jewish Law. *Alon Shevut: Tehumin* 23, 325–333 (in Hebrew).
Eretz Hemdah (2003). Internet Trade on the Internet and Sabbath Observance. *Shut B'Bmarei Habazak*, 5, 89–95 (in Hebrew).
Gabel I (2006), *The Modern Religious Community and the Media: A Love-Hate Relationship*. Tel Aviv: Herzog Institute, Tel Aviv University (in Hebrew).
Ginzberg, Y. and Branover, Y. (n.d.). How Beautiful Are Your Creations. In: A. Gotfryd (Ed.), *Science & Technology in the Light of Hassidus*. Kefar Habad (in Hebrew).
Goldberg, Z. N. (1986). Copying from a Cassette without Permission. *Alon Shevut: Tehumin*, 6, 185–207 (in Hebrew).
Goodman, Y. (2010). The Modern Religious Youth and the Internet. *Tzohar, Tammuz*, 5770 (in Hebrew).
Horowitz, N. (2000). Internet Haredim and the Internet. *Kivunim Hadashim*, 3, 7–30 (in Hebrew).
Micolson, M. (1990). The Haredi Press in Israel. *Kesher*, 8, 11–20.
Ringler, S. A. (1989). *The Streams of Judaism*. Jerusalem: Sharett Center (in Hebrew).
Romm, D. (1998). *The Jewish Guide to the Internet*. New Jersey: Jason Aronson.
Schwartz, Y. (2005). *The Computer Era and What We Can Learn From It*. Jerusalem: Yeshivat: Dvar Yerushalayim Zichron Tvi (in Hebrew).
Stern, Y. and Friedman, S. (Eds.) (2011). *Rabbis & Rabbinate: The Challenge*. Tel Aviv: Am Oved and the Israel Democracy Institute (in Hebrew).

# Contributors

**Nathan Abrams** is a professor of Film Studies at Bangor University, UK. He has written widely on Judaism, politics, popular culture and film. His work has focused on Judaism in contemporary culture and appeared in *Journal of European Popular Culture, Shofar: An Interdisciplinary Journal of Jewish Studies* and the *Journal of American Studies*. His most recent book, *The New Jew in Film: Exploring Jewishness and Judaism in Contemporary Cinema* (2012), also explores Jewish identity in film. His current work looks at the presentation of Jewish identity in video games and social media.

**Wendi Bellar** is a PhD candidate at Texas A&M University. She is also a research associate with the Network for New Media, Religion and Digital Culture Studies. Her scholarly research has focused on a variety of issues related to religion and media, with current extensive work being done on Jewish, Christian and Muslim mobile apps. Her research has appeared in *Mobile Media & Communication* and the *Journal of Religion, Media and Digital Culture*.

**Menahem Blondheim** is a professor and the chair of the communication department at Hebrew University in Jerusalem and serves as head of its Truman Institute. A scholar of old and new communication technologies, he is a former vice president and scientific manager in the high-tech industry, and was one of the first scholars to study and teach Judaism on line (in the mid-1990s). His research explores the role of communication in American and in Jewish history, as well as the history of media. He has published extensively in academic journals and is author of two books including *News Over the Wires: The Telegraph and the Flow of Public Information in America, 1844–1897* (1994) and three edited collections including *Telling News Stories: Perspectives on Media Discourse in Israel* (2008). He is currently completing a two-volume work on communications in Jewish history and culture, which also deal with the Jewish encounter with the internet and new media.

**Heidi A. Campbell** is an associate professor of communication at Texas A&M University, where she teaches in media studies. She has researched and published extensively on themes related to religion and the new media, especially on themes of social shaping of technology, internet studies, religious community and authority online. She is considered an expert on Judaism and Christianity online and is the author of *Exploring Religious Community Online* (2005) and *When Religion Meets New Media* (2010), editor of the *Digital Religion: Understanding Religious Practice in New Media Worlds* (Routledge, 2012) and the coeditor of *Playing with Religion in Digital Gaming* (2014). She is also the director of the Network on New Media, Religion and Digital Culture Studies (digitalreligion.tamu.edu).

**Yoel Cohen** is an associate professor in the School of Communication (school chairman 2009–2011) at Ariel University in Israel. He has done extensive work on media and religion in Israel, Judaism and mass media and religion news. His scholarship has appeared in *Gazette, Journal of Media & Religion; Encyclopedia of Religion, Communication & Media; International Handbook of Media and Mass Communication Theory*; and *Encyclopedia Judaica*. He is also author of *God, Jews and the Media: Religion and Israel 's Media* (2012).

**Oren Golan** is a lecturer in the Faculty of Education at the University of Haifa, Israel. His research expertise is in internet studies and sociology of youth in Israel. His work draws from research conducted while a Fulbright Fellow at New York University exploring the practices of Jewish digital entrepreneurs within the Brooklyn ultra-Orthodox community. He also served as a postdoctoral fellow in Sociology and Jewish Studies at Northwestern University. His works has appeared in such publications as *Media, Culture & Society* and *Israeli Sociology*.

**Owen Gottlieb** is an assistant professor at the School of Interactive Games and Media, at the B. Thomas Golisano School of Computing and Information Sciences at the Rochester Institute of Technology. He is the founder and director of ConverJent: Jewish Games for Learning (www.converjent.org), whose mobile GPS game for teaching Jewish history, Jewish Time Jump: New York was nominated for Most Innovative Game, 2013 by the 10th annual Games for Change Festival. Gottlieb is a Reform rabbi and resident faculty member at Clal: The National Jewish Center for Learning and Leadership.

**Tsuriel Rashi** is the head of the mass communication department at Herzog College of Education in Jerusalem, a lecturer in the School of Communication at Bar-Ilan University and a prime researcher at the Center for the Media and Judaism. His research expertise is in media studies and communication/legal rhetoric in the Israeli context. His research on Judaism and Media Ethics received the Yoav Prize for Significant Academic Work in Media Criticism and his articles are being presented internationally and published in and significant media scholars' journals.

**Michal Raucher** is an assistant professor in Judaic Studies at the University of Cincinnati. Her research interests include the anthropology of Judaism, women in religion, Israel, moral agency, ethics, medical ethics and technology. Raucher's most recent manuscript is based on two years of ethnographic research among Haredi women in Jerusalem, Israel, looking at their reproductive ethics and their development of moral agency during pregnancy. Her studies have been interdisciplinary, as she has combined theories and methods from religious studies, anthropology, bioethics and gender studies.

**Rivka Ribak** is an associate professor and the chair of the Department of Communication at the University of Haifa. Her work on political and gender identities through the media has been published in high ranking journals such as the *Journal of Communication, Communication Research* and *New Media & Society*. She is on the editorial board of the *Journal of Children and Media*. Her current research focuses on the domestication of technologies (computers, telephones) in cultural contexts (the home, the kibbutz) as well as issues of privacy and other technological threats from an intercultural perspective. Her joint research project with Michele Rosenthal is titled *Media Ambivalence and Avoidance in Everyday Life* and focuses on the ways in which users negotiate communication technologies in an age of media saturation.

**Michele Rosenthal** is an assistant professor in the Department of Communication at the University of Haifa. Her research focuses on religion, media and culture, and theoretical issues in the study of popular culture. She is author of two books, *American Protestants and TV in the 1950s: Responses to a New Medium* (MacMillan, 2007) and *Mediating Religion, Sanctifying Media: Exploring the Nexus of Media Practice and Contemporary Religious Revival in Israel* (De Gruyter, forthcoming) and numerous articles. Her joint research project with Rivka Ribak is entitled *Media Ambivalence and Avoidance in Everyday Life* and focuses upon the ways in which users negotiate communication technologies in an age of media saturation.

**Hananel Rosenberg** is a PhD candidate at the Department of Communication and Journalism at the Hebrew University of Jerusalem. His dissertation deals with the impact of using cell phones in isolated settings (for instance, backpacking experiences), in total institutions (such as armies and schools) and in cultural enclaves (such as the ultra-Orthodox Jewish community). His work has appeared in journals including *The Communication Review* and *Social Semiotics*.

**Aya Yadlin-Segal** is a PhD student at Texas A&M University. She is also a research assistant in the Network for New Media, Religion and Digital Culture Studies. Her research interests include the representations of the "Other" in mass media, identity construction in online environments and the flow of culture across globalized mediascapes. Her research has appeared in the *Journal of Religion, Media and Digital Culture* and *Journalism History*.

# Index